The Violence Volcano

Reducing the Threat of Workplace Violence

The Violence Volcano

Reducing the Threat of Workplace Violence

David D. Van Fleet
Arizona State University

Ella W. Van Fleet
Professional Business Associates

INFORMATION AGE PUBLISHING, INC.
Charlotte, NC • www.infoagepub.com

Library of Congress Cataloging-in-Publication Data

Van Fleet, David D.
  The violence volcano reducing the threat of workplace violence / David D. Van Fleet, Ella W. Van Fleet.
      p. cm.
  Includes bibliographical references.
  ISBN 978-1-60752-343-7 (pbk.) – ISBN 978-1-60752-344-4 (hardcover) – ISBN 978-1-60752-345-1 (e-book)
  1. Violence in the workplace. 2. Bullying in the workplace. I. Van Fleet, Ella W. II. Title.
   HF5549.5.E43V36 2009
   658.4'73–dc22
                                                              2009043796

Volcano graphics were prepared by Wendy Renee Vinzant, WuRVe Graphics, Redondo Beach, CA 90278 (www.wurve.com)

Copyright © 2010 Information Age Publishing Inc.

All rights reserved. No part of this publication may be reproduced, stored in a retrieval system, or transmitted, in any form or by any means, electronic, mechanical, photocopying, microfilming, recording or otherwise, without written permission from the publisher.

Printed in the United States of America

Contents

Preface xiii

The Authors xv
   Joint Publications xvi

Prologue xix

PART I

Introduction

1 How Workplace Violence Has Grown 3
   Violence in Organizations 4
      Violent Events in Organizations, 1981–1990 4
      Violent Events in Organizations, 1991–1994 6
      Violent Events in Organizations, 1995–2000 8
      Violent Events in Organizations, 2001–2005 13
      Violent Events in Organizations, 2006–2009 16
   Violence in Education 21
      Violent Events in Education, 1989–1999 22
      Violent Events in Education, 2000–2004 24
      Violent Events in Education, 2005–2009 27
   Summary 32

2 Costs and Definitions 35
    Types of Costs 36
        Immediate and Direct Costs... 36
        Delayed and Hidden Costs 36
        Prevention Costs... 38
    Magnitude of Costs to Business 38
    Imprecise Definitions Affect Accuracy of Statistics....................... 40
    Defining and Classifying Workplace Violence................................ 40
        Definitions Widely Used But Limited......................... 41
        Where and When May Not Be the Defining Factors................ 42
        The Intent May Be More Defining than the Act...................... 44
        Definition Should Include Target, Perpetrator, and Intent...... 44
    Summary.. 48

3 How Violent Behavior Builds: The Volcano Analogy 49
    Can We Predict Violent Behavior? 50
    The Volcano Analogy.. 52
        Level 1 53
        Level 2 54
        Level 3 55
    Summary.. 56

PART **II**

The Environment

4 Environmental Influences on Workplace Violence 59
    Changing Sociocultural Environment 60
        Changing Norms of Behavior 60
        Changing Relationships 61
        Work and Family Interdependence 62
        Drugs, Gangs, and Organized Crime.......................... 62
    Changing Economic Environment: The Over–Under Society 64
        Changing Business Conditions 64
        Shrinking Job Market 65

Contents **vii**

    Political-Legal Changes 66
    Changing Nature of Jobs (Including Technological Changes) 67
    Changing Nature of Workforce 67
        Increased Diversity and Presence of Women 68
        Sexual Preference, Age, and Other Forms of Diversity 69
    Summary 71

5 Management's Dealing with Environmental Influences 73
    Handling Changes in the Sociocultural Environment 74
    Responding to the Increased Use of Drugs and Alcohol 76
    Responding to Changes in the Economic Environment 77
    Responding to Changes in the Nature of the Workforce 78
    Responding to Ineffective or Problem Supervisors 79
    Summary 81

PART **III**

The Workplace

6 How the Workplace Affects Behavior 85
    Occupations Traditionally Considered Hazardous 86
    Vulnerable Organizations Not Traditionally Considered
        Hazardous 86
    Organizations Disliked By Fanatics 90
    Any Organization 92
    Summary 93

7 Dealing with Workplace Influences 95
    Recognize Potential Problems 96
        In Occupations Traditionally Considered as Hazardous 96
        In Vulnerable Organizations Not Traditionally Considered
            Hazardous 97
        In Organizations Disliked by Fanatics 99
        In Any and All Organizations 100
    Identify, Prioritize, and Protect Organizational Assets 103
        Define and Prioritize Organizational Assets 103
        Perform a Needs Assessment 104

Correct Security Problem Areas 104
Establish Necessary Administrative Controls 105
Develop an Early Warning System 105
Train and Familiarize All Employees with Security
   Procedures 106
Summary 107

PART **IV**

Employees

8 Employee Factors That Influence Violent Behavior 111
   Financial Factors 112
   Personal Motivations 112
   Job and Work Expectations 114
   Manager and Supervisor Expectations 115
   Job Security 115
   Personal Identity 116
   Dysfunctional Behavior of Bosses and Coworkers 116
   Personal and Personality Factors 117
   Summary 119

9 Dealing with Employee Factors Related to Violence 121
   Train to Recognize Personal Characteristics and Personal
      History 122
      Was Recently Disciplined 122
      History of Violence 122
      Suspicious Job History 122
      Unfavorable Military Record 123
      Fascination with Guns and Weapons 123
      Fanatical Behavior or Extremist Views 123
      Substance Abuse 124
      Emotional Instability 124
      Blaming Others 124
      No Healthy Way to Express Rage 125

Contents

- Heightened Anxiety 125
- Psychosis 125
- Personality Magnification 126
- Personality Disorders or Lack of Social/Family Support 126
- Poor Self-Esteem and a Defensive Posture 127
- Problems in Credit and Driving Records 127
- Train to Recognize Work Behaviors and Relationships 127
  - Loss of Interest in Work 128
  - Threatening Behavior or Words 128
  - Malicious Gossip 128
  - Disgruntled Complaints 128
  - Attendance Problems 129
  - Property Destruction or Theft 129
  - Labor–Management Disputes 129
  - Uncontrollable Temper and Outbursts 129
  - Concentration Problems 129
  - Requires Much Supervision 130
  - Change in Behavior or Personal Appearance 130
  - Inconsistent Work Habits 130
  - Decline in Productivity or Performance 130
  - Bullying and Abusive Behavior 130
- Train to Recognize How Violence Builds Through Different Levels 131
- Take Special Precautions with Computers 132
- Train to Diffuse Potentially Violent Situations 133
- Provide an Adequate Support System to Prevent Violence 134
  - Behavioral Observation Programs (BOPs) 135
  - Employee Assistance Programs (EAPs) 135
  - Reduce Social Stigma 137
  - Eliminate Bullying 137
  - Exhibit Post-Violence Patience 137
- Train for Emergencies When Violence is Not Preventable 137
- Summary 138

PART V
The Organization

10 Organizational Influences on Workplace Violence 143
    Inappropriate Management Styles/Behaviors 144
        Abusive Management 144
        Intentional Mismanagement 145
        Management Fads 146
        Inappropriate Management Policies 146
    Poor Communication 147
    Management's Poor Relationship with Employees 147
    Disagreeable or Distressful Job Factors 148
    Pressures from Downsizing/Reorganizing 149
    Negligent Attitude Toward Safety/Health of Personnel 150
    Negative Organizational Culture 150
    Job Overload and High Turnover 151
    Summary 152

11 Dealing with Organizational Influences 153
    Develop and Maintain Security 154
    Establish A Positive, Hostility-Free Workplace Environment 154
    Balance Rights of Troubled Workers and Other Employees 156
    Select and Train Positive Managers and Supervisors 156
    Eliminate Sick Work Environments 157
    Summary 159

PART VI
General Approaches to Workplace Violence

12 Administrative Ways of Reducing Risks 163
    Establish Anti-Violence Policies 164
    Improve Asset Security 165
        Conduct Security Needs Assessment 165
        Consider Facility Design and Provide Security Devices 166

Address Security Personnel Needs 167
Provide Access Control 169
Improve Communication 170
Establish Procedure for Reporting Behaviors and Threats 170
Follow Established Disciplinary Procedures 171
Practice Non-Exacerbating Termination Procedures 172
Prepare for Bomb Threats 173
Minimize Negative Effects of Reorganization 174
Provide Outplacement Services 174
Assist with Stress Management 175
Establish a Crisis Management Team 176
Establish an Organizational Crisis Plan 178
Establish Distress Signals and Procedures 178
Set Up Early-Detection System 179
Identify and Communicate Who Handles Problems 179
Train Personnel in Well-Defined Procedures 180
Prepare a Post-Violence Trauma Plan 180
Summary 181

13 Legal Issues and Law Enforcement 183

Legal Issues 183
Responsibility and Liability 184
Harassment 185
Stalking 186
Domestic Violence 186
Mental Disabilities and the ADA 186
Approaches to Reduce Liability 187
Law Enforcement 188
Jurisdictional and Other Limitations 188
Pre-Incident Happenings 188
When Violence Occurs 189
Employee Rights 189
Summary 190

APPENDICES

A Organizations That Assist in Learning About Workplace Violence 195

B Example Documents 201
      Incident Self-Report 202
      Violence Prevention Checklist 203

C An Evaluative Instrument 205
      Identifying Your Organization's Propensity to Elicit Violence 205

D A Training Outline Using the Violence Volcano Metaphor 211

Bibliography 213
Additional References 219

Preface

David D. Van Fleet
Ella W. Van Fleet

All members of organizations clearly need to be knowledgeable about workplace violence and ready to act in advance so as to reduce the threat of violent incidents. For the same reasons, students and teachers in business, education, criminal justice, and law enforcement also need to understand workplace violence—how to reduce the threat and how to respond to it if it occurs. Numerous books, articles, workshops, seminars, and the like proffer information and advice on the perplexing subject. However, virtually all that advice comes from psychologists, physicians, lawyers, and law enforcement personnel. What has been lacking is knowledge that would not only reduce the threat of workplace violence but also enable organizations to develop the core competencies of personnel and productivity that can be achieved when members of the organization feel they can function in a safe, secure environment.

We believe that this book fills that need by offering advice and information from a purely managerial point of view. The managerial point of view is important for even non-managers to understand because it is only through managerial action and decisions that effective control and prevention of workplace violence can occur. Those in consulting, criminal justice, and law enforcement can achieve greater results if they, too, approach workplace violence from a managerial perspective. The authors have spent their careers intimately involved with the practice, teaching, and research on management and organizations and now apply that knowledge and experience to the issue of workplace violence.

The Authors

Dr. David D. Van Fleet, Professor of Management at Arizona State University and an Associate with Professional Business Associates, has over 35 years of experience including full-time graduate and undergraduate teaching experience, extensive editing work, over 200 publications and presentations, numerous officer roles in professional associations, extensive executive education experience, and active consulting both in the United States and abroad. His work focuses on leadership, strategy, workplace violence and terrorism, and management history.

His books include *Contemporary Management, Behavior in Organizations, Military Leadership, Organizational Behavior,* and *Workplace Survival*. He is a past Editor of both the *Journal of Management* and the *Journal of Behavioral and Applied Management*. He has been President of several professional organizations in management. He has been a member of the Board of Governors, Academy of Management, Southwest Federation of Academic Disciplines, and the Southern Management Association; and was national Chair of the Management History Division of the Academy of Management.

Because of the extensiveness of his endeavors, David was named a Fellow of the Academy of Management and a Fellow of the Southern Management Association, and is listed in *Who's Who in America* (5th ed.) and *Who's Who Among America's Teachers* (Vol. V).

Dr. Ella W. Van Fleet, Founder and President of Professional Business Associates, has an impressive background that includes more than 35 years of experience in teaching, training, managing, and consulting, plus three interdisciplinary degrees in Business and Higher Education. She focuses on entrepreneurship and workplace violence and terrorism. Ella moved to Arizona in 1989 after sixteen successful years as a practicing and teaching entrepreneur in Texas for which the Texas House of Representatives passed H.R. No. 746 honoring her for outstanding professional contributions to the State of Texas.

Early in her career, Ella gained a unique perspective on violent behavior while interviewing prison inmates for the U.S. Department of Justice. Then as Associate Director of the Texas Institute for Ventures in New Technology, she managed diverse teams of engineering and business consultants in projects involving a diverse clientele and subcontractors. Under contract to the U.S. Department of Commerce, she gained experience interacting with a variety of business owners. Her consulting with new and expanding businesses has been in strategic planning, marketing, and developing human resources for the future.

Ella was also a founding member of the Board of Governors of the Houston Enterprise Alliance, a member of the International Council of Small Businesses, and a member of the SBA Advisory Council for Region IV. In addition to her research and business experience, she has designed and taught courses and seminars for six different universities in five states. At Texas A&M University, her course in Entrepreneurship won regional and national recognition for creativity and innovation and was also named by the students as the "Best Class at Texas A&M."

In 1991–92, Ella conducted a study of sexual harassment in the workplace. More recently, she has focused her attention on valuing and managing diversity in a changing work force, with special emphasis on workers who differ in age or gender, as well as the problems of workplace violence and terrorism. This latter led to her book (co-authored with David), *Workplace Survival: Dealing with Bad Bosses, Bad Workers, and Bad Jobs*.

Joint Publications

Among their many publications authored individually or with others, the Van Fleets have also authored the following publications together: "Preventing Workplace Violence: The Violence Volcano Metaphor," in the *Journal of Applied Management and Entrepreneurship* (2007); *Workplace Survival: Dealing with Bad Bosses, Bad Workers, and Bad Jobs* (2007, PublishAmerica Press); "Internal Terrorists: The Terrorists Inside Organizations," in the *Journal of Managerial Psychology* (2006); "Closing the Performance Feedback Gap with Expert Systems," in the *Academy of Management Executive* (2005); "How Terrorism

Affects Companies," in the *Scottsdale Airpark News* (2001); "Terrorism and the Workplace: Concepts and Recommendations," in *Dysfunctional Behavior in Organizations* (1998, JAI Press); and *Workplace Violence: Moving Toward Minimizing Risks* (1996), a Project Minerva publication funded by OSHA.

Prologue

Violence in the workplace is not a new phenomenon. It is probably as old as workplaces themselves, but its documentation has been relatively poor and limited primarily to those incidents in which one or more fatalities occurred as necessary or collateral damage in a robbery, usually by someone outside the company. For the most part, documented American experiences started in the late 1970s when American businesspeople were kidnapped in several South American countries and held for sizable ransom payments before being released, which sometimes took years. Then during the 1980s, American citizens working abroad were kidnapped in Lebanon for political purposes. Chained and beaten in the dark, some were murdered while others languished for years.

August 19, 1986, however, marked the first significant incidence of what most people would consider workplace violence. At the U.S. Postal Service in Edmond, OK, postal employee Patrick Henry Sherrill shot 14 former coworkers and himself because of the way he had been disciplined the previous day. This incident seems to have been the beginning of the use of lethal weapons as tools of employer-directed violence in the United States. Suddenly, workplace violence became a problem that could occur anywhere and anytime. After that, no matter how one categorized the incidents, the list began to grow both in the type of violent act and in the type of workplace in which it occurred. By the mid-1990s, the list was getting uncomfortably long. This was especially true in United States Postal Service facilities, where between 1986 and 2001 postal workers and former postal employees "went postal," shooting and killing 39 people at U.S. Postal Service facilities across the country. And the list continued, greatly increasing in the 1990s and spreading to a totally different group of workers in a familiar worksite where violence was once unthinkable: the nation's schools. In addition, the nation suffered through enormously damaging violence committed by foreign terrorists at our workplaces within our country. Then in 2008, as workplaces had became more and more mobile with the advent of portable technology and satellites, one of the oldest forms of workplace violence returned: piracy on the high seas, where man is less in control than when on land.

When, you may ask, is a violent event an act of workplace violence and when is it just another crime? Also, since students are not employees, is violence at any educational level within our school systems a form of workplace violence? The answer is yes and yes. Crimes in the workplace are hazards that can and do cause death or serious physical harm to employees, and schools are workplaces for teachers, administrators, cafeteria workers, janitorial workers, and students.

For many years the Department of Labor's OSHA regulations have required organizations to furnish a place of employment "free from recognized hazards" that may cause death or serious physical harm to employees. In other words, managers and employees need to be proactive in reducing the threat of workplace violence within their organizations. This means that organizations must be prepared for any form of violence and should take actions to reduce the risks of any and all forms of violence that affect workers during the time they are carrying out their duties as employees and at other times if the violence is a result of their being employed at that company. The workers themselves must cooperate and take all possible responsibility themselves to help the company provide this protection. That is what this book is all about.

In this book we expand on the Violence Volcano metaphor introduced in our *Journal of Applied Management and Entrepreneurship* article to illustrate how societal, organizational, and personal pressures build to the point where the individual explodes by performing a violent act. The challenge for management and employees is to recognize the early warning signs, enabling them to stop the volcano from erupting, thus providing a place of employment free from perils that lead to decreased productivity or increased turnover or result in serious physical harm and even death to employees.

PART I
Introduction

1

How Workplace Violence Has Grown

Violence in society at large is not new. After all, incidents of violence are mentioned in The Bible and in ancient hieroglyphics and literature. For centuries piracy by groups of bandits was a familiar form of violence faced by sailors who traveled on the high seas for their employers, far away from their homeland and more helpless to defend themselves on water than on land. Various religious and political groups have frequently resorted to violence—and still do. A larger and more organized group, the Mafia, has been around since its origination in Sicily during the 9th century. Street gangs have been fighting one another for at least 400 years. Earlier in the last century there were instances of violence committed by "The Mob" or other criminal elements in places where people work. However, virtually all of these violent attacks were tabulated as criminal acts, not workplace violence; and they had little direct impact on most citizens in the United States.

Violence in the workplace increased rapidly, however, in the last quarter of the 20th century. Initially it seemed to be an aberration—such an uncommon or far-removed occurrence that, while unfortunate, failed to capture the attention of either managers in organizations or the general public. In the 1970s and 1980s violence events for the most part were still limited to the kidnapping of businessmen in South American countries and holding them for ransom payments from their employers. These were followed by the kidnapping of American citizens in Lebanon for political purposes. Some of those businessmen were tortured and at least three were murdered. Yet the kidnappings did not capture the attention of the American public, either, perhaps because they occurred in foreign countries and involved relatively few workers.

Violence in Organizations

Public and managerial indifference began to change when violence struck closer home in the 1980s and 1990s. To illustrate what was happening, we are highlighting below some of the incidents that occurred in that more recent time period. From 1997 to 2007, for example, the most recent year for which data are available, there were more than 7,000 occupational homicides nationwide, according to the U.S. Bureau of Labor Statistics. Most involved robberies, but more than 1,000 involved work associates. ["Recession fuels worries of U.S. workplace violence," Wed Apr 22, 2009 1:00pm BST: uk.reuters.com/article/marketsNewsUS/idUKN2150174520090422?pageNumber=3].

The following incidents and discussion should not be taken as an inclusive effort to present all of the occurrences of workplace violence. Indeed, we deal exclusively with incidents in the United States or involving U.S.-based organizations and, in addition, we are highlighting only the more violent incidents—those that made headlines in local, if not national, newspapers. There are many other incidents in the rest of the world.

Violent Events in Organizations, 1981–1990

On August 19, 1983, in Johnston, SC, Perry Smith, a former 25-year veteran of the U.S. Postal Service, marched into the facility with a shotgun and began firing at workers, wounding two and killing the local postmaster. Later that year, on December 2, 1983, James Howard Brooks walked into the office of the Anniston, AL postmaster, shot him dead, and then wounded another supervisor. Brooks had been involved in a long dispute with supervisors.

Then in July of 1984, an out-of-work security guard killed 21 people at a McDonald's Restaurant. But Americans began to really pay attention when, in 1984, Denver talk-show host Alan Berg was killed in his driveway because of his on-air comments. The following year, on March 6, 1985, in Atlanta, GA, Steven W. Brownlee opened fire in a mail-sorting area of the main Atlanta post office, killing two fellow employees and wounding a third. Brownlee had worked for the postal service for 12 years. Two months later, in New York City (May 31, 1985), letter carrier David Perez, age 45, pulled a rifle from a mailbag and aimed it at supervisor George Grady. A postal clerk who came to the supervisor's aid was shot and wounded. Perez, who had been suspended several times, held Grady hostage for two hours before surrendering.

And then on August 19, 1986, former Marine Patrick Henry Sherrill shot 17 coworkers and himself at the U.S. Post Office in Edmond, OK. He killed people he knew, not strangers, because of the way he had been disciplined the previous day and threatened with being fired. At that point, violence in the workplace began to take on a different character; it was no longer an aberration.

The list began to grow both in the type of violent act and in the type of workplace in which it occurred. On December 7, 1987, David Burke, fired by USAir for petty theft of in-flight cocktail receipts, followed his boss onto Flight 1771, shot him and then the pilots. This caused the plane to crash in California, killing forty-three people. Two months later, on February 16, 1988, Richard Wade Farley, an ex-employee at ESL Corp. in Sunnyvale, CA killed seven people indiscriminately with a shotgun after he had been terminated for terrorizing a female engineer who had not returned his affection. In June 1988 a clerk in Chelsea, MA killed a co-worker before committing suicide. Six months later, December 1988, a New Orleans mail handler held his ex-girlfriend hostage during a 13-hour siege, killed his supervisor by shooting him in the face, and also wounded four others. Then on December 21, 1988, 250 passengers on Pan Am flight 103 were blown to pieces over Lockerbie, Scotland, by terrorists whose complaints and motives were unknown to the victims—the crew and passengers.

In 1989, the violence continued when on January 17, Patrick Edward Purdy, using a Chinese-made semi-automatic rifle, opened fire on the Cleveland Elementary School schoolyard in Stockton, CA. He fired 106 rounds that killed five and wounded 30 Cambodian immigrant students and one teacher before taking his own life. The victims were unknown to the perpetrator, who disliked members of the Asian race. Two months later, on March 25, 1989, in Poway, CA, 44-year-old letter carrier Donald Mace walked into the post office and killed himself with one 38-caliber shot to his head. Two months later a 42-year-old Boston mail handler and Vietnam vet, Alfred J. Hunter, murdered his ex-wife, then stole a two-seater Cessna airplane and strafed the city's streets with an AK-47 for three hours. Then in early August 1989, postal worker John Taylor in Escondido, CA shot and killed his wife at their home, then drove to the Orange Glen, CA post office, where he shot and killed two colleagues and wounded another before killing himself. In September in Louisville, KY a former employee of a local firm killed eight and wounded 12 others before killing himself.

The following year, on June 18, 1990, a Jacksonville, FL man, whose car had been repossessed by General Motors Acceptance Corp (GMAC), went on a shooting spree, killing 10 GMAC workers and wounding four others before killing himself. Also that year a Merrill Lynch employee in Boston killed the supervisor who had fired him.

By this time workplace violence in the United States was receiving world-wide attention, particularly because incidents were occurring repeatedly in one organization: the U.S. Postal Service. The similar location and modus operandi resulted in the coinage of a new term, "Going Postal," to describe a worker's mental snapping and explosive reaction.

Violent Events in Organizations, 1991–1994

Similar isolated incidents continued to make front-page news. As shown by the following list of the more violent workplace incidents, the pace accelerated in the early 1990s, making workplace violence "a household word":

> *October 11, 1991, Ridgewood, NJ*—Joseph M. Harris, a fired postal worker and 35-year-old Navy veteran, killed a former supervisor and her boyfriend at their home, then went to the Ridgewood NJ post office where he killed two mail handlers as they arrived for work.
>
> *October 16, 1991, Killeen, TX*—George Hennard drove a Ford Ranger pickup truck through the glass front of a Luby's Cafeteria and executed 22 people randomly before shooting himself. He had not worked at Luby's but had lost his job as merchant seaman 2 years previously and half a continent away.
>
> *November 8, 1991, Royal Oak, MI*—At a USPS facility, a 31-year-old letter carrier and former Marine, Thomas McIlvane, hunted down and shot 3 supervisors, then wounded 14 others and killed himself after being dismissed the previous year for insubordination. Another employee indicated that McIlvane had been "needled" to the breaking point.
>
> *May 1, 1992, Oliverhurst, CA*—Hewlett-Packard employee, Eric Houston, who had just been terminated, used a shotgun and a .22-calibre rifle to kill 4 people and wound 10 in a siege at his former high school. He killed people he said had not prepared him well in high school.
>
> *June 3, 1992, Citrus Heights, CA*—A 60-year-old postal worker, Roy Barnes, killed himself in front of co-workers in the post office.

In 1993 the following and other workplace incidents added up to 1,063 homicides (an average of three per day) and more than 22,000 injuries that were serious enough to cause employees to miss work (Toscano & Weber, 1995). The most shocking incident, of course, was the February 26th bombing in New York City:

January 25, 1993, Langle, VA—Two people were murdered and three others seriously injured by a young Pakistani firing an AK-47 assault rifle into cars waiting at a stoplight to enter the grounds of the Central Intelligence Agency headquarters.

January 27, 1993, Tampa, FL—Eight months after being terminated, Pat Calden returned to the office and shot and killed three former managers, wounded 2 others, and killed himself at Fireman's Insurance.

February 26, 1993, New York, NY—Terrorists struck the heart of the largest city in the United States. A truck-bombing in the basement of the World Trade Center resulted in six dead, about 1,000 injured, and millions of dollars in damage. This violent act confirmed our worst fears that someday international terrorists would find their way into our cosmopolitan centers, bringing a new kind of "imported violence" to the workplace.

May 6, 1993, Dearborn, MI—In the garage area of a USPS facility, 45-year-old postal mechanic, Larry Jasion, brought a .38-calibre handgun in a doughnut box to murder a pre-selected co-worker, wound another, and wound his supervisor before killing himself. He had at least 13 guns. He complained about loud music at the plant and was upset that another employee got a job he wanted.

May 6, 1993, Dana Point, CA—At another USPS facility later that same day, fired postal employee, Mark Richard Hilburn, shot two of his fellow workers, one fatally, after having killed his own mother at her home.

July 1, 1993, San Francisco, CA—Gian Luigi Ferri, a 55-year-old businessman and former (10 yrs. before) client of Pettit & Martin Law Firm entered their legal offices on the 34th floor and opened fire, injuring six people and killing eight, plus himself.

December 2, 1993, Oxnard, CA—An unemployed computer engineer killed four and injured four others, at an unemployment center before police fatally shot him.

July 1994, Bethesda, MD—Mark Craft, a hotel security guard, was shot and killed by his superior.

According to Department of Justice reports, in 1994 approximately one million people were victims of violent workplace incidents at work, not including another 2.2 million who experienced theft at work (Bachman,

1994). Altogether, 879,000 assaults, 13,000 rapes, and 80,000 robberies were reported and together on average resulted in five days of missed work per person. These figures do not include the numerous incidents and threats that went unreported, which has been estimated to be more than 50 percent. Incidents that do not result in loss of work time are not required to be reported (BLS, 1996).

Violent Events in Organizations, 1995–2000

The whole nation was surprised on Wednesday, April 19, 1995, when an explosion occurred at 9:02 a.m. outside the Federal Building in Oklahoma City—this time at the hands of someone who neither worked for that organization nor lived in that state. Again, the perpetrator's complaints and motives were unknown to the victims, who included Federal workers, their children, and the general public. That massive workplace killing really directed our attention to the vulnerability of innocent people at work or at play, everywhere—even in the nation's non-cosmopolitan heartland—and at the hands of our own people.

Regardless of how the incidents are categorized, the list continued to grow both in the type of violent act and in the type of workplace in which it occurred. For example, in 1995 assaults and violent actions in the workplace resulted in 1,262 deaths, of which 10 percent were caused by coworkers or former employees. In addition, 45,800 workers reported nonfatal injuries resulting in time away from work (Toscano & Windau, 1996). That same year saw toxic gas released in Japanese subways and a continued rash of attacks on abortion clinics in the United States. Among the shootings and killings that year were the following:

> *April 3, 1995, Corpus Christi, TX*—A former oil refinery employee wounded five workers and then killed himself.
> *April 19, 1995, Oklahoma City, OK*—At 9:02 a.m., Timothy McVey carried out a well-planned bomb explosion outside the Federal Building killing at least 1,168 people, including children.
> *April 27, 1995, Richmond, CA*—A Richmond Housing Authority employee who had been fired from his job returned to shoot and kill a supervisor and a coworker.
> *April 29, 1995, Littleton, CO*—Distraught over marital problems, a man opened fire in a crowded grocery store, killing his wife and two others before he was subdued by a bystander.
> *May 18, 1995, Asheville, NC*—A man who had just been fired from his job at a machine tool company returned and killed three workers and wounded another four before quietly surrendering to police.

June 19, 1995, Los Angeles, CA—Willie Woods, a normally soft-spoken ex-Marine who had a history of good performance as a city worker, at the C. Erwin Piper Technical Center, tracked down, shot, and killed four supervisors after his declining performance had led to unsatisfactory performance evaluations.

July 9, 1995, City of Industry, CA—In a USPS mail processing center, Bruce Clark, a "quiet, unassuming" postal worker who had been on the job for 22 years, pulled a handgun from a paper bag and killed his supervisor.

July 19, 1995, Los Angeles, CA—A 42-year-old city electrician, of 12 years, shot and killed four supervisors when he learned he was facing possible dismissal for poor work performance.

August 17, 1995, Portland, ME—A 46-year old Postal Service project engineer, with 12 years of experience, killed herself by overdosing with her diabetic insulin. Judith Coffin had been unsuccessful in getting postal officials to help with her complaints of harassment by male supervisors and those who worked under her.

August 29, 1995, Palantine, IL—A 53-year-old USPS worker reported to work with a handgun and shot two coworkers.

October 7, 1995, San Jose, CA—A young accountant, on the job for only six weeks, shot and killed his female supervisor, then committed suicide with the same gun, one day after receiving his first performance counseling session.

October 9, 1995, Hyder, AZ—In the early morning hours the twelve-car Amtrak "Sunset Limited," bound from Miami to Los Angeles, derailed outside Phoenix on tracks that had been "tampered with." Of the 248 people on board, one was killed and another 78 were injured.

October 21, 1995, Carmel, IN—A man entered a bank office where his wife worked, shot and killed her, and then committed suicide with the same weapon.

November 19, 1995, Columbus, OH—Jerry Hessler forced his way into at least two homes of former coworkers, fatally shooting four individuals (including a 4-month-old girl) and wounding two others. He had been fired from his job at a bank credit card center in October 1994, following charges of sexual harassment against coworkers.

December 8, 1995, Harlem, NY—Roland Smith, Jr., 51, walked into a Jewish-owned clothing store on West 125th Street, pulled out a gun, ordered all the black customers to leave, spilled paint thinner on several bins of clothing and set them on fire, killing 8 people, including Smith himself. Apparently he had been incited to protest the closure of a Radio Shack store leased to a Black tenant by a Jewish owner.

December 15, 1995, Evendale, OH—Gerald Clemons, 53, returned to the Trans-Continental Systems offices from which he had been recently fired and shot and killed three employees and wounded a fourth.

In 1996, assaults and violent actions resulted in the deaths of 1,144 individuals while at work (BLS, 1997). The violence saga continued in 1997, including at U.S. postal facilities, where a former employee at a Denver postal facility took seven hostages and held them for ten hours on December 24, 1997. A few other events during those two years included:

January 3, 1996, Clearwater, FL—A 52 year-old secretary shot, but did not kill the company's president after being terminated.

April 24, 1996, Jackson, MS—A disgruntled firefighter killed four superiors.

July 27, 1996, Atlanta, GA—A pipe bomb exploded at the Olympics, killing one person, causing another to die of a heart attack, and injuring over 100 others.

August 29, 1996, Palatine, IL—Dorsey Thomas, a 23-year-old mail clerk veteran, suddenly shot and killed two coworkers with whom he supposedly had a good working relationship.

June 5, 1997, Santa Fe Springs, CA—Following an argument with co-workers, Daniel Marsden, got a gun from his car at Omni Plastics and returned to fatally shoot two co-workers, wound four others, and then kill himself

September 1, 1997, Miami Beach, FL—A 64-year-old postal employee with 20 years of service shot his ex-wife, a friend, and then himself in the post office.

September 1, 1997, Aiken, SC—A 38-year-old, fired worker, killed four.

September 15, 1997, Aikens County, GA—After telling a security guard that he "had work to do," an individual wounded the security guard, then went into the plant and killed four people and injured two others.

October 7, 1997, San Antonio, TX—Charles Lee White killed two employees and himself at a paging company where his ex-girlfriend worked.

December 1, 1997, Milwaukee, WI—A 37-year-old employee, angry about being turned down for a schedule change, wounded two and killed another before killing himself.

December 1, 1997, Orange, CA—A former maintenance yard employee killed four others before police killed him.

December 3, 1997, Barstow, FL—Three employees at Erie Manufacturing were killed.

December 18, 1997, Orange, CA—A shipyard worker killed four workers before being killed by police.

December 18, 1997, Milwaukee, WI—While on the job, postal worker Anthony DeCulit, age 37, suddenly shot his supervisor in the eye, killed another postal worker, wounded still another, and then shot himself in the mouth.

December 24, 1997, Denver, CO—A former postal employee, David Jackson, entered the Denver General Mail Facility with a weapon, taking seven postal employees hostage for 10 hours before surrendering.

Violence in the workplace continued throughout 1998–2000 and included a variety of workplaces and relationships. For example:

March 1, 1998, Connecticut— A 35 year-old employee killed four supervisors and then himself.

April 1, 1998, Dallas, TX—A postal worker killed a co-worker.

June 1, 1998, Washington, DC—Two policemen at the U.S. Capitol were killed.

October 6, 1998, Riverside, CA—Former Air Force sergeant and 49-year-old letter carrier, Joseph L. Neale, Jr., shot and wounded the mayor, two councilmen, and three police officers. Neale allegedly snapped under the strain of working two jobs to earn a decent living.

January 14, 1999, Salt Lake City, UT—An employee killed one and wounded another.

March 6, 1999, Newington, CT—A lottery workers killed four other workers before killing himself.

March 15, 1999, Johnson City, TN—A man killed a lawyer and a client in a dispute over his ex-wife's will.

April 15, 1999, Salt Lake City, UT—A 71 year-old killed two and wounded four others at the Mormon library before being killed by police.

June 1, 1999, MI—A mental patient killed his doctor and another patient and wounded four others before killing himself.

July 11, 1999, Southfield, MI—Joseph Brooks, Jr. killed two, wounded four others, and then killed himself at his former psychiatrist's clinic.

July 29, 1999, Atlanta, GA—Mark Barton, a day trader who became angry after losing a great deal of money, went on a rampage, slaying nine workers and wounding twelve more in two brokerage firms after killing his own family.

August 5, 1999, Pelham, AL—A delivery truck driver shot and killed two coworkers at a heating and air conditioning company, then drove to the site of his previous job and killed a third person.

September 1, 1999, Fort Worth, TX—After virtually destroying his family's house, Larry Gene Ashbrook burst into Wedgwood Baptist Church, shot and killed seven worshipers, wounded seven others, then killed himself.

***November 2, 1999, Honolulu, HI**—*A Xerox Corp. copier repairman shot and killed seven coworkers at a Xerox warehouse.

***November 3, 1999, Seattle, WA**—*A former employee of Northlake Shipyard shot and killed two men and wounded two others at his former workplace in downtown Seattle. He was reportedly angry over terminated disability benefits.

***December 30, 1999, Tampa, FL**—* A hotel employee opened fire at Radisson Bay Harbor hotel, killing five coworkers there and another person in an attempted carjacking.

***February 1, 2000, Pittsburgh, PA**—*Three people were killed and four others wounded at a McDonald's restaurant.

***March 8, 2000, Memphis, TN**—*A man killed a women, set the house on fire, and then killed three and wounded two firefighters as they attempt to control the fire.

***March 20, 2000, Irving, TX**—*Three days after being fired for exposing himself to two women, Robert Wayne Harris entered his former place of employment, a car wash, and began shooting co-workers. Five people were killed during the shooting.

***April, 2000, Pittsburgh, PA**—*Five were killed and two were wounded in two synagogues and a minority-owned business.

***April, 2000, Sandy, UT**—*At Chevy's Restaurant a 21 year-old went on a shooting spree, killing two and wounding three.

***April 18, 2000, Lincoln Park, MI**—*At a retirement center two people were killed and another wounded by a retired country music singer and guitar player who had been accused of sexual harassment by two of the residents.

***April 25, 2000, Washington, DC**—*A feud between 11–16-year-olds at the National **Zoo** ended with one boy wounding six youngsters, leaving one of them brain dead.

***May 25, 2000, New York City**—*A Wendy's ex-employee killed five and wounded two others.

***June 12, 2000, Florence, AL**—*Three workers were shot by a fellow employee.

***December 26, 2000, Wakefield, MA**—*Brandishing a .12 gauge shotgun and a semiautomatic rifle, a 42-year-old software tester opened fire at the Edgewater Technology firm, killing seven. Michael McDermott supposedly snapped because the company planned to attach his wages to collect back income taxes he owed.

Violent Events in Organizations, 2001–2005

The real wakeup call came when the workplace and American national security found themselves jointly vulnerable. On September 11, 2001, the whole world witnessed society's worst case of workplace violence as terrorists took the lives of thousands of workers in their office buildings in multiple locations, or in jet planes en route to and from their workplaces. Again, the victims did not know the perpetrators, who were terrorists from outside the country. Military personnel and government employees were no longer the sole targets of people who were anti-American. The lives and the responsibilities were changed forever—Government officials, first responders, managers and workers, and citizens in general. Everyone had now been touched; nowhere, not even our schools (more on this later) and workplaces, could promise a safe harbor.

In the nine months (September-May) following the 9–11 terrorist attack, at least 18 separate workplace violence incidents occurred across the nation resulting in the deaths of 34 people and the wounding of 23. Some of those incidents along with others that made the front pages of newspapers in 2001–2005 are listed below:

January 1, 2001, Houston, TX—A man killed five at a wholesale distributor because they sold to one of his competitors.

January 26, 2001, Jackson, MS—At a daycare center, a man killed his girlfriend and was then killed by the girlfriend's teenage son.

February 5, 2001, Chicago, IL—At a Navistar International engine plant, 66-year-old William D. Baker shot and killed four people and wounded four others before killing himself. Terminated seven years earlier for attempted theft, this former employee forced his way past security with a golf bag full of weapons.

June 23, 2001, Lansing, MI—The wife of a state trooper was killed by the single shot of an unknown sniper who was hidden in the woods near the zoo.

July 23, 2001, Palm Beach Gardens, FL—Construction worker Keith Adams walked to his truck, pulled out an AK-47 machine gun and killed two coworkers. Police recovered more than 80 live rounds from the truck.

September 11, 2001, New York, Washington, and Pennsylvania—In this country's worst act of violence to date, in New York City, the Pentagon, and Pennsylvania, terrorists took the lives of more than 3,000 people in high-rise buildings and aboard airplanes en route to and from their workplaces.

September 12, 2001, Denver, CO—A distraught fire department officer allegedly gunned down his supervisor before turning the gun on himself.

September 26, 2001, Detroit, MI—A man killed his former girlfriend and then turned the gun on himself at an automobile parts company.

November 5, 2001, Tallahassee, FL—A fire department supervisor shot and wounded a fellow employee in a love triangle situation.

December 6, 2001, Goshen, IN—Robert Wissman killed one co-worker and wounded six before taking his own life at the Nu-Wood factory.

January 3, 2002, Addison, TX—A worker killed a female co-worker.

January 18, 2002, Ft. Lauderdale, FL—A man shot dead his ex-girlfriend and killed himself at Broward Community College near Ft. Lauderdale.

January 26, 2002, Pittsburgh, PA—In a restaurant shooting, three were killed, including a man in a wheelchair and an 8-year-old girl.

February 5, 2002, Mobile, AL—A mailroom worker at a newspaper office shot a fellow employee to death and fled, but was later caught.

March 1, 2002, Silicon Valley, CA—A worker at a Silicon Valley biotech company shot and killed his former boss, then turned the gun on himself.

March 22, 2002, Southbend, IN—A factory worker killed four others and later himself after wounding two police officers on a high-speed chase.

April 19, 2002, Miami Beach, FL—A fired temporary worker returned to a construction site and shot his former supervisor in the chest with a spear gun.

May 29, 2002, Milwaukee, WI—A 20-year old defendant in a criminal case grabbed a bailiff's gun and wounded the bailiff before being shot to death by a plain-clothes police officer.

September 16, 2002, New York, NY—An insurance executive called two employees into his office, shot and killed both of them and himself. Police found two semi-automatic handguns (a .9mm and a .45 caliber) as well as another gun in his office.

September 24, 2002, Indianapolis, IN—A police officer at Butler University was shot and killed while responding to a report of a disruptive stranger on campus.

February 25, 2003, Huntsville, AL—An employee shot and killed four people at Labor Ready Inc., a temporary employment service. A fifth person was wounded.

June 29, 2003, Irvine, CA—A bagger at Albertsons Grocery used a sword to kill two people and injure three others before being fatally shot by the police.

July 1, 2003, Jefferson City, MO—An employee at the Modine Manufacturing Co. used a semiautomatic pistol to kill 3 co-workers and wound 5 others. He then drove to the local police station, where he exchanged fire with an officer and shot himself to death in front of the police station.

July 8, 2003, Meridian, MS—A worker at the Lockheed Martin aircraft parts plant attended an annual ethics training class at the plant, then shot and killed six coworkers and wounded eight others before killing himself.

July 23, 2003, San Antonio, TX—A man walked into his real estate office and tried to kill his supervisor, fatally shot his closest competitor plus another woman he had not intended to kill, then later shot himself in the head. Police indicated that the man was known as a control freak who did not like having female peers or competitors, and had very different personal and public personas.

July 28, 2003, Boynton Beach, FL—A worker at the Golf Leaf Nursery used a semiautomatic weapon to kill his estranged wife and two other employees, and then killed the man with whom he believed his wife was having an affair.

August 19, 2003, Andover, OH—Armed with four handguns, an angry 32-year-old employee at an automotive injection molding plant shot and killed a co-worker, then wounded two others before killing himself.

August 27, 2003, Chicago, IL—A former employee shot and killed the two owners and four employees of the auto parts warehouse from which he had been fired 6 months earlier for absenteeism and causing trouble at work. He had been arrested dozens of times for weapons violations and beating his girlfriends.

November 4, 2003, Fort Pierce, FL—Aaron Anderson, a mentally challenged male with an IQ of 67, walked into a church service at the End Time Tabernacle Church and shot Rev. Benjamin Mobley in the chest with a handgun, shouting "You took my wife!"

November 6, 2003, West Chester, OH—Former employee Tom West went on a shooting rampage at the Watkins Motor Lines Trucking Company, killing two people and wounding three others.

November 10, 2003, Riviera Beach, FL—Fred Keller shot and killed his fifth ex-wife and attempted to kill her brother at the Riviera Beach office of Keller Trust Co..

February 2, 2004, Pleasant Grove, UT—A week after being suspended for violating company policy, Louis Darrell Kinyon chased his co-workers with a handgun, fatally shot his supervisor, and then shot himself.

January 29, 2004, Seminole, FL—James A. Webb killed two plus himself and wounded one other at a real estate office from which his longtime girlfriend was fired.

July 3, 2004, Kansas City, KS—In a 10-minute rampage, a 21-year-old ConAgra meat-packing plant worker used two handguns to shoot seven co-workers, killing five of them, before killing himself. The killings were not random, as the worker passed by some co-workers, telling them, "You haven't done anything to me, so you can go."

February 18, 2005, Romulus, MI—Gustabo DeJesus Vanegas returned to the International Paper Co. plant to shoot the supervisor who just fired him. In the process, Vanegas fatally shot a coworker who tried to translate for him.

February 21, 2005, Pascagoula, MS—An angry employee at Northup Grumman shipyard opened fire with a Smith & Wesson 9 mm handgun, shooting two supervisors.

February 25, 2005, Los Angeles, CA—A city worker killed another employee and then himself after being reprimanded.

May 5, 2005, Houston, TX—A lawyer working for an oil-services company walked into an office armed with two handguns and shot a co-worker to death before turning the gun on himself.

May 9, 2005, San Francisco, CA—A year after being fired from a mental health center, Gregory Gray returned to his former place of employment armed with a shotgun and killed one employee before others could take him down.

September 16, 2005, Oak Lawn, IL—After a work-related dispute, a restaurant employee entered the back door of the restaurant and shot and killed two of his coworkers.

September 27, 2005, New Windsor, NY—A former employee, fired after he was arrested on child pornography charges, returned and shot the two co-owners and a manager at the factory where he worked, then killed himself.

November 23, 2005, Glen Burnie, MD—A truck driver who had been fired a few weeks earlier returned to the H&M Wagner food distribution business and shot two supervisors before killing himself with a .38 caliber handgun.

Violent Events in Organizations, 2006–2009

Unfortunately, incidents of workplace violence did not cease. In a study reported by the Bureau of Labor Statistics in November 2006, half of all employers with 1,000 or employees in the United States, more than 28 percent of respondents with 250 to 999 employees, and 5 percent of all establishments including state and local governments, had an incident of workplace violence within the 12 months prior to completing a new survey on workplace violence prevention. [hr.blr.com/news.aspx?id=19318] A sampling of the violent workplace incidents in 2006 and later includes the following:

January 30, 2006, Goleta, CA—Jennifer Sanmarco, a 44-year-old former postal worker who had been discharged three years earlier as being unfit for duty, returned to Goleta and shot her neighbor, then drove to her former worksite and shot six postal workers before killing herself.

April 4, 2006, Baker City, OR—Feeling harassed by his supervisor, 41-year-old Grant Gallaher, a letter carrier with 18 years of service, ran over his supervisor in the parking lot, searched unsuccessfully for the postmaster, then returned to the parking lot and shot the supervisor's body several times.

April 18, 2006, St. Louis, MO—After raping a woman and killing another at separate non-work locations, Herbert Chalmers, Jr. shot two people and then himself at his place of employment, Finninger's Catering. Chalmers apparently went on the rampage because he was being charged too much for child support.

April 21, 2006, Pine Bluff, AR—Two weeks after Tyson Foods Inc. suspended him from his job, Julian English returned to the poultry processing plant with two pistols and shot and seriously wounded a co-worker.

June 25, 2006, Denver, CO—At a Safeway warehouse, a gunman killed one person, wounded five others, and set several fires before being killed by police.

January 11, 2007, Indianapolis, IN—At 6:30 a.m. an employee brought a semiautomatic handgun into Crossroads Industrial Services, a company employing mostly people with disabilities, and shot three people in the cafeteria plus one in an office. The gunman, who was on medication for bipolar disorder, said that his shooting of the three production workers and an office manager was "over respect."

February 12, 2007, Salt Lake City, UT—Eighteen-year-old Sulejman Talović began a deadly shooting spree in Trolley Square shopping area, resulting in the wounding of four persons plus the deaths of five bystanders. He was then killed by the police. No motive for his actions was known.

February 14, 2007, Houston, TX—A warehouse worker at Service Wire Co. entered the break room and fatally shot a co-worker's husband who was waiting for his wife. Co-workers restrained him until police arrived. Police found two other ammunition magazines at the scene.

March 5, 2007, Signal Hill, CA—Three employees at a menu printing company were injured when an employee opened fire because his hours at the plant had recently been reduced to zero. He then killed himself with the 9mm Beretta semiautomatic gun as a SWAT team entered the building.

March 9, 2007, Miami, FL—A man walked into the back offices of the company where his former girlfriend worked, shooting at her repeatedly while chasing her through the cubicles. He then turned the gun on himself, but the semiautomatic handgun was empty.

April 2, 2007, Atlanta, GA—A woman at work was killed by her former boyfriend.

April 9, 2007, Troy, MI—A terminated accountant killed one person and wounded two others.

April 20, 2007, Houston, TX—William Phillips, an employee of NASA contractor Jacobs Engineering, requested a meeting with his superior about his performance review, then brought his new .38-caliber revolver and shot the superior and another person. He then duct-taped a female employee to a chair and held her hostage for three hours before killing himself.

April 27, 2007, Santa Cruz, CA—An employee of the Lode Street Wastewater Facility entered the administrative building, killed his estranged wife and a supervisor, then killed himself.

Spring 2007, Hollywood, FL—Arriving at work with a fully loaded AK-47 assault rifle in the trunk of his car, a disgruntled employee warned his co-workers at the BrandsMart USA warehouse that he would "take them out" if anyone "messed" with him. The employee was escorted off the premises and fired because BrandsMart has a company policy prohibiting guns on the premises, including inside cars.

August 30, 2007, Bronx, NY—A man walked into his former workplace and opened fire, killing his ex-supervisor and shooting two other workers. He tried to shoot other employees but reportedly ran out of bullets.

September 10, 2007, Sheboygan, MI—A former employee killed a coworker and then himself at a Rockline Industries manufacturing plant.

October 5, 2007, Alexandria, LA—John Ashley, a retired Alexandria Public Works employee who witnesses said has been depressed the past few years, took several hostages at a downtown law office, killed one attorney and a USPS mail carrier, and shot three other employees before being shot by the police after an all-night standoff.

October 9, 2007, Simi Valley, CA—A gunman burst into a tire shop at 7:30 a.m., killed a female customer, wounded the manager plus one employee, then killed himself.

October 11, 2007, Phoenix, AZ—An argument between two employees at a bakery escalated to the point where one employee walked out of the bakery, returned with a firearm, and shot the other employee several times before running away.

December 9, 2007, Colorado Springs and Arvada, CO—Two people were killed at the New Life Church in Colorado Springs and two others at a training school in Arvada. The gunman then killed himself.

December 19, 2007, Jackson, MS—An argument between two employees at an engineering company triggered one man to walk out to the parking lot, retrieve a gun he kept in his car, return to the building, and shoot the other employee.

January 12, 2008, Baltimore, MD—In a discussion with the supervisor about not being hired by the asphalt company, an applicant became angry, took out a revolver, and shot the supervisor in the leg.

March 3, 2008, West Palm Beach, FL—A well-dressed gunman opened fire inside a Wendy's during lunchtime, killing a firefighter who'd gone back to fetch his child's toy and wounding five other diners before killing himself.

March 12, 2008, McComb, MS—Robert Lanham killed two people, his ex-wife, and then himself at the bank where his ex-wife worked.

March 18, 2008, Santa Maria, CA—Lee Leeds entered the family-owned auto salvage yard and shot and killed his father, two coworkers, and a customer.

March 27, 2008, Columbus, GA—Bearing a grudge over his mother's treatment at the hospital where she died of natural causes, a retired school teacher fatally shot one of her nurses, another employee, and a man outside before police shot him.

April 1, 2008, Louisburg, NC—Jarold Obrien Lee, 26, on probation for a 2006 residential burglary conviction, entered Phelps Temporary Staffing Service and shot two women in a domestic-related event, then killed himself.

April 1, 2008, Chester, VA—A personal argument at the 7:00 a.m. shift change at Pre Con Industrial ended with one employee dead in the parking lot.

April 1, 2008, Randolph, MA—At Alloy Fabricators of New England, 48-year-old Howard Trang shot a coworker, then killed himself.

April 4, 2008, San Antonio, TX—A man upset with his wife's care shot and killed her doctor outside her medical office.

April 30, 2008, Chicago, IL—At the O&G Spring & Wire Form Specialty Company, an older man quarreled with a coworker, then left the factory and returned with his sons, one of whom shot the victim fatally in the head.

June 24, 2008, Henderson, KY—A disgruntled 25-year-old worker shot his supervisor outside the plastics plant where he worked, then went inside and shot five other co-workers before taking his own life.

June 25, 2008, Henderson, KY—After an argument with his supervisor about wearing safety goggles, an angry 25-year-old employee opened fire at Atlantis Plastics, fatally shooting a supervisor and four others before committing suicide.

August 1, 2008, Bristol, PA—Robert Diamond, 32, killed two co-workers outside a Simon & Schuster warehouse. Diamond told authorities he was upset about getting a severe reprimand in March for calling a black coworker "boy" and more recently at being harassed by coworkers.

August 22, 2008, Niagara, NY—William P. Rosati, acting supervisor at the Niagara Maintenance Contracting Corp., shot into the floor, the wall, a briefcase, a desk, and a water cooler, then pointed a gun at a co-worker. Rosati reportedly had been drinking but was not upset or angry at anyone.

November 14, 2008, Santa Clara, CA—Engineer Jing Hua Wu, 47, requested a meeting with SiPort Company officials about his recent layoff. During that meeting he shot and killed the chief operating officer and two other officers of the 4-year-old semiconductor start-up company.

January 29, 2009, Cambridge, MA—After several months of arguing, custodian Clyde Howard chased, fired several shots, and killed a male coworker at Baystate Pool Supplies.

February 17, 2009, Lakeland, FL—In an attempted murder-suicide in the parking lot of a Publix fresh produce plant, one male worker attempted to kill a coworker before shooting and killing himself.

March 10, 2009, Samson, AL—Michael McLendon, 28, shot and killed 10 people, including five family members, before taking his own life at a metals plant where he formerly worked.

March 21, 2009, Oakland, CA—Four police officers were killed by convicted felon Lovelle Mixon, 26, after a routine traffic stop revealed he was wanted for parole violation. Mixon, who worked sporadically as a plumber and custodian, was killed in a barrage of gunfire with other officers.

March 29, 2009, Carthage, NC—Robert Stewart went to Pinelake Health and Rehab Center to kill his recently estranged wife, but instead shot and killed seven residents and a nurse before a police officer shot him.

April 3, 2009, Binghamton, NY—Jiverly Voong aka Jiverly Wong shot 18 people, killing 14, in a three-minute shooting spree at a civic association building that caters to immigrants. His suicide note indicated he felt persecuted by law enforcement.

April 4, 2009, Pittsburgh, PA—Three police officers were killed and another two wounded when 23-year-old Richard Poplawski opened fire on them as they responded to a 911 call. Friends said that the gunman was upset about losing his job recently.

Violence in Education

During these years workplace violence gradually spread to a totally different group of workers in a worksite that had always been considered safe: the nation's schools. The earliest and by far the deadliest incident of school violence happened as far back as 1927 in Bath Township, MI. A disgruntled member of the Bath school board, Andrew Kehoe, shot and killed seven adults and 38 children (www.schoolviolenceresources.com/). Another early incident of a school shooting was by a young student on January 29, 1979, at Cleveland Elementary School in San Carlos, CA (San Diego County). In that case, 16-year-old Brenda Spencer stood inside her home across the street from the school and fired a .22 rifle to kill her principal and the head custodian in addition to wounding nine others. The reason she gave was that she didn't like Mondays.

Unfortunately, the violence at the school workplace took a sudden turn in the 1980s and 1990s. "From 1992 to 2001, 35 incidents occurred in which students showed up at their school or at a school-sponsored event and started shooting at their schoolmates and teachers. These incidents left 53 people dead and 144 injured" (Moore, Petrie, Braga, & McLaughlin, 2003). While some have suggested that school violence is on the decline, recent data suggests otherwise, noting that from 1996 to 2008 at least 44 schools had school shootings (www.cdc.gov/yrbss). There appeared to be a decrease from 2001–2005, but from 2006–2008 13 schools witnessed a shooting and 2008 saw an increase in shootings over the previous seven years (www.cdc.gov/yrbss). As shown in Table 1.1, school-related deaths reached almost 300 in the ten-year period from 1999 to 2009.

TABLE 1.1 School-Associated Violent Death Summary Data

School Year	Total Deaths
2008–2009[a]	12
2007–2008	16
2006–2007	32
2005–2006	27
2004–2005	39
2003–2004	49
2002–2003	16
2001–2002	17
2000–2001	31
1999–2000	33
Total:	**272**

[a] (8/1/08 to 7/31/2009)
Source: Trump, K.S. (2009). *School Associated Violent Deaths and School Shootings.* Cleveland, OH: National School Safety and Security Services (www.schoolsecurity.org)

Below are some examples of incidents from 1989 to 2009, including the first multiple school shooting in Jonesboro, AR (1998), the infamous Columbine, CO incident of 1999, and the Virginia Tech Massacre of 2007. Please note that this list excludes most school shootings that involve only student-to-student confrontations—of which there were at least 65 such incidents between August and December 2003 alone, and the trend appears to continue.

Violent Events in Education, 1989–1999

January 17, 1989, Stockton, CA—A 24 year-old killed five children, wounded 29 other children and a teacher, and then killed himself.

May 1, 1992, Oliverhurst, CA—Armed with a semiautomatic weapon, 20-year-old Eric Houston killed four people and wounded 10 in an armed siege at his former high school in retribution for a failing grade.

January 18, 1993, Grayson, KY—Scott Pennington, 17, walked into an English class at Carter High School, shot the teacher in the head, and then shot the janitor.

October 12, 1995, Blackville, SC—A high school teacher was left dead and a second critically wounded after an expelled student returned to the school building and starting shooting before turning the gun on himself.

February 2, 1996, Moses Lake, WA—A 14-year-old freshman, Barry Loukaitis, opened fire on his algebra class at Frontier Junior High School. Armed with a hunting rifle, two handguns and 78 rounds of ammunition, he killed a teacher and two students and wounded another student.

February 19, 1997, Bethel, AK—A 16-year-old student, Evan Ramsey, armed with a shotgun, killed the principal and a student and wounded two other students at Bethel High School.

October 2, 1997, Pearl, MI—After stabbing his mother to death, 16-year-old, Luke Woodham wounded seven students with a .30-.30 rifle and killed two at Pearl High School.

December 1, 1997, West Paducah, KY—A 14-year-old freshman, Michael Carneal, killed three students and wounded five others at Heath High School as they participated in a prayer circle before school.

December 15, 1997, Stamps, AR—Teenage sniper, Colt Todd, 14, hid in the woods and shot two students as they stood in the parking lot at Stamps High School because he was tired of being picked on.

March 24, 1998, Jonesboro, AR—Two boys, Mitchell Johnson (13), and Andrew Golden (11), set off a fire alarm, then hid in the woods in camouflage clothing and fired upon students and faculty of Westside Middle School as they evacuated outside,. They killed four and wounded ten others.

April 24, 1998, Edinboro, PA—A 14-year-old student at James W. Parker School, Andrew Wurst, shot and killed John Gillette, the science teacher who had organized the student dance where the incident occurred.

May 21, 1998, Springfield, OR—After killing his parents, 15-year-old Kip Kinkel shot and killed two students and wounded 24 others at Thurston High. He had been arrested and expelled the previous day for bringing a gun to school.

June 15, 1998, Richmond, VA—A 14-year-old male freshman at Armstrong High School wounded one teacher and one guidance counselor in the school hallway.

April 20, 1999, Littleton, CO—At Columbine High School, Eric Harris (18) and Dylan Klebold (17), killed 12 students and a teacher and wounded 23 others before killing themselves in a long and bloody rampage that stirred the entire nation.

May 20, 1999, Conyers, GA—A 15-year-old sophomore, Thomas "T.J." Solomon Jr., armed with a handgun and a .22 rifle shot and wounded six students at Heritage High School.

September 1, 1999, Los Angeles, CA—A man shot and wounded five children at a Jewish Community Center school before killing a mail carrier on a nearby street.

November 19, 1999, Deming, NM—A 12-year-old 7th grader, Victor Cordova Jr., killed one student when he brought guns to Deming Middle School to "make history blasting this school."

December 6, 1999, Fort Gibson, OK—Armed with his father's 9mm semiautomatic handgun, a 13-year-old boy walked out to a tree and opened fire on his classmates at Fort Gibson Middle School, wounding four.

Violent Events in Education, 2000–2004

By the year 2000, violence in our schools had become a national problem that had parents and students everywhere feeling that any educational institution was now just another unprotected site in our daily world—or maybe even the most vulnerable of places since the participants were "housed" in relatively large numbers in classrooms and school events.

February 29, 2000, Mount Morris Township, MI—Taking a handgun from his pants pocket, a 6-year-old boy shot and killed a 6-year-old girl at Buell Elementary School.

March 24, 2000, Lisbon, OH—A 12-year-old student took his teacher and classmates hostage before being disarmed by another teacher at McKinley Elementary School.

May 26, 2000, Lake Worth, FL—After having been sent home the previous day for disrupting class, a 13-year-old student at Lake Worth Middle School shot and killed his popular male teacher on the last day of school.

July 23, 2000, Glendale, CA—A 15-year-old boy was charged with bludgeoning to death two boys whose bodies were found on an elementary school lawn.

August 21, 2000, Mesa, AZ—A Mesa High junior was caught with an unloaded, holstered gun which he brought to school for protection because he heard that other students planned to beat him up.

August 28, 2000, Fayetteville, AR—James E. Kelly, a 36-year-old graduate student recently dropped from a doctoral program, shot and killed the professor overseeing his work before killing himself.

October 24, 2000, Glendale, AZ—Reportedly upset with his home life, a teenage former student with a 9mm handgun held a teacher and 32 students hostage for an hour before surrendering at Pioneer Elementary School.

January 31, 2001, Cupertino, CA—A 19-year-old was arrested in a plot to plant bombs on the De Anza Community College campus.

February 2, 2001, Detroit, MI—Two students and a teacher at Osborn High School were grazed by gunfire that came from off-campus.

February 2, 2001, York, PA—A man wielding a bat and a machete attacked the principal, two teachers, and five students at Winterstown Elementary School.

February 6, 2001, Hoyt, KS—Three high school students were arrested in a plot to bomb their school.

February 8, 2001, Fort Collins, CO—Two teenagers were arrested in a plot to bomb their school and attack students on the anniversary of the Columbine attack.

February 15, 2001, Littleton, NJ—Two 14-year-olds were arrested after bringing a pipe bomb to school.

March 4, 2001, Santee, CA—A 15-year-old freshman killed at least two students and injured 13 others, including a security guard, at Santana High School.

March 7, 2001, Williamsport, PA—An 8th-grade girl at a Roman Catholic school, Bishop Neumann Junior-Senior High, shot another 8th-grade girl because of repeated teasing.

March 25, 2001, El Cajon, CA—After being rejected when he tried to enlist in the U.S. Navy, high school senior Jason Hoffman, 18, tried to murder his Granite Hills High School principal, then shot three students and two teachers before being wounded by a police officer.

July 30, 2001, Los Angeles, CA—An off-duty police officer was shot while acting as a security guard for summer school classes.

October 17, 2001, New Bedford, MA—Modeling after Columbine, three teen-age boys plotted to kill faculty and students at New Bedford High School. They were charged with conspiracy to commit murder, conspiracy to commit assault and battery with a dangerous weapon, and possession of ammunition.

December 5, 2001, Springfield, MA—A teacher was stabbed to death by a student who was angry after being told to remove the hood from his coat during class.

January 11, 2002, Raymond, MS—A 17-year-old suspended student returned to school and held the principal and assistant principal at gunpoint for about three hours. He released the hostages unharmed after talking with police negotiators.

January 16, 2002, Grundy, VA—A 43-year-old foreign exchange student opened fire with a .380 semiautomatic handgun at the Appalachian School of Law, killing the Dean, another professor, and one student, and wounding three other students. The failing student had been dismissed from law school.

February 2, 2002, Zanesville, OH—A school employee shot a school bus driver and then killed himself.

April 30, 2002, Villisca, IA—A 15 year-old was arrested for plotting to spike the punch with poison at the Villisca High School prom.

October 28, 2002, Tucson, AZ—A 41-year-old male student who was flunking out of the University of Arizona nursing school shot three of his professors to death in their classrooms, then killed himself.

April 7, 2003, Natchitoches, LA—A student who had stopped attending classes at Louisiana Technical College opened fire in a classroom, killing one student and wounding another.

April 14, 2003, New Orleans, LA—In a gang-related shooting by four non-student teenagers, one 15-year-old student was killed and three students were wounded by gunfire at John McDonogh High School.

April 24, 2003, Red Lion, PA—A 14-year-old student armed with several handguns shot and killed his principal before shooting himself at Red Lion Area Junior High.

September 17, 2003, Dyersburg, TN—Student Harold Kilpatrick Jr. was shot and killed after he took a dozen people hostage, including a teacher, at Dyersburg State Community College.

September 22, 2003, Spokane, WA—Armed with a 9mm handgun, a distraught 16-year-old student shot a hole in the wall of his science classroom at Lewis and Clark High School and demanded that the teacher and students leave the room. A Rapid Response plan and a statewide crisis plan enabled the school to evacuate the entire school and avoid injuries except to the armed student.

September 26, 2003, Cold Spring, MN—Fifteen-year-old John Jason McLaughlin of Rocori High School killed two other students who had teased him about his acne problem.

October 1, 2003, Sacramento, CA—Mario Rodriguez, 19, used a shotgun and a handgun to hold an administrator hostage until he was taken down by local law enforcement at Rio Cazadero Alternative High School.

January 27, 2004, San Jose, CA—A 15-year-old male high school student was stabbed and killed on the way to school by another 20-year-old male, in a gang-related incident.

February 3, 2004, Palmetto Bay, FL—A 14-year-old Miami-Dade Middle School male student bled to death in a second-floor restroom after being cut with a sharp object around 8:30am. A 14-year-old fellow student was charged.

February 20, 2004, St. Martinville, LA—A 41-year-old part-time city police officer and school custodian at a city junior high school, allegedly called his 19-year-old girlfriend outside of her father's church and school where she worked, then shot her to death just feet from the school full of children.

March 29, 2004, Pharr, TX—A 15-year-old female student was stabbed to death at PSJA High School around 7:30 p.m. A 16-year-old male was taken into custody.

May 24, 2004, Salt Lake City, UT—A 39-year-old female high school cafeteria worker was shot in the chest and head as she walked in the faculty parking lot at the school around 6:00 am. Her 52-year-old estranged husband then shot and killed himself.

June 25, 2004, Omaha, NE—A 16-year-old female special-needs student died after reportedly being jumped and beaten by a group of females in the parking lot after she left a Burger King, where she had gone for lunch during summer school. The victim had reportedly been the victim of bullying and harassment during the school year and the school had taken action upon the report of such activity.

Violent Events in Education, 2005–2009

The number of major incidents in our schools seemed to be heading downward in 2006 and 2007 but increased markedly in 2008.

March 2, 2005, Cumberland City, TN—A 14-year-old boy who allegedly had been reported for chewing tobacco on a school bus was charged with first-degree murder for the shooting death of a 47-year-old female school bus driver. None of the students on the bus was injured.

March 21, 2005, Red Lake, MN—After killing his grandparents, 17-year-old Jeff Weise killed seven people at Red Lake Senior High School, including a principal and a security guard, and injured more than a dozen others before committing suicide.

July 24, 2005, Brownsville, TX—A 15-year-old male was beaten to death near the track area of Lopez High School. Two teen suspects, ages 17 and 18, were subsequently acquitted of the crime but a third pled guilty to attempted murder.

October 26, 2005, Moulton, AL—A 55-year-old female 1st-grade teacher at a Head Start facility was beaten by a 15-year-old 8th-grade student. She subsequently died of her injuries.

November 8, 2005, Jacksboro, TN—A 15-year-old student, Kenneth Bartley Jr., shot the principal and two assistant principals with a .22-calibre handgun at Campbell County Comprehensive High School.

May 5, 2006, Miramar, FL—Devon Sutton, a 19-year-old student at Parkway Academy Charter High School, was shot in the head and died after an altercation in the school parking lot following a dance.

August 14, 2006, Moreno Valley, CA—A security guard was killed at an elementary school.

August 25, 2006, Essex, VT—An elementary school teacher was shot to death in her classroom.

September 27, 2006, Bailey, CO—A 53-year-old male entered a high school where he took six female high school students hostage. As police closed in, he shot one student and then committed suicide.

September 29, 2006, Cazenovia, WI—The principal of a school was killed by a 15-year-old male student who believed that teachers and administrators were not acting to protect him from being harassed by other students.

October 2, 2006, Paradise, PA—A 32-year-old man took control of a one-classroom rural Amish school and shot 10 girls, aged 6 to 13, killing five of them before committing suicide.

December 12, 2006, Springfield Township, PA—Shane Halligan, a 16-year-old high school student unhappy and upset over his grades, shot and killed himself with an AK-47 in the school hallway.

January 19, 2007, Framingham, MA—A high school men's-room fight that spilled into a hallway led to a 15-year-old being stabbed to death by a 16-year-old.

May 2, 2007, Newark, DE—A bus driver was stabbed to death on her school bus soon after she left to begin picking up students.

April 16, 2007, Blacksburg, VA—In one of the largest school shootings to date, a Virginia Tech student shot two students in a dorm, then killed 30 others in a classroom building.

October 10, 2007, Cleveland, OH—A 14-year-old student, who allegedly had warned others that he was going to shoot people, wounded two teachers and two students at Success Tech Academy before killing himself.

January 15, 2008, Putnam City, OK—A 17-year-old was shot three times in a Putnam City High School parking lot after a basketball game.

January 16, 2008, Cleveland, OH—A 16-year-old boy pulled a gun from his locker and aimed it into a crowd of students when a fight erupted at South High School.

January 16, 2008, Charlotte, NC—A student at Crossroads Charter High School was shot in the parking lot after an early-scheduled dismissal.
January 18, 2008 Las Vegas, NV—A 16-year-old shot at another student outside a basketball game at Cheyenne High School. Nobody was injured in the incident.
January 22, 2008, Washington, DC—Four Ballou High School students were shot as they were leaving school at the end of the day.
February 4, 2008, Memphis, TN—A 16-year-old student shot another 16-year-old in the leg while in class at Hamilton High School.
February 8, 2008, Baton Rouge, LA—A female student killed herself and two others in a classroom at Louisiana Tech.
February 11, 2008, Memphis, TN—A 17-year-old shot another student multiple times before handing the gun over to the teacher during gym class at Mitchell High School. The two students had argued over the weekend.
February 12, 2008, Oxnard, CA—A 14-year-old fatally shot another student in the head while in class at E .O. Green Junior High, allegedly because he admitted he was gay.
February 14, 2008, DeKalb, IL—Six persons were killed and 18 wounded in a massive shooting incident on the campus of Northern Illinois University. Steven Kazmierczak, 27, had been a good graduate student but had had psychological problems and had reportedly stopped taking some of his medications.
February 23, 2008, Jonesboro, AR—A student was injured when a bullet from an unidentified shooter ricocheted off a building and hit him in the leg on the campus of Arkansas State University.
February 27, 2008, Little Rock, AR—A student was shot on the campus of the University of Arkansas at Little Rock.
February 28, 2008, Miami Gardens, FL—A bullet grazed the ear of a 17-year-old student as he was leaving band practice at Norland Senior High School.
March 6, 2008, Mobile, AL—One student shot and killed himself in front of 150 other students in the gym of Davidson High School.
March 7, 2008, Chicago, IL—A 15-year old fatally shot an 18-year-old student outside Crane High School.
March 29, 2008, Chicago, IL—An 18-year-old died after being shot by a 17-year-old and a 19-year-old outside Simeon Career Academy after Saturday classes. Several fights had led up to the shooting.
March 31, 2008, Hayward, CA—A 17-year old boy was shot in the leg at Royal Sunset Continuation School. Three other students are believed to have been involved in the shooting.

April 16, 2008, Fresno, CA—A 17-year-old male high school student attacked the school resource officer from behind, hitting him in the head with a baseball bat. The officer then shot and killed the student.

April 24, 2008, Omaha, NE—An 8th-grader was shot in the face during a soccer game at King Science and Technology Magnet Middle School.

April 29, 2008, Washington, DC—A student shot two people at Excel Institute, a vocational school, then stole two cars and fled from the police.

April 30, 2008, Boca Raton, FL—One person was injured at Florida Atlantic University when a man pulled a gun and fired twice during a fight at a party. The University was locked down until the shooter was arrested.

July 24, 2008, Phoenix, AZ—A former student shot three people in a computer lab at South Mountain Community College. The gunman had a longstanding disagreement with the intended victim.

August 21, 2008, Knoxville, TN—A 15-year old fatally shot a fellow 15-year old classmate in the cafeteria at Central High School.

August 26, 2008, Opelousas, LA—Three students were arrested after shots were fired at the T. H. Harris campus of Louisiana Tech. No one was injured.

August 29, 2008, Portland, OR—An unidentified shooter fired five or six shots into a crowd leaving a football game at Madison High School. Shortly before the shooting, police arrested a 14-year old carrying a gun in a separate incident nearby.

September 2, 2008, Willoughby, OH—A 15-year-old student fired two shots in a hallway at Willoughby South High School. The boy apparently had planned to kill himself in front of his girlfriend.

October 13, 2008, San Antonio, TX—A 38-year-old librarian was shot and killed by a part-time librarian, age 62, at Northeast Lakeview Community College Library, where both men worked.

October 26, 2008, Conway, AR—Several men in a car drove up to a dormitory at the University of Central Arkansas and opened fire, killing two students and injuring a third person.

October 29, 2008, Big Bear, CA—Five teenage boys were arrested for plotting to shoot students, teachers, and staff at Big Bear High School. Other students overheard their plans and alerted authorities.

November 12, 2008, Fort Lauderdale, FL—A 15-year-old female student shot and killed a 15-year-old classmate in a hallway at Dillard High School. The two girls had been friends for years but had issues recently.

November 15, 2008, St. George, UT—A 15-year-old student died from injuries after the gun he was holding discharged at Desert Hills High School. The gun was a prop for the school play and was loaded with blanks.

November 21, 2008, Savannah, GA—A 19-year-old student shot a fellow student twice after the two argued at Savannah State University.

December 4, 2008, Montco, PA—A 15-year-old was institutionalized after stealing three guns and hundreds of rounds of ammunition from his father and plotting to shoot other students and himself at Pottstown High School. Police began investigating when the father reported the guns stolen.

December 18, 2008, North Manheim, PA—A 17-year-old was arrested for plotting to shoot students at Blue Mountain High School. Police found multiple weapons and paramilitary gear at his home.

January 8, 2009, New Castle, DE—One person was shot and injured outside of William Penn High School after a basketball game.

January 9, 2009, Chicago, IL—A gunman began shooting indiscriminately from a car into a crowd of people that were leaving a basketball game at Paul Laurence Dunbar Vocational Career Academy. Five people were injured.

January 27, 2009, Clayton, NC—Two teenagers were arrested for firing a gun in the parking lot of Clayton High School. A bullet struck the outside wall of the gymnasium, where a basketball game was in progress.

February 11, 2009, El Monte, CA—A third-grader accidentally fired a gun while showing it to friends on the playground of Baker Elementary School. Nobody was injured, even though there were approximately 100 other kids on the playground at the time of the shooting. The boy says he took the gun from his grandmother.

February 12, 2009, Wake County, NC—A boy pulled a pistol out of his backpack and accidentally shot a 14-year-old classmate in the leg while the two were on the bus to Zebulon Middle School.

February 17, 2009, Detroit, MI—A former student snuck into Central High School and was shot by another non-student at the end of the school day.

March 10, 2009, Jacksonville, FL—At least one shot was fired during a fight that erupted among several students at Ribault High School before classes began. Nobody was injured, but the school went into lockdown and two guns were recovered.

March 23, 2009, Rocklin, CA—A 22-year-old male student stabbed a former male student and acquaintance on the campus of Sierra College in what appeared to be a premeditated attack.

April 9, 2009, Dove Creek, CO—Two Dove Creek High School teens arrested in New Mexico for burglary had planned a shooting spree to kill the school's principal and the superintendent as well as the County Sheriff and Undersheriff. Police found three guns in the teenagers' possession and seven more guns at the younger boy's home.

April 10, 2009, Dearborn, MI—A man shot and killed a female classmate and then himself at MacKenzie Fine Arts Center on the campus of Henry Ford Community College.

May 5, 2009, Canandaigua, NY—Thomas Kane, a 17-year-old male student at Canandaigua Academy, committed suicide with a modified shotgun in a men's bathroom at the school.

So, as you can see, at the time this book goes to press, violent incidents continue to invade what were once considered the safest of workplaces, disrupting the business of learning from preschool through higher education, both private and public. Many other incidents have no doubt been thwarted by new security measures. Yet despite the cameras and other controls at Yale University, for example, the murder of graduate student Annie Le in September 2009 by a fellow worker should have convinced us that workplace violence is a very real problem in all types of workplaces in the United States.

Summary

In just a few short years, workplace violence has become a serious and all-too-common problem for all organizations, including our educational system. A pervasive fear of violence at work has become one of the more significant threats faced by people in all walks of life, including current workers and future workers whose current job is learning in the nation's school system. Indeed, this realization of ubiquitous vulnerability has led to still another new stress on the job. The prospect of violence at work has given us a new level of anxiety and uncertainty. Not only must people perform well in a highly competitive, shrinking job market in a complex society functioning in a global economy, but now they must fear death or injury on their jobs unrelated to the nature of their work.

And remember, the above incidents cover only a few of the more deadly incidents that actually have occurred. The non-deadly ones may be just as costly in many ways. But so long as we are not personally impacted, why should we care? Aside from humanitarian reasons, we should also care because the cost associated with workplace violence is ultimately borne by everyone in the country. The cost of violence at work is the topic of the next chapter.

2

Costs and Definitions

The most serious impacts of workplace violence on the organization and its employees are decreased productivity, increased stress, time away from work including time spent on police or similar related activities, and increased employee turnover (Morash, Vitoratos, & O'Connell, 2008). Identifying precise costs can be difficult because many companies are reluctant to reveal private information as it might be seen as less than positive by the organization's stakeholders. In addition, the costs associated with violent incidents would tend to vary according to whoever is presenting the statistics. First of all, different authors or agencies use varying definitions or time frames and so report different amounts. Also, some of the costs associated with workplace violence are readily discernible and reported while others are not. Still other costs are less tangible and so quite difficult to estimate even though their impact can be considerable. Thus, the immediacy of the impact and the discernable nature of the impact seem to be a reasonable approach to identify the costs.

Types of Costs

Using the immediacy of impact, two types of costs can be readily identified: those that are the immediate and direct consequences of workplace violence, and those that are hidden or delayed and are not so immediately apparent.

Immediate and Direct Costs

The readily identifiable, immediate, and direct costs of workplace violence to an organization include, but are not limited to, the following:

Death or injury
Cleanup, repair, and replacement
Increased absenteeism and/or turnover
Increased personnel costs associated with turnover (hiring, training, etc.)
Increased insurance premiums, including Workers' Compensation
Increased security costs
Decreased productivity (general malaise, compulsory or voluntary unpaid leave, etc.)
Medical treatment
Lost wages to workers
Investigations (outside experts, management consultants, etc.)
Litigation
Prevention costs

The comparable costs to society include:

Law enforcement for the immediate incident
Follow-up investigation(s)
Risk assessments
Increased presence and security by law enforcement or other public safety agencies

Delayed and Hidden Costs

Some of the greatest delayed and hidden costs of violence in the workplace stem from the stress created by the events and from the threat of such events. Perpetrators may attack only where it hurts most (i.e., computers or product safety), or they may simply engage in harassment to the point where employees lose confidence in the company's ability to protect them. The resulting stress not only reduces productivity within the organization but also can affect the family unit outside of work and destroy the worker's social life. There are numerous other important costs that are often are not attributed to workplace violence because they are less immediate, less recognizable, and/or less measurable:

  Decreased efficiency, morale, productivity, quality
  Business interruption
  Diversion of management and employee attention from the business of the organization
  Decreased reputation and credibility of the organization (through its impact on employees, customers, and financial backers)
  Additional sick days resulting from heightened stress
  Side effects of fear
  The price of a life that is taken
  Future prevention costs

These hidden or delayed costs to organizations are especially characteristic of the fallout from psychological or stress-related problems that are experienced by victims of workplace violence. For example, excessive stress often results in turnover, absenteeism, conflicts with co-workers, decreased morale, blaming management, and survivor guilt, as well as tension and fear. Even if not physically harmed, employees can experience a drop in job satisfaction and morale, emotional scarring that erupts later, and a decreased sense of well-being. Medical claims on the average are more costly for stress-related problems than for physical injuries. Further, employees with stress-related injuries stay away from work longer.

Total damage to the mental health of survivors may never be fully recognized, as the impact on their mental health does not show up for extended periods of time. Some of them may even become potential perpetrators to vent the rage that begins to build in them. "Early retirement" and "buy out" employees resulting from workplace violence also are not reflected in most workplace violence statistics.

Furthermore, the costs of workplace violence are not always easily expressed in dollar terms. Morale and productivity impacts, for example, are not readily measured. Besides the reduction in productivity within the organization, an employee's psychological damage also affects the family unit outside of work and destroys the worker's social life. It's hard to concentrate on the job when worried about your life or your family, but the actual financial cost is difficult to assess. Some costs, of course, are simply not capable of being estimated. For example, what is the real cost to a family when a member is murdered? What happens to the productivity of an employee when he or she is abused or bullied by a supervisor? Consider also the psychological and future health costs to the harassed worker who must take prescription anti-anxiety drugs that result in substantial, undesirable weight gain. Finally, these costs are primarily borne by the organizations directly and indirectly impacted, but society also bears costs as noted above. The increased costs of law enforcement and public safety must also be recognized.

Prevention Costs

Minimizing the risk of workplace violence generates its own costs, too. Many organizations mistakenly conclude that prevention is the responsibility of law enforcement and public safety agencies. In addition, others may conclude that prevention is probably not worthwhile as they compare prevention or security costs only with immediate, direct costs weighed by the probability of their occurrence. Invariably, those organizations are neglecting the hidden and delayed costs and/or assigning too small a value to human life. Nevertheless, there are very real costs associated with prevention. They include the actual costs of security (physical and electronic) as well as hidden costs such as having management's attention diverted from other important matters.

Magnitude of Costs to Business

Just looking at commercial enterprises, it is easy to conclude that company owners and top executives should pay serious attention to the possibility of workplace violence because there are sufficient incidents and the subsequent cost of those incidents demands it. Numerous estimates of the costs of workplace violence have been made. One estimate claims that over $270 billion annually is lost in employee productivity due to the personal problems of employees and their mismanagement by organizations (Health Alliance, 2004). Another source suggests that $100 billion is lost to companies each year due to alcohol and drug abuse owing to decreased productivity and quality of work, increased incidence of job injuries, property damage, theft, and increased payout of medical benefits to and for the benefit of employees (Buddy, 2003). The U.S. Department of Justice, in its National Crime Victimization Survey, tallied the costs this way:

> While working or on duty, U.S. residents experienced 1.7 million violent victimizations annually from 1993 to 1999 including 1.3 million simple assaults, 325,000 aggravated assaults, 36,500 rapes and sexual assaults, 70,000 robberies, and 900 homicides. (BJS, 2008, www.ojt.usdoj.gov/bjs/cvict_c.htm)

Obviously, these statistics do not attempt to include the more subtle costs associated with the impact of bullying managers. Nor do they include losses suffered from the more recent and larger acts of terrorism such as

9/11 and the Oklahoma City bombing. Nevertheless, based on these data alone, violence represents a substantial risk that managers in all organizations must attempt to minimize.

A survey conducted by Northwestern National Life Insurance in 1993 revealed that 25 percent of all workers say that they had been harassed, threatened, attacked, or otherwise endangered on their job in that one year alone. Another 15 percent say they were attacked physically—pushed or shoved, slapped or hit—at some point during their working lives. The study also estimated that more than two million workers are physically attacked at work each year in the United States (Northwestern National Life Insurance Company, 1993). Between 1993 and 1999, workplace violence accounted for 18 percent of all violent crime and it affects over one million individuals annually (Bureau of Justice Statistics, 2006). In 2004, ten percent of all workplace fatalities were homicides (BLS, 2005). The costs of much of this behavior is borne by individuals, but organizations also incur costs, as mentioned earlier—decreased productivity, medical and legal expenses, lost work time, lowered quality, and a damaged culture and public image, for instance.

If we use the U.S. Department of Labor's figure of more than a thousand workplace deaths a year, this would mean that an average of more than three persons dying at the workplace each and every workday of the year (U.S. Department of Labor, 2005). Federal and state OSHA regulations require an employer to "furnish to each of his employees employment and a place of employment which are free from recognized hazards that are causing or are likely to cause death or serious physical harm to his employees" even though most workplace violence is committed by organizational outsiders (OSHA, 2006, SEC. 5(a)).

Another source (Nixon, 2009) attempts to report the indirect costs more precisely:

- According to the Bureau of Justice Statistics, about 500,000 victims of violent crime in the workplace lose an estimated 1.8 million workdays each year. This represents a $55 million impact as a result of loss of productivity and increased healthcare expenses.
- Domestic violence costs businesses approximately $6 billion annually in healthcare costs, lost productivity, and missed work time.
- The average out-of-court settlement for 'negligence' litigation is approximately $500,000 and the average jury award is around $3 million.
- For 6 to 18 weeks after a violent incident, there is a 50% decrease in productivity and a 20% to 40% turnover in employees.

Imprecise Definitions Affect Accuracy of Statistics

Documenting this increased threat and related costs is not so simple, as the statistics are none too accurate for a variety of reasons. In the first place, the reporting of incidents is more likely to occur nowadays because documenting crime has become more important to many law enforcement agencies and because more techniques are in place for reporting and confirming crime. In fact, reporting is so easy and so expected or demanded that some incidents may be unintentionally double-counted. The statistics, then, may be somewhat overstated. Statistics in some other cases are based on telephone surveys with all the inherent problems associated with that approach. In spite of the limitations in the statistics, some data should prove illustrative of the size and therefore the importance of the problem.

It is interesting to note that "front-page" examples of workplace violence originating inside the workplace actually decreased after the terrorist attacks of September 11, 2001. We had met the enemy, so to speak, and he was not us. Nevertheless, the National Crime Victimization Survey, while showing a recent decrease in violent crimes, still shows that workplace violence is of increasing concern to managers. In 2002 that survey indicated that almost 32% of all crimes occurred at work or on the way to or from work (BJS, 2006). The number of crimes committed that year was in excess of 22 million. Clearly, crime in the workplace is a major problem.

A larger problem with the limitations of statistics is that some incidents are not reported at all because there is no clear consensus as to what constitutes workplace violence. Lacking a clear definition of workplace violence, for example, law enforcement has not always reported some incidents appropriately and therefore investigators have arrived at different estimates of the costs problem. For that reason, we need to develop a definition of workplace violence. Incidents are undoubtedly more widespread and costs are greater than indicated above. Regardless of the varying estimates, workplace violence is a serious problem that requires attention and prevention. A clear definition can produce more accurate statistics and help us to better understand and deal with the problem, including the costs.

Defining and Classifying Workplace Violence

In the past researchers and criminologists have used various methods of classifying violent occurrences, including the following:

- Legal description—categories such as homicide, stalking, theft, sabotage

- Motive—why the perpetrator wants to commit violence
- Degree of harm—scaring someone, minor injury, major injury, death
- Time and place of harm—when and where did the incident occur
- Targets—supervisors, customers, coworkers, family member, strangers

The latter approach generally identifies four types according to the relationship between the perpetrator and the organization or victim:

Type I—No relationship
Type II—Customer/client/patient relationship
Type III—Both are members of the organization
Type IV—Personal relationship but only one is a member of the organization.

Most of the statistics used in business publications today reflect one or more of these classifications as required by or used by government agencies such as the Department of Justice, the Federal Bureau of Investigation, the Bureau of Labor Statistics, NIOSH (National Institute for Occupational Safety and Health), or OSHA (Occupational Safety and Health Administration). Some of these classifications are simple and permit researchers to obtain data that are already available from law enforcement agencies; but, at the same time, they also limit our ability to understand and minimize the risk of workplace violence.

Definitions Widely Used But Limited

Many law enforcement agencies define workplace violence to include only a proscribed criminal act or coercive behavior that occurs in work settings. Some government agencies (BLS, NIOSH, and OSHA) seem to have broader definitions, but researchers sometimes remove those cases that are not clearly and directly related to work, such as personal disputes. For reporting purposes, the U.S. Postal Service categorizes violence as homicides, injuries, property damage arising from anger or violence, aggravated assault or serious verbal threats, abusive and threatening acts, and acts of sabotage related to violence. Other organizations have long lists as well.

But what about violent work-related incidents that occur away from work? Do those not constitute workplace violence? Just where do we draw the line between workplace violence and terrorism that comes to the workplace? Because of the inter-relatedness of work and personal life, plus the increased usage of telecommuting and other forms of non-traditional work sites, classifying violent acts by any of the traditional criminal classification methods is severely limited. For example, if a man is angry at this supervisor and kills him at work and then continues his rage by going home and killing his wife, children, and himself, which of these violent acts should be reported as a workplace incident? If a Right-to-Life extremist accidentally kills the owner next door when he explodes the Planned Parenthood facility, is that workplace violence or an accident statistic?

Regardless of its legal interpretation, violence has come to have a rather broad meaning to the general public. The general public usually thinks of "substantial" acts of violence—phenomena such as homicide, injury from assault and/or battery, and acts of terrorism. They think about destructive, vindictive, and violent employees who commit workplace assault or homicide. They may also include theft, arson, burglary, and vandalism. Computer sabotage and data destruction are also usually included. Finally, upon reflection, the public may also include psychological trauma and stress-related mental disorders stemming from assault, verbal abuse, or sexual assault.

Not all workplace violence is so substantial, though. Many times it involves only nuisance problems for the organization—stopping up toilets, parking housecleaning carts in one location while the maids loaf elsewhere, re-routing telephone messages, and so on. Other times it may be damaging but subtle—stealing from hotel guests; damaging a part or component on an assembly line; dropping a nut, bolt, or washer inside a unit on an assembly line so that it rattles when later used. Workplace bullying is yet another act of violence that generally has been overlooked but is receiving greater attention as jobs have become scarce and as companies have begun to realize the costs of such psychological damage to employees.

In other words, which is the determining factor for classifying the crime as a workplace incident: where the act occurred, where the provocation originated, where the crime began, where the crime ended, or some other factor?

Where and When May Not Be the Defining Factors

The place and time where violence occurs may not provide a clear answer as to whether the incident should be classified as workplace or non-workplace violence. Again, statistics may differ according to who is counting, as the field is too new to have an established, completely agreed-upon definition of who should be included. For instance:

- Should workplace violence include a *business dispute* that starts at work and ends in a violent act away from the workplace?

- If a *personal dispute* erupts from the amount of time a spouse is spending at work, or because one spouse is jealous of the other spouse's work partners, does it constitute workplace violence when he shoots her as she walks in the door at home—or only if he follows her to work and shoots her on the company premises?
- Is it workplace violence when a person walks into his own workplace and shoots whomever he sees first because he had an argument before leaving his home two hours earlier?
- Or if he goes to his spouse's place of work and does the same thing for the same reason?
- Is it workplace violence when a worker commits suicide at home on Saturday because he knows he will be terminated on Monday?
- Or if he commits suicide at his desk on Monday because he is despondent over his wife's filing for a divorce?

Similar questions can be raised about crimes other than assault or homicide; e.g., hate crimes.

Do the earlier kidnappings and the more recent school shootings represent workplace violence, or are they merely crimes and acts of terrorism? Are terrorism, stalking, harassment, and physical molestation crimes but not workplace violence even if they occur at or in conjunction with someone's job? There should be no question that Americans who were kidnapped abroad were in their workplaces at international companies. As for the schools, it is important to note that schools have traditionally been thought of as places where children learn rather than workplaces in the usual sense. But schools are workplaces, so any violence committed in that setting must be classified as workplace violence. Even if committed by youngsters below the age of 10, violence at educational workplaces cannot be explained away as "boys will be boys," ignored as merely a "playground incident," or tallied as just another thug or criminal act.

As shown in Figure 2.1, it may be theoretically possible to separate violent acts that occur at the workplace into different categories according to motivation or type of incident. However, from a managerial perspective it makes little sense to do so. OSHA regulations require organizations to furnish a place of employment "free from recognized hazards" that may cause death or serious physical harm to employees; schools are not excluded. The organization must be prepared for any form of violence and should take actions to reduce the risks of any and all forms of violence that affect workers during the time they are carrying out their duties as employees and at other times if the violence is a result of their being employed at that company.

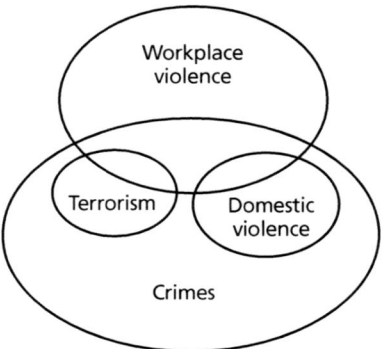

Figure 2.1   Forms of violence occurring in the workplace.

The Intent May Be More Defining than the Act

When company equipment or facilities are intentionally damaged or destroyed, we can safely assume it is workplace violence rather than "just an accident." But what about the mental anguish inflicted by a psychologically battering coworker, a sexual harasser, or a bully boss whose actions prohibit the employee victim from being productive? What about the employee or manager who contaminates computer files in an attempt to sabotage the company or to ruin the reputation of an individual or a company? Mere words in the form of vicious lies, innuendoes, and ugly rumors may be more damaging to morale and productivity than some forms of physical violence but are not generally considered to be crimes. If a worker detonates a fuse to blow up a company building, we would consider it to be workplace violence. But suppose, instead, that the same worker sabotages his coworker's work and drives him to commit suicide or to commit an overt act of violence against the boss or against the coworker who is causing the problem. Is that different?

Definition Should Include Target, Perpetrator, and Intent

Many people think that workplace violence refers only to incidents where an employee lashes out because of a work-related event, but both managers and employees need a broader definition to help ensure a safe workplace. All incidents of violence that transpire on company premises—regardless of the motivation behind them—can be considered workplace violence. Some incidents occurring elsewhere may also constitute workplace violence. And as noted in the Preface, while it may be theoretically possible to separate violent acts that occur at the workplace into different categories according to motivation or type of incident, it makes little sense to do so.

Instead, we need to consider not only the *place* and the *act* but also the *target*, the *perpetrator*, and the *intent*. With that in mind, then, the following definition of workplace violence is used throughout the remainder of this book:

> Workplace Violence refers to willful or negligent acts, including either proscribed criminal acts or coercive behavior, that occur in the course of performing any work-related duty and that lead to significant negative results, such as physical or emotional injury, diminished productivity, and/or property damage.

This definition includes but is not limited to physical assaults (beatings, stabbings, shootings), homicides, suicides and near suicides, kidnapping, robbery, forcible sex offenses, reckless endangerment, disorderly conduct, and psychological traumas (threats, obscene phone calls, harassment) that are work-related. It also includes coercive behavior committed without the use of physical force. It could include implied threats, such as in sexual harassment and in managerial assignments to perform work that jeopardizes the safety of employees because it is inferior but tolerated or demanded in order to protect the manager's job and/or the company's "bottom line." It also includes work-related acts that occur off the work premises.

Note that our definition of violence and indeed virtually all other definitions are very broad. As such, it is easy to envision some sort of continuum of violence ranging from behaviors or actions that cause little hurt to those that end with the greatest of hurts: the death of someone. The concept of a continuum or levels of violence has appeared in various forms, from family violence (Steinmetz & Straus, 1974; Gelles, 1991; Straus, Hamby, Boney-McCoy, & Sugarman, 1996) to school violence (Zimman, 1996; Bryngelson, circa 2000) to the Silence-to-Violence concept (see, for example, McMillan, 1999). Baron (1993) had a similar concept in mind when he described three-levels of violence indicators. Those continua seem to be built around either the intensity of the violence or the degree of harm/hurt that could occur as a result.

Such violence could also involve a variety of means or categories—oral, visual, or physical. And, of course, the result of the violence could be emotional harm, social harm (in terms of their group acceptance), or physical harm. Thus, to fully comprehend violence, the relationships shown in Figure 2.2 below must be understood. Rather than trying to specify a precise continuum of violence, we have chosen to simply use a scheme similar to that of Baron and employ three levels of violence. To better understand the forms of violence associated with these stages, Figure 2.2 is opened and then expanded here as Figures 2.3, 2.4, and 2.5, including examples for each of the cells to further illustrate the full nature of violence.

46 ▪ *The Violence Volcano: Reducing the Threat of Workplace Violence*

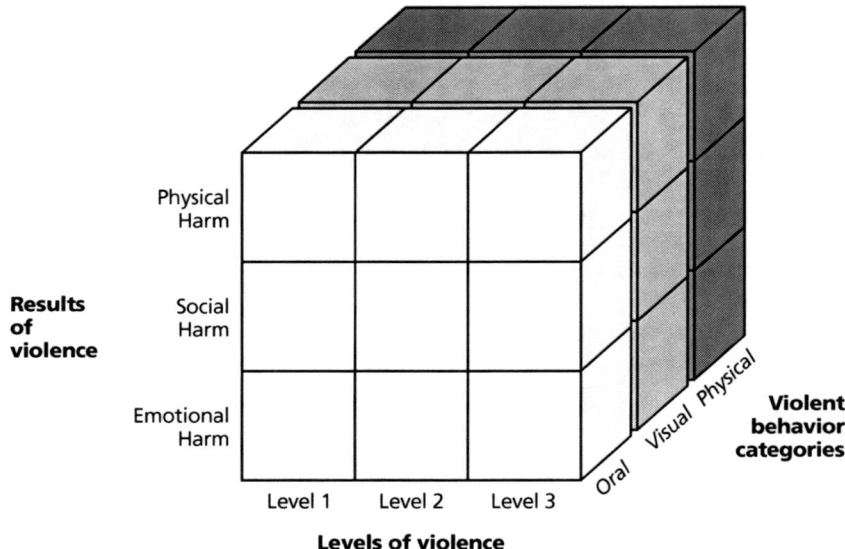

Figure 2.2 Relationships among major workplace violence factors.

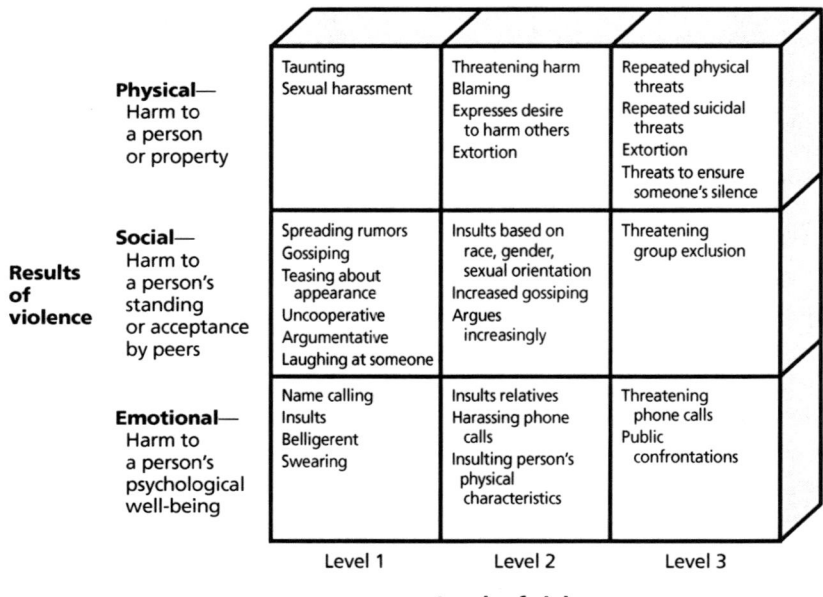

Figure 2.3 Relationships among major *oral* violence factors (expansion of Fig. 2.2).

Costs and Definitions ▪ 47

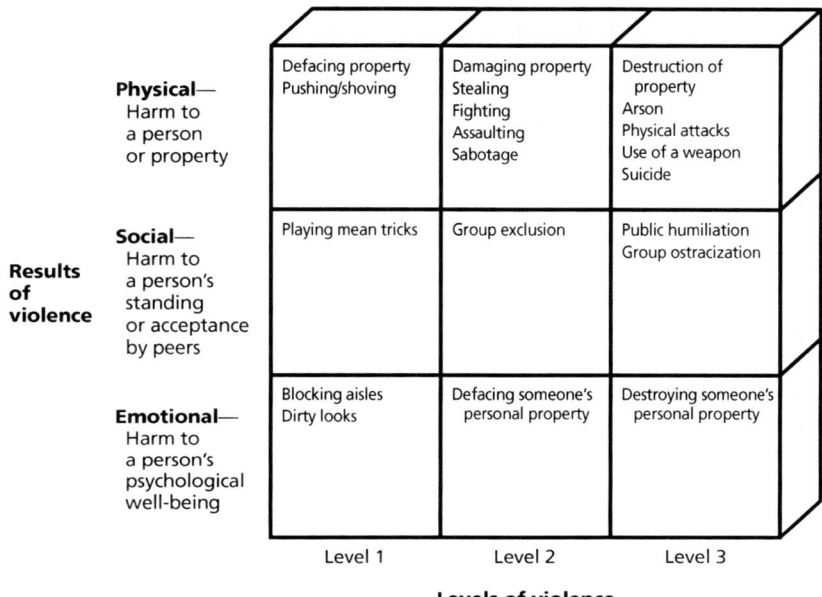

Figure 2.4 Relationships among major *physical* violence factors (expansion of Fig. 2.2).

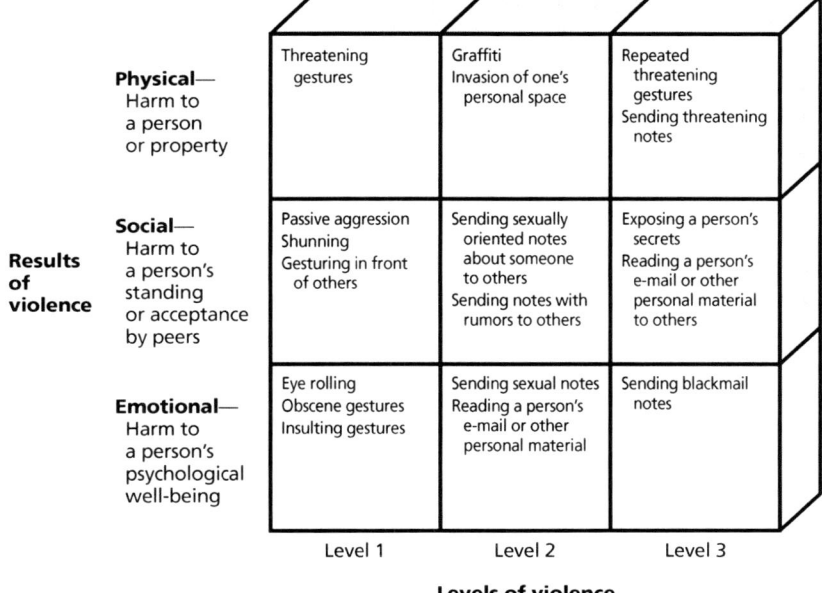

Figure 2.5 Relationships among major *visual* violence factors (expansion of Fig. 2.2).

Summary

To fully understand the consequences of workplace violence, one must first appreciate its costs, and the costs of workplace violence are considerable. There are three major types of those costs: direct costs that are readily identifiable; immediate, indirect or hidden costs; and prevention costs.

Defining workplace violence through the use of categories of one sort or another may not be entirely satisfactory. The use of legal descriptions, motives, targets, degree of harm, or the time and place of harm all have limitations. A truly complete definition should include the target, the perpetrator, and the intent. One such definition has been developed in this chapter.

Using that definition, a complex picture of workplace violence emerges. That picture involves categories of violent behavior, levels of violence, and the result of the violence. Most people when thinking about violence of any kind have in mind the higher levels identified in this chapter. Indeed, many people would not even consider Level 1 behaviors as violence. However, the important point to remember here is that low levels of violence that do only emotional harm can escalate to higher levels that do physical harm. Thus, everyone in an organization needs to be mindful of low-level incidents of violence as those may be an indicator of the potential for increased levels in the future. Law enforcement and public safety agencies may not become directly involved until Level 3 violence occurs, but their work may be made quicker and easier if the organization has carefully documented any Level 1 and 2 incidents.

How or why does Level 1 behavior escalate to Level 3? That is explored in the next chapter.

3

How Violent Behavior Builds: The Volcano Analogy

As described in Chapter 1, changes in work and workplaces can have substantial impacts on the behavior of people. Offshoring, reorganizing, budget cutting, and downsizing are up, while job security, loyalty, and staffing are down. These plus lean-and-mean manufacturing, illegal immigration, and threats of mass disaster and terrorism cause employees to feel overstressed, overloaded, and over-watched physically and electronically. Many employees feel under-titled, underutilized, underpaid, underappreciated, underemployed or, in far too many cases, already unemployed. When work imposes such stress, interpersonal conflicts rise and dysfunctional behavior at work can be anticipated; indeed, it can almost be guaranteed. Whether it occurs because of work-related changes, social or environmental pressures, in conjunction with a crime, or as a carryover from domestic or substance abuse problems, the costs are large and long lasting.

In this chapter we identify the conditions and events within society that can cumulatively push a person to exhibit violent behavior, including economic and political forces; the organization, including the workplace itself and the climate/culture of the organization; and the individual. We also introduce our analogy of the volcano to explain how violent action or reaction builds within an individual. In subsequent chapters, we look at what managers, employees, and the organization can do to intervene, hopefully preventing these emotions from building in intensity and erupting in an act of high-intensity workplace violence.

Can We Predict Violent Behavior?

All individuals enter organizations with some potential tendency to exhibit dysfunctional behavior (Denenberg & Braverman, 2001; Griffin & Lopez, 2005, 2004; Van Fleet & Griffin, 2007). Fortunately, physical assault of a worker by a coworker is relatively rare. The majority of dysfunctional behaviors involve only shouting, spreading rumors or malicious gossip, or other forms of aggressive but low-level violent behavior, which may and too frequently does, however, escalate to higher levels of violence (Coleman, 2004). The greater that potential tendency is, of course, the more likely the individual will actually "erupt," becoming dangerously violent, under some set of circumstances (Innes, Barling, & Turner, 2005). Thus, individual or personal factors as well as organizational and environmental factors are useful in predicting who is most likely to engage in unacceptably aggressive behavior in the workplace.

Considerable research has focused on the backgrounds and personalities of individuals with a high tendency for violent behavior so that those individuals can be identified by the organization in an effort to prevent or minimize violence (Kelloway, Barling, & Hurrell, 2006; Griffin & O'Leary-Kelly, 2004; Sommers, Schell, & Vodanovich, 2002; Neuman & Baron, 1998). Other individual factors (e.g., alcohol consumption, hostile attributional bias) also seem to help predict which organizational members are most likely to engage in aggression (LeBlanc & Barling, 2004). In addition to individual factors, there are also organizational factors (e.g., the workplace itself, overcontrolling supervision, perceived injustice) and environmental conditions that can increase the potential for eruptions of violent behavior. As shown in Figure 3.1, the total influence on workplace violence consists of combinations of those individual factors, organizational influences, and environmental conditions.

Since most organizational members and even some law-enforcement personnel do not know how to recognize these early warning signals of possible violence, this book should help stem workplace violence by giving them a better understanding of the way violence builds (Workplace Violence, 2004).

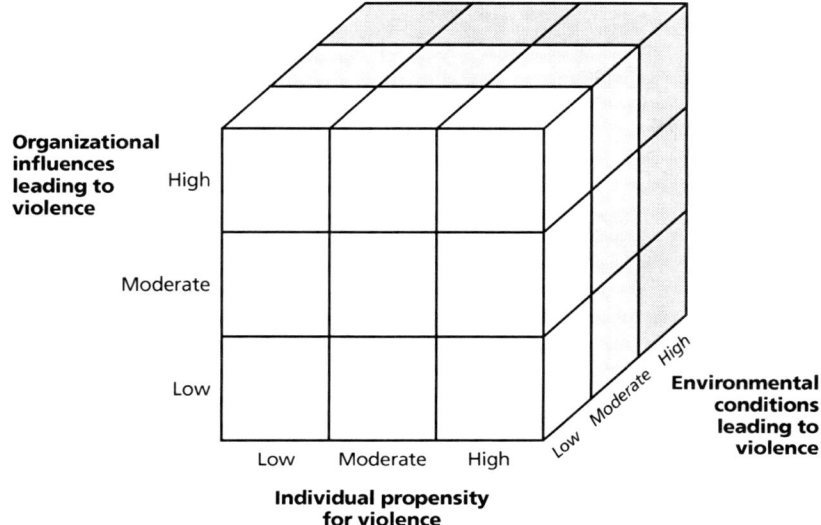

Figure 3.1 Individual, organizational, and environmental influences on workplace violence.

Most of us are not familiar with violent behavior, so we think that we cannot predict it, even though we find ourselves predicting many other behaviors of individuals around us and even animals. We're actually quite good at predicting, in fact. Our relationships begin with a stranger and are based on the early predictions that we make as to how acceptable or unacceptable are the characteristics and behaviors of that individual. We generally decide whether we can trust a person only after he or she has passed some of our "tests," albeit those tests may often be subliminal or intuitive. In other words, we can and do actually predict behavior if we read the signals that others give us.

First, we need to recognize that people don't just snap. Violence is a process. For example, a violence incident starts long before the spouse attacks his partner at her workplace, before a worker shoots his former boss on the factory floor, or before a student guns down his fellow students or school personnel. Thus, violence is not really so much cause-and-effect steps as it is an up-ramp with each footstep leading to a decisive end unless the path is blocked. Pre-incident indicators build like a mound of dirt or the rising temperature of boiling water, so in effect they are simply an early part of the incident itself.

Second, predicting behavior requires trying to see a situation not only your way but also the same way the subject does. You think you know how you would feel and what you would do if you were turned down for a promotion, but you must instead look at it from the other person's circumstances and personality, which are perhaps quite different from your own.

Third, context is more important than content in predicting whether threats will be acted upon. For example, a would-be bomber's threat is most likely a way of getting attention or some degree of control; otherwise he would never tell you ahead of time so you could avoid his consequences. An exception to this would be someone, such as a terrorist, who wants credit for placing a bomb. A person who threatens to kill has, at least for the moment, stopped short of that violent act and resorted instead to threatening words. So threats are an attempt to obtain what the person desires without his needing to resort to violence. Our job is to determine how to give him what he needs or to satisfy his needs in some other way. Threats spoken to a third person, however, are more likely to be acted upon; they are not being spoken simply to scare the victim (de Becker, 1997).

The Volcano Analogy

An easy way to conceptualize the process by which seemingly simple events escalate to violent acts of behavior is to use the analogy of a volcano. A volcano sits dormant until events occur that lead to its eruption. So, too, many individuals appear to be relatively unruffled by actions or events until stress and anger build up, leading to dysfunctional behavior and eventually a violent eruption.

Like a volcano in which the seismic pressure increases so drastically that it causes an eruption of explosive ash or lava, the problems and stresses build up in an individual to the point where sometimes a single final action or event ultimately causes an eruption in the form of unacceptable behavior or violence. Although people, like volcanoes, tend to give warning signs of impending threat, predicting when and how violently their behavior will erupt is still as inexact as predicting the eruption of a volcano. Learning how the Violence Volcano operates, though, can help us prepare for, and hopefully prevent, a full-scale eruption.

Volcanoes contain molten rock in some form and at some temperature, but only the ones with adequately boiling lava create enough pressure to erupt or explode. If scientists truly understood how magma movement, surface and temperature changes, water, gas emissions, earth movement, dust and lava ejections, etc. combine or interact to create temperature or other changes to cause volcanic eruptions, they would be able to warn people in the affected area, and someday we may even be able to weaken the impact. Toward that goal, volcanologists use a combination of monitoring techniques, including seismic, geodetic, hydrological, geochemical, and remote satellite analysis, etc. Although exploding volcanoes differ in the way they behave, potentially they all can inflict heavy damage on nearby property, on the atmosphere near and far, and on people living in the "line of fire" at the erupting volcano as well as those living anywhere else in the world near a volcano site. Even travel into and out of nearby airports is interrupted.

Similarly, individuals come to the workplace with some potential tendency for unacceptable aggressive behavior and violent outbursts. To defuse that tendency or cut short that potential bad act, we need to be able to recognize when an individual is moving toward explosive behavior, or eruption. So just as volcanologists use multiple tools—seismometers, tiltmeters, and gas spectrometry in particular—multiple indicators must also be used within organizations to identify the potential for an individual to become an erupting "Violence Volcano." In our volcano analogy, we don't permit people to live too close to the volcano or we try to convince them to move out of the danger zone—or they leave the area for their own safety.

One preventive or "monitoring" technique is to screen out the more likely problem employees during the hiring process. Unfortunately, hiring personnel sometimes spend more time qualifying an applicant than disqualifying him, which leads to hiring the wrong person. Once the person is hired, they must rely on the eyes and ears of management and other personnel to observe the temperature changes, the rumblings, and the bubbling before the Violence Volcano begins to spew its way to an all-out eruption. Sadly, they never expand the information they know about that person. As a result, they have very little information to help them see pre-incident indicators.

The signs of impending trouble generally progress through five stages—reaction, rejection, expression, escalation, intensification – finally ending with eruption (Van Fleet & Van Fleet, 2007). These stages overlap the levels of violence previously discussed.

Level 1

Reaction. Just as the volcano initially undergoes some type of changing conditions that cause its molten rock to heat and the pressure to increase, in the beginning individuals also experience one or more "conditions" or annoyances that frustrate and aggravate. This could be physical pain, emotional hurt by a friend or family member, fear of losing a job or home, etc. Even if these separate conditions or hurts are minor, their cumulative effect can really sets things off. Or there could be a single, major event (e.g. involuntary termination) that starts the Violence Volcano to bubble. In either case, the individual sees this as a provocation and begins to react. Level 1 forms of violence begin to emerge. The individual may become argumentative and uncooperative. He may also start swearing and rolling his eyes when "target" individuals (supervisors or coworkers) communicate.

Rejection. As the heat and pressure continue to build, the volcano begins to rumble. Depending upon whether this was a series of events or a single, major one, the individual begins the rejection stage by reacting in a relatively quiet way. He may try to hurt or annoy individuals who are believed to be the cause of the troubles, perhaps by refusing to do what is needed or expected. This may take on one or more forms such as playing dumb ("I didn't know what you wanted"), playing only by the rules ("But that's not my job"), or slowing down ("I'm working on it"). The individual is then rejecting others by refusing to cooperate and may even cut off people or psychologically deny their existence by refusing to acknowledge them (giving them the "cold shoulder"). The individual becomes increasingly defiant over time. Level 1 forms of violence occur with increasingly frequency and intensity.

Level 2

Expression. At the Expression phase, Level 2 forms of violence begin to appear. The volcano begins to release a few bursts of steam, which may cause some concern but also enables it to delay actual eruption. Similarly, as the Violence Volcano builds, the individual begins to reveal his or her anger and frustration through verbal or behavioral expression. He or she may spread rumors and gossip to harm others; make unwanted sexual comments or innuendo; argue with co-workers, customers, vendors, and management; exhibit bullying behavior, or blame others in an attempt to create a scapegoat, to enlist support from neutral parties, or to transfer blame from self. These sorts of articulations or demonstrations act as manifestations of the growing problem. Others become increasingly aware that something is wrong with the individual, that he or she is hurt, upset, or very angry. The individual may begin to blame others, particularly management, for her problems. She may send notes, frequently anonymously, that spread rumors or threaten individuals.

Escalation. In the escalation phase, the volcano sends signals that are noticeable not only to experts but also to people in the surrounding area. The various pieces of monitoring equipment pick up more intense signals. More intense steam or even the glow of flames may be visible at night. Likewise, the individual escalates his or her behavior. Bullying behavior may mushroom. There may be a proliferation of negative feelings toward the organization or some members of management—the individual may express feelings of being victimized by management or begin openly to defy company policies and procedures. He may argue more often and heatedly with customers, vendors, coworkers and management. The individual may swear, yell at others, or send sexual or violent notes to co-workers or management. He or she may express a desire to hurt co-workers or management and threaten retaliation if demands are not met. Unknown to anyone else at the time, the troubled individual may purchase a gun or explosives, or display more negative behavior at home while still managing to maintain composure at work. All of this is an amplification of the process and pushes the Violence Volcano toward its ultimate outcome. As the name implies, Level 2 forms of violence begin to escalate. The individual may damage or steal property in addition to increasing his negative comments and negative notes or memos.

Intensification. As the pressure intensifies, the volcano deep inside the mountain will start to release some pressure, perhaps allowing some lava to flow slowly, tossing some rocks from its belly, or occasionally belching forth some ash. As the Violence Volcano intensifies, the individual also begins to "lose it." He or she begins to display dysfunctional behavior, to go ballistic or berserk. The individual may physically limit another person's activities as to where to go, what to do, or with whom to talk. He may block the path of another in the workplace or actually grab and hold them while berating, threatening, or making sexual suggestions to them. He may stalk a perceived enemy or display intense anger resulting in abusive or threatening language, suicidal threats, physical fights, or destruction of property. Coworkers may comment that he or she needs a day off, is "going postal," or is about to "snap." Level 3 violence is about to begin.

Level 3

Eruption. Extreme Level 3 violence occurs. We all know what happens when a volcano finally erupts, spewing its fiery lava in a killer rage. Similarly, the Violence Volcano eventually erupts—the individual acts or reacts in a forceful, reprehensible manner, such as seeking revenge by sabotaging equipment or stealing property, or using weapons to harm or even kill others. Personnel or other company assets are now at stake, and the consequences of the individual's action will be costly and long lasting. Suicide, rape, and murder may occur, sometimes involving individuals with whom the person has no connection.

According to Gavin de Becker (1997), a world-renowned expert on violent behavior, whether an individual progresses to the eruption stage—actually committing an act of violence—depends on how that individual perceives four simple issues:

1. Justification: Does he believe he is justified in using violence?
2. Alternatives: Does he see any alternative to using violence?
3. Consequences: Does he view the consequences as favorable or intolerable?
4. Ability: Does he believe that he will prevail if he uses violence?

Summary

A volcano does not just spring up on its own, suddenly deciding to send out its lava, rock, and ash in a violent explosion that tears away a mountain or burns its way into the ocean. Numerous factors influence the development of the volcano, such as surface and temperature changes, internal pressure, water, magma movement, gas emissions, earth movement, etc. Neither do individuals suddenly erupt into violent behavior without having given some signals of impending problems. Just as the forces causing eruptions in physical volcanoes are complex and not yet well understood, so, too, the causes of the Violence Volcano are complex and only just beginning to be understood. Some are environmental (economic, social, political); some are organizational, occupational, or managerial; some are the result of interpersonal interactions; and some spring from individual characteristics. It is clear, though, that the major forces underlying any escalation in the Violence Volcano are the environment, the workplace, members of the organization, and the organization itself. The following chapters explore these in detail and provide suggestions for dealing with each of them.

PART II

The Environment

4

Environmental Influences on Workplace Violence

What causes workplace violence? As noted earlier, some of the perceived increase in workplace violence may be simply the result of better record keeping and reporting by law enforcement and public safety agencies. However, there are numerous changes in society that also have an impact. Like dropping a bomb or other explosives inside a volcano crater—especially an already rumbling, steaming crater—they can cause dangerous rock spewing if not an all-out magma eruption.

Many times it is difficult to differentiate between causes that stem from work factors and those that come from personal and environmental factors. Today's worker operates in a world characterized by change, innovation, uncertainty, and therefore stress. If not destroyed by the stress itself, the worker's performance and behavior may still be negatively affected by physical or mental overindulgence in the lifestyle or the quick fixes. The worker's problems then stem from the general environment as well as the company's internal environment, as each individual's personal life and his work are symbiotically related.

Among the environmental influences on employee behavior are such things as changes in the sociocultural environment that make violence more acceptable and workers more vulnerable, changing economic conditions that make all jobs less secure, changing political pressures and policies, restructuring in organizations that leads to fewer and more complex jobs, and increased diversity with its inherent increases in problems of communication and other complications. An awareness of these causes can help organizations move toward minimizing the risks of workplace violence.

Changing Sociocultural Environment

To a large extent, we have been transformed into a violent society by shortcomings in our general environment. Violence is "forgiven" or overlooked in a judicial system supported by large legal fees, rationalized and glamorized in our entertainment industry, "practiced" through computer and video games, provoked by the failure of the world's greatest economic system to provide enough good jobs, worsened by an economy that reflects increasing internationalization and technological change, and left largely unchecked by an inefficient legal system and an unwillingness to discipline abusive citizens, employees, or employers.

In our sociocultural environment, changes that have led to increased workplace violence include the norms that regulate behavior and the support systems that once could be counted on to help us get through troubled times.

Changing Norms of Behavior

One of the reasons for increased violence has been the acceptance of violence in defense of one's needs or sense of justice. Violence is the subject in TV shows, news, and movies, and it is sometimes glamorized so that criminals are heroes rather than contemptible characters. While debatable, there are some studies showing a positive relationship between the depiction of violence in the media and increased incidents of violence in society. On the other hand, others argue that this is not the case, pointing out that millions of others view the same materials and do not resort to violence. Perhaps the truth lies somewhere in between: that "Each act of violence has a way of legitimizing similar acts of violence by emotionally fragile people" (Kinney, 1995, p. 162). We all become desensitized to some degree, but emotionally fragile persons can become totally desensitized.

Traditionally, guns have been the weapon of choice for violence because people have access to them and experience with them. However, in the past guns for violent purposes were primarily used by criminals and low-class thugs whereas guns are now increasingly viewed by ordinary citizens as a means of leveling the playing field or seeking justice. Even more troubling, the new twist is the use of guns by children and by adults to resolve conflicts or disputes in a work environment. And in the hands of young people, guns are an even greater problem because youths are less mature about their use and hence more violent and lethal in their actions. Guns used by youngsters in their schools are sometimes erroneously explained away as "boys will be boys" or simply identified as "just another criminal act." Schools are places of work, however, and so violence committed at a school clearly should be classified as workplace violence.

The newest weapon in the workplace violence arsenal is the computer. The availability of computers outside the workplace and the increased dependence on computers inside the workplace have resulted in harmful acts by individuals who might never think of using a traditional weapon such as a gun. For example, employees who might never use a traditional weapon may perhaps justify inflicting damage on the company, the boss, or coworkers through computer sabotage or vicious e-mail. Individuals outside the company, including youngsters in school and adults who are relatively untrained, can shut down company or school workplaces for days for no reason at all except to demonstrate their computer skill or their power. The recovery costs of such attacks and the increased costs to protect computers have created a financial burden on organizations that in turn affects the already-stressed worker and results in cost-cutting moves by management. The result is even more stress for the workers who remain.

The computer can play a role in school violence as well. Consider the case of Megan Meier, the 13-year old who thought she had a new online boy friend. When he turned on her and criticized her, she committed suicide. The "new boy friend" was fictitious—an online creation by the mother of a jealous schoolmate. While this did not happen at school, it was a result of interactions among the teens at school that led to the charade and then to the untimely death of this young girl.

Changing Relationships

Another reason why people turn to violent solutions to their problems is because they have become detached from family, church, and community. Those institutions are no longer there to pull them through in times of trouble. In single-parent homes the parent who is present may feel overburdened, under-financed, or unfairly tied down. The absent parent may feel socially isolated and unfairly treated by the court system through custody rulings or financial expectations. Even in homes consisting of two parents, many parents are not taking responsibility for teaching and supervising their children. Social organizations also prove fallible and ineffective; e.g., teachers are already overworked and criticized for low-performing students; religious institutions are run by disordered, unstable, and even criminal people; and our "cowboy spirit" and desire for individual freedom allow those who would try to solve the problem to be shouted down instead by cries of "free speech" and "right to bear arms."

Work and Family Interdependence

Work and non-work roles are mutually dependent. Increasing the time demand or the level of stress at work tends to result in work-family conflicts that in turn carry back over to the workplace, thus creating a vicious cycle. Job hopelessness and frustration also lead to stress and then to changes in physical condition that spill over into family life. This is a growing problem in our society today due to the increased number of single-parent homes, where time is already stretched to the limit. Perhaps the overlap in stress is also one reason why suicides are increasing along with other violence.

Drugs, Gangs, and Organized Crime

Violence has also increased because of the increased presence of, and access to, both alcohol and legal and illegal drugs. By the late 1980s various national news media reported that over $150 billion was spent yearly on illegal drugs. Prescription drugs and over-the-counter remedies probably equal that amount. In recent years, significant attention has been directed toward the use of illegal drugs among employees because of the tremendous productivity cost of drug-impaired employees and also because of other problems which result: theft of company property, high absenteeism, errors on the job, and increased accident rates. The percentage of our workforce that has some form of alcohol or drug abuse problem has been estimated at upwards of 15 percent with annual productivity losses of $50 billion. For example, between about 1975 and 1986 more than 50 train accidents resulted from the impaired judgment of employees while working under the influence of drugs. In 1989, the relapsed alcoholic captain of the Exxon-Valdez super-tanker accidentally caused the most devastating man-made environment disaster ever at sea, costing his company more than a single year's profit and causing both short- and long-term economic effects. In 1990 an oil spill in New York harbor was attributed to a crew member operating under the influence of liquor or drugs. Indeed, drugs and alcohol are frequently involved in boating accidents. In addition, public transportation is not as safe as it once was. A search on the Internet will quickly confirm this as one finds numerous references to bus and train wrecks in the last few years.

One form of crime that has impacted workplaces is gangs. Gangs are nothing new; as a social problem they can be traced back to the 1600s. Their relationship to workplace violence is primarily from two standpoints. For one thing, gangs are associated with drugs. For another, even if its employees are not members of a gang, a company may nevertheless experience significant monetary losses from neighborhood gangs through payoffs for protection or through theft, robbery, hijacking, assaults, and manslaughter. The peer-pressure-driven gang member will undertake whatever violent activity he must to advance his or her standing in the gang.

Organized crime has also been around for some time. Its toll on the workplace has not previously been thought of as workplace violence even though it does occur in the workplace. One workplace area in which organized crime has long been involved is cargo-related crimes. These include cargo theft, insurance fraud, drug trafficking, and the transportation of illegal weapons and illegal immigrants into the United States. Increasing violence and criminal involvement of cargo and transportation operations make the U.S. transportation infrastructure more vulnerable than most of us expect. Despite concerted law enforcement efforts, organized criminal activity continues to grow in both frequency and consequence. Meanwhile, businesses are feeling the secondary effects resulting from the crackdowns that have been necessitated by "Coyotes" and others engaged in human smuggling, including a reduction in low-skilled labor force as well as consumers for their products.

Piracy, the it-happened-long-ago "romantic" topic of children's books and films, is a form of centuries-old workplace violence that has recently reared its ugly head again. Although piracy on the high seas affects relatively few employees directly, it nevertheless can take a high toll on human life and cost shipping companies incredible amounts of ransom money that in turn raises the price of goods shipped between countries. Dealing with piracy is more complicated than some other forms of workplace violence since the pirates are individuals from other societies (often lawless) who are not subject to our laws or ethics, and not officially aligned with a legitimate government with which we can deal on an international level.

Changing Economic Environment: The Over–Under Society

Our modern economy has been described as techno-Darwinian, which means that the weapons have changed but still only the fittest survive. The fittest apparently are those companies that adhere to the "five contemporary commandments of business:" make money, save money, increase production, cut costs, and solve problems (Baron, 1993, p. 31). To this we would add a sixth commandment: Be politically correct. In the recent economic environment, adhering to these commandments is not easy and can directly or indirectly cause or contribute to workplace violence.

Global economic competitive pressures have resulted in numerous changes in business. Offshoring, outsourcing, reorganizing, reengineering, budget-cutting, downsizing, just-in-time delivery, and similar organizational changes have increased while at the same time job security, loyalty, dedication, staffing, and esprit de corps have decreased. "Under" has become a key descriptor of most members of organizations—they are undertitled, underutilized, underpaid, underappreciated, underemployed, or even unemployed. All this plus lean-and-mean manufacturing, illegal immigration, and the threats of mass disaster and terrorism (often on top of increasing mortgage payments and credit-card debt) have led also to "over" as another key descriptor—people feel overstressed, overloaded, and overwatched physically and electronically.

Organizations seem to be causing more stress than they are providing support. Under those conditions over time, employees and managers can expect to face increasing problems of coping, interpersonal conflicts, and workplace violence.

Changing Business Conditions

Downsizing, restructuring, just-in-time inventorying, and re-engineering are more than merely well-known buzzwords created in the late 20th century. Generally these are intended to reduce system costs by reducing administrative costs, inventory expenses, or time for product development and manufacturing cycles. The bitter reality is that all of these terms are almost automatically equated with massive layoffs, in keeping with two of the 21st century business commandments: cutting costs and saving money. As such, they are also the source of momentous, stressful changes in worker's lives and frequently the cause of workplace violence.

While job layoffs are not new, the inability to get another job is. In the 1960s and 1970s, 80 percent of workers who lost jobs were able to find jobs with comparable wages; in the 1980's and 1990s, some estimates were that only 10–25 percent were able to easily replace their jobs (Kinney, 1995, 35). Despite favorable labor market conditions in the 1990s, between 1995 and 1996 2.2 million workers aged 20 years and older lost jobs they had held for 3 or more years because their plants or companies closed down or moved, their positions or shifts were abolished, or their employer did not have enough work for them to do (Hipple, 1999). The prolonged economic downturn that began in 2008 has intensified these trends.

Furthermore, the loss of millions of jobs by high-performing workers is unprecedented. Traditionally, workers have felt that, if they worked hard and "kept their noses clean," they would remain with their companies for life. Losing jobs without cause breeds a deep mistrust by employees at all levels, creating great personal stress and destroying the loyalty that companies and all levels of their management have enjoyed for ages. After workers have "busted their butts" day in and day out, when the layoff finally comes, the resentment may boil to the surface, erupting in the form of violence toward some level of management. To the extent that those laid-off workers have problems getting new, comparable positions, the ranks of those embittered against their organizations may grow.

Layoff-related stress is not limited to the laid-off workers; it is also felt by the "survivor" employees and some levels of management. Employees and supervisors who have been lucky enough to be spared this time around may feel overwhelmed by the new expectations of them, by the overload that they are now expected to carry, and by the perceived threat of further layoffs. By raising productivity expectations or asking the survivors to assume overloads and/or overtime work, the company may thus create stress outside the job as well by, in effect, requiring workers to choose between family and job. The survivors may become cynical about their association with the company and withdraw their loyalty to the company because they perceive their company as being disloyal to good workers.

Shrinking Job Market

Throughout our history workers have vocalized their anger at being stuck in boring, unchallenging, or underpaid jobs. They have sometimes carried the verbalization a step further by engaging in minor mischief such as dropping a few pebbles inside a car door as it passed down the assembly line. Or with the help of their union, they walked out on strike when they perceived the work situation as intolerable. In the 1980s and 1990s, despite being paid relatively high wages, they fretted about being unable to make economic progress at work like their parents had done.

Now these stressed workers have a larger problem: keeping any job. The greatest stress is felt by the laid-off millions who cannot find a job—any job—even with college degrees and years of impressive work experience. When men and women are losing their possessions and cannot afford proper food and medical care for their families, the understandable reaction is depression or anger, either of which can lead to attacking the cause of their problem: the company or the supervisor.

Many other workers experience a sense of hopelessness because of their inability to replace their existing jobs with new positions offering equal pay and benefits, which could mean losing everything they have worked for—car, house, etc. Stress is inevitable when a worker is forced to take a job with less pay, less benefits, less security, less prestige, less desirable duties, and perhaps farther away from home and in an entirely different kind of company. For example, moving to a job that does not provide the customary medical benefits not only results in stress due to a loss in financial benefits but also a loss in status and also may necessitate taking two jobs, thus creating even greater problems with relationships and stress.

Political-Legal Changes

Many citizens feel that our pursuit of justice, together with our cry for individual freedom and free speech, has left our criminal justice system comparatively inefficient so that it is not very threatening to many criminals and potential criminals. The emphasis on criminal rights deters some crime prevention efforts so that we do not have a legal system that emphasizes crime prevention, apprehension, and swift punishment for violators. Our overriding emphasis on criminal rights rather than personal responsibility for one's own actions means that crime is too seldom equated with punishment and therefore individuals are not held responsible for their actions. For the most part, criminals can seemingly operate with impunity while the rest of society lives in fear of being victimized. Even in prisons that are supposedly equated with punishment, armed gangs and religious cults often operate without interference. Because of crowded court dockets, the prison population may have more access to the courts than the law-abiding victim and may also be able to force the tax-paying public to provide amenities inside "the walls" that are denied the citizen "outside" who is working two jobs at minimum wage.

Changing Nature of Jobs (Including Technological Changes)

Making the transitions necessitated by technological or other changes can be intensely stressful for some individuals. Employees whose job prospects are jeopardized because their skills or knowledge have not kept pace with changes in the work environment are understandably stressed when they cannot qualify for a new job. Corporations have had to bear the costs of retraining many workers, especially in the use of computers and constantly changing software. The government has also provided some re-training programs for individuals, but many people feel embarrassed to "go back to school," cannot support their families while undergoing new training, or perceive other barriers such as transportation.

Even those who are relatively secure in their job skills face other technology-based changes. It has been suggested that our information base is doubling about every eight years (Naisbitt, 1984). Our mental and physical faculties are being constantly bombarded with perceptual "noise" and "information"—cognitive, behavioral, and environmental stimuli that serve to maintain, enhance, or injure our well-being and states of equilibrium. The effect of this is to put even more stress on the worker. Workers who have been accustomed to working at a slower pace can be overwhelmed, for instance, by the rapid feedback through e-mail or on-line messaging. Knowing that you are constantly under camera surveillance or that your phone calls are monitored can be stressful, especially for workers with some borderline personality problems. And in jobs where a slip-up can have drastic consequences (flight controllers, nuclear workers, surgeons, anesthesiologists), it is difficult to believe that the worker is not constantly feeling maximum stress.

Changing Nature of Workforce

We live in a world of accelerated change and increasing pressures. Some people react by trying to eat right and exercise; some resort to drugs and alcohol; others try to cope without changing their lifestyle; some reach emotional overload. They come to the workplace with little or no job security, retirement seems attractive, and many are quick to place blame and to question authority. They may feel trapped in a job for which they are overqualified or otherwise ill-suited because of economic conditions or the changing nature of the workplace, and then be faced with perplexing problems that are caused by poor management or by management's attempts to comply with government regulations and to cut costs.

Some workers are emotionally affected when they find themselves working in close proximity to workers from other cultures, races, sex, sexual preference, or age. They may resent having to change for the sake of new hires who upset that comfort zone. They may be uncomfortable with their relationship with coworkers, their coworkers' personalities, work patterns, communication styles, etc. In such cases the worker may elect to act out his/her displeasure either by attacking the employee directly, by attacking the employee indirectly, or by absolving the employee from the blame and striking out at management instead (for a fuller discussion, see Van Fleet & Van Fleet, 2007).

Another irritant for many workers and managers alike is the emphasis on political correctness, not so much because of the mixed workforce it creates but because they feel it causes reverse discrimination and further jeopardizes their job security. Not much has changed since the term was first introduced and used to describe "a growing intolerance, a closing of debate, a pressure to conform ... or risk being accused of a commonly reiterated trio of thought crime: sexism, racism and homophobia" (Bernstein, 1990, p. 4).

Increased Diversity and Presence of Women

Diversification and stratification of the workforce are two environmental changes that affect employee relationships both inside and outside the organization. Workers can feel cheated by management when they learn or even suspect that they are being paid less than a minority worker who was recruited to fill a perceived quota, or when they see themselves being replaced by minority workers who are lesser qualified. Some workers are emotionally affected when they find themselves working in close proximity to workers from other cultures, races, sex, sexual preference, or age, regardless of qualifications or pay equality.

The increasing presence of women in the workforce has created bias and resentment in both sexes. As solutions, women have generally sought counseling whereas men often have become aggressive. With more women entering the workforce, men have less "support" at home, which may make them inclined toward violence—and women are frequently the objects of that violence at home or in the workplace. Traditionally, the critical anchor for women is the relationship; for men, it has been the chosen job or profession. Both are being lost in today's culture. As women began to gain ground in society and in the workplace, more men attacked women because that secondary anchor for women was a challenge to male authority and potency. While such feelings might ordinarily be kept relatively in check, when the job situation regresses, their entire anchor is gone and they may totally lose control.

Men are more likely to feel threatened when they already harbor negative attitudes toward either females or males of other colors, races, or cultures. In particular, white males are frustrated and angered when they perceive these groups being hired, promoted, or given undeserved raises at the expense of white males. At the same time, women and minorities feel they are the ones not being treated fairly in job opportunity and rewards. They find themselves in lower-wage, higher-risk jobs in the service industry, which because of its openness to customers is also more vulnerable than factory work to violence perpetrators from the outside.

In addition, women often feel sexually harassed by males who simply are not accustomed to relating to women as coworkers, supervisors, or subordinates in the workplace. Others find themselves having to deal with males who prefer supervising, reporting to, or working alongside other males, or other females who feel threatened by other females. Males have their own problems in these new workplace relationships because some women are so defensive that they consider almost any remark (even an innocent compliment), touch, joke, or glance as "threatening" harassment. This is not to say that sexual harassment is acceptable—it is not and should be dealt with immediately and forcibly; but the umbrella of sexual harassment has been opened so wide that it is punching innocent workers in the face and even being used as a weapon without cause. On the other hand, women often experience a very different problem when they work under a female supervisor who seems less supportive of women than men.

Managers at the top, supervisors, and co-workers can create problems as great or greater when they go overboard in attempts to promote diversity. The resulting reverse discrimination can create a backlash and unintentionally do more harm than good for the deprived person and for the organization. As one example, in 1999, Patricia Steffes was awarded $2.6 million in a reverse discrimination suit. She was a white woman who PepsiCo Inc. passed over for a management promotion in favor of a less-qualified black man. Not only did PepsiCo Inc. suffer from bad publicity, it suffered monetarily as well.

Sexual Preference, Age, and Other Forms of Diversity

Another change in the workforce that provokes strong feelings is the employment of individuals whose sexual preferences differ from the majority. Placing a homosexual worker among heterosexual workers can elicit fear and dissension among uninformed workers and unprepared managers, especially if one or more of the homosexuals has acquired immune deficiency syndrome (AIDS).

Age is another form of diversity that can lead to problems. Most older workers feel cheated by management when they see themselves being replaced by less-expensive younger workers. It is also common for an older, more experienced worker to resent a younger boss who lacks that experience, or a younger coworker with a degree who is paid almost as much as the older worker but does not have equivalent experience. Sabotage is about the only weapon the older worker has in his arsenal.

Some workers may feel ill-at-ease working closely with or interacting with a handicapped individual, and that reaction may be wrongly interpreted as a dislike of the individual. Occasionally, an employee will feel that he or she has to "take up the slack" for a handicapped person or an unqualified person who is not contributing 100 percent. Feelings on both sides tend to grow more intense so that the situation may become hostile.

The unfortunate fact is that so-called "political correctness" (PC) has accelerated to the point where workers are under constant threat of violating PC. Many employees can remember when everyone laughed along with a blonde, Polish, or Italian joke; today, the worker may be afraid of being reprimanded or even dismissed for trying to lighten the day with a smile. Men remember when opening a door was a chivalrous, not a discriminatory, act and when issuing a compliment was not a sexual come-on. Today, because another employee may complain of being insulted or offended, both men and women risk being labeled and reprimanded even when they hug a coworker of the same or opposite sex in a gesture of expressing sympathy.

To be sure, adverse treatment of individuals on the basis of age, sexual orientation, physical features, etc. is unacceptable and should not be tolerated in the workplace. The issue is in defining "acceptability." Using "politically correct" definitions based on what is acceptable to only a few overly sensitive persons creates unnecessary stress in the workplace and is detrimental to teamwork. Rather than expecting everyone to develop some tolerance, such definitions fail to take into account the feelings and norms of the majority by demanding that everyone adopt the standards of the overly sensitive few, or even a single employee. This extreme political correctness has in fact hindered the process of training workers of all types to work together in harmony and, rather than promoting equality and acceptance, has in many cases creating greater rifts between the different groups.

Summary

Each of the environmental factors discussed above can lead to violence. Clearly, anyone experiencing one of these will react, possibly by beginning to reject his or her situation. Whether or not they begin to express their stress and frustration and then have their feelings and behavior escalate and intensify may well depend on what job options they have and whether the organization is aware of the growing potential for violence and acts appropriately. If it does not, eruption becomes more and more likely.

How to reduce environmental influences and manage their consequences is the subject of the next chapter.

5

Management's Dealing with Environmental Influences

Managers and supervisors have little if any direct control over the environmental changes and pressures that may drive their employees toward acts of violence at the workplace. They may therefore assume that society through its law enforcement and public safety organizations is responsible for dealing with environmental influences on workplace violence. As the "front-line" of contact with most employees, however, managers can have a significant effect on whether the work environment will contribute further to the external stresses with which the employee is trying to cope. Because they interface with employees and spend a relatively large amount of time with them, supervisory personnel can play a vital role in identifying workers whose environmentally-influenced problems (Chapter 3) may be escalating toward a violent eruption. This chapter will focus on how supervisory personnel can deal with those environmental changes and pressures.

Handling Changes in the Sociocultural Environment

Managers cannot be expected to undo the values and mores held by an individual employee after years of socialization in a particular direction, but management should be able to avoid accelerating the problem. For instance, trying to convince a gun owner that all guns should be outlawed is not only fruitless but probably detrimental to current and future workplace relationships. However, management does have an obligation to make it clear that all guns are prohibited in the workplace and to see that that policy is enforced by installing metal detectors or other security devices.

Managers also can hold employees fully responsible for using violence in any form to resolve issues. This requires that the company take a strong anti-violence stance, heavily communicate it, and rigidly enforce it. Managers must know, though, that there are at least five potentially serious problems if this no-nonsense approach is handled improperly.

First, an accusation must be confirmed before action is taken. Management must be careful to gather all the facts, not just the apparent details. If an accusation is not investigated and confirmed objectively, the employee may be wrongfully accused. If contributing factors are overlooked, the wrong person may be deemed at fault. To respect the concerns raised by some employees while at the same time discouraging false allegations or gossip, some managers ask complaining employees to "go with me to H.R. so we can file an official report" rather than listening alone to complaints. This technique tends to discourage reports of petty tattling to the boss, as most employees will file a report only if there is a genuine problem.

Second, the manner in which the supervisor disciplines or terminates a worker can unintentionally trigger an act of workplace violence. All it takes sometimes is a careless choice of words, an improper tone of voice, or a perceived unfairness of the penalty. Sometimes an understanding talk with the supervisor and/or coworkers may be all that is needed to help the employee through the crisis, whereas a tough stand would have been all that was needed to trigger a violent reaction. Just knowing that someone cares can make a big difference in a person's attitude and ability to see the light at the end of the tunnel. When an employee is being terminated, the insult is greater when that message comes indirectly and cowardly through e-mail (as it did at Radio Shack in the summer of 2006), interoffice mail, or postal delivery. The insult is exacerbated when employees are told to clean out their offices under the eyes of a hovering manager or security personnel, then escorted out of the building like a criminal. Chapter 9 on Dealing with Employee Influences discusses the training of managers to identify workers who are experiencing serious problems from various causes and how to discipline or terminate them without triggering violence.

Third, the company may need to forego a rigid application of the uniformly prescribed discipline to avoid triggering an act of violence. When an employee is experiencing relationship problems at home or in the workplace, for example, a penalty may be the worst possible way to resolve a work issue. For the sake of the company and the employee, management may need to give more careful consideration to the employee's overall record. Is this worker dependable and productive or is he prone to causing problems or violating rules? Is this a first-time incident or is it habitual? Is it something that could be corrected through retraining, or is there evidence that this person will never change?

Fourth, the definition of what constitutes a violent act in the workplace may not always be clear, as behavior norms differ from person to person. We need to define violence explicitly (see Chapter 2), not leave it to the interpretation of each individual. Planting a virus or a worm may be regarded by the computer jock as "no big deal" or simply a way to get even with the company, but it can be seen by others as a disastrous act of violence to the company that bears the costs of the damage. What may have been basically a "joy ride" to one coworker who conspires with another to "teach someone a lesson" is nothing short of sabotage to the coworker who lost his or her job because of it. Acts such as these are harmful to the worker and as such constitute acts of violence.

Fifth, if management is not trained to recognize when an employee is in need of help, regardless of the cause, the timing of the penalty may serve as a trigger for workplace violence. Supervisors need to spend ample time with each employee to get some sense of the kinds of problems exist in the employee's life. If contemplating a harsh penalty, especially firing an employee, the supervisor should first know whether that employee lacks a proper support group such as a family to help him through the crisis, has a medical problem for which he would lose insurance coverage if terminated from the job, has just added a baby to the household budget, has just experienced a divorce or loss of custody of a child, or similar circumstance. Indeed, a crisis might explain the deficient behavior, suggesting that it is a one-time occurrence and that termination is too harsh a penalty under the circumstances. Furthermore, because most workers are serious about supporting their families, just warning an employee that his job is at risk may forestall the need for termination.

Responding to the Increased Use of Drugs and Alcohol

The use of drugs is an example of a major change in behavior norms that is seriously affecting the workplace. Some companies have experienced problems in enforcing their substance-abuse policies because of the lack of cooperation by workers' unions. Union support for all policies should be sought to assure a cooperative work atmosphere.

Alcohol is a long-standing problem, but the company's obligation to the employee has changed over the years. Employers are significantly more receptive to helping an otherwise acceptable employee overcome a substance-abuse problem if the employee does not attempt to use these substances while at work. In some instances, medical rather than punitive intervention is in order. How best to handle workers with drug and alcohol problems is a subject that should be discussed with medical and legal experts as well as with unions, if applicable. In other instances, especially when an employee abuses prescription drugs or illegal substances on the job, punitive action is generally the rule, following use of progressive discipline and other forms of due process. More and more organizations are both using drug testing for new hires and randomly testing all employees to prevent substance abuse problems.

When safety is a profound concern, as on some assembly lines and medical jobs, the only choice may be to conduct random drug testing and enforce zero drug tolerance through swift termination. In other cases, management may elect to bear the cost of drug counseling or provide for the costs through employee insurance deductions. In still other cases, management will argue that it should address only those problems that appear to interfere directly with the employee's ability to perform the job effectively or adversely affect his interactions with management and coworkers. One of the problems with that approach, though, is that it may be difficult to know when the substance-abuse will affect performance. Another problem is that the worker could still test positive on a workday because of drugs that he says were used on a previous non-workday.

An organization should have a drug and alcohol policy that clearly and strongly states that it has a drug- and alcohol-free work environment. Drug testing, as a condition of employment, which has become common in many organizations, should be among the first considerations. Testing after employment should be done where safety concerns or accidents so dictate. Then the EAP and/or health plan should provide for treatment for those for whom drug use is a problem, and the organization should conduct training on its drug policy, treatment options, and the importance of confidentiality. The policy should also indicate that drug testing may be used if conditions so indicate and that refusal to comply with testing can lead to termination.

Drug screening and testing should not be entered into lightly, however. It is sensitive and it is not simple. Questions that must be considered include the drugs that will be tested for, the tests that will be used, sampling procedures, and how security for confidentiality will be provided. Working with local law enforcement agencies should be done to assure that testing and screening satisfy local legal restrictions.

Many indicators of employee stress are similarly possible indicators of drug or alcohol problems. These include sudden, pronounced, or unusual changes in mood, aggressiveness, performance, absences, accidents, disciplinary problems, and interpersonal relationships. The presence of one or more of these might well indicate the necessity for action. Any employee who is suspected of having a drug or alcohol problem should be counseled and encouraged to seek assistance. It is important that the problem be regarded as a health, not a legal, issue.

Responding to Changes in the Economic Environment

As mentioned in the previous chapter, employees whose skills do not fit the current job market are under much stress as they continually face not only layoffs but also a low probability of finding another job. Even highly trained and experienced employees suffer similar stress in times of economic downturns or shrinking job markets. Under these economic conditions, employees know that organizations will resort to tightening their belts by reducing their benefits, their perks, their salaries, and even their jobs. Management may not be able to do anything about the conditions leading to the belt-tightening, but they can help soften the impact on the already stressed workers.

For many people, working is about more than just money; it is their self-identity. Having a job, even a part-time job, is more desirable psychologically and financially than being unemployed. Theoretically at least, organizations could sometimes reduce the dire consequences of economic downturns for some employees by resorting to more creative ideas such as shared jobs, rotating jobs, or shorter workdays. Such arrangements would reduce the number of hours for some people but enable more people to stay employed.

Even when the organization has no choice but to terminate employees during adverse business conditions, the decision must be delivered in a timely and sensitive manner to avoid pushing an employee over the edge.

Chapter 9 talks about training supervisors to be sensitive to workers' worries and to deliver the bad news carefully. Chapter 12 discusses other tools that may be available to the manager, such as outplacement and other programs available through the Human Relations department.

Responding to Changes in the Nature of the Workforce

The changing nature of America's workforce has been discussed as an important contributor to workplace violence. For some workers and some supervisors, diversity is the root of all their problems in the workplace. They have a problem with diversity either because their unfamiliarity with a particular group makes them feel uncomfortable working with such persons, or because stereotyping leads them to dislike or feel superior to a worker of a particular class or sex or age, or because they fear being replaced as the organization attempts to meet diversity quotas.

Because different sexes, generations, and cultures have different supervisory styles, both workers and supervisors need training to avoid problems with "new" arrangements that include women, minority, or younger supervisors. Women and men are more-or-less accustomed to having male supervisors, and both tend to distrust or dislike women supervisors or younger supervisors. Women supervisors need to recognize and avoid displaying the disliked, stereotyped behavior attributed to females, and frequently directed toward other females. Similarly, male supervisors need to know more about how to effectively supervise females and mixed gender workplaces. The company must insist on sensitivity training for both workers and supervisors to avoid serious problems that can result from racial or cultural biases.

There is no going back to homogeneous, "separate and unequal" workplaces. Adaptation is mandatory, and the alternative is to train workers and supervisors to understand, communicate with, and not stereotype people whom they perceive as different from them. Such training must center around taking the focus off the differences and concentrating instead on the team's solidarity, which relies on the total of each individual's assets. Many how-to books are available to managers, as are consultants, training materials, and training seminars.

Problems due to age differences in the workplace have received less attention than other forms of discrimination. Younger management needs special training to avoid generation-gap problems that can result when older workers have years of experience that in some ways make them better qualified than the young supervisor. It is easy for the inexperienced supervisor to hopelessly alienate his more seasoned employees on the first day of his assignment. The younger manager needs to be taught to tap into the experience that older workers could share with coworkers and supervisors.

When discrimination is reported or observed, the manager must exercise his duty to handle it properly. Managers must be trained to confront with care, as the manner in which an employee is approached will either improve his or her chances for getting help or will provoke additional anger. The incident must be documented properly. That means writing specific, thorough details regarding observable behaviors. It also entails recording the details in appropriate records, such as the OSHA 200 Log, internal assault records, insurance records, worker's compensation records, and medical records. It requires the supervisor to prepare for and meet with the appropriate personnel to fill in the details and note what is documented and what is not. And the problem must be followed up through additional conferences as necessary and through observation—especially to check on the emotional response of the employees involved.

Responding to Ineffective or Problem Supervisors

Managers and supervisors exert a profound influence on the immediate work environment and, hence, on the daily job experiences of their subordinates. Sometimes they are the source of the problem instead of the solution. Poorly chosen or poorly trained, they can create sick environments. The organization has a serious obligation to provide training for its managers and supervisors, especially diversity and sensitivity training and other legal issues. Some of the problem areas in which training can be most helpful are discussed below.

Abusive, authoritarian supervisors can create dissatisfaction and hostile environments. Taking a tough top-down approach does not mean the manager must play a tough-guy role. Often such managerial behavior will intensify the problem.

Managers must understand that behavior is a reaction to stimuli in a situation *as that person perceives it*, which is not necessarily the way the manager sees it. So, ignoring a problem or blaming the victim may be interpreted as being disinterested in, uncaring about, or unsympathetic to the needs of the worker. Even worse, the supervisor who carelessly and erroneously blames the victim is really accepting and encouraging bad or devious behavior.

With all the emphasis on diversity and discrimination, managers can become overly focused on the well-being of one or a few disadvantaged workers to the detriment or exclusion of others. Also, managers may overlook improper behavior or inadequate performance on the part of minorities, perhaps mistakenly believing that letting minorities get by with behavior or performance that would not be tolerated from others is part of a diversity policy. However, this is reverse discrimination and may cause even more problems for the organization. It should not be permitted. Reverse discrimination, like any form of discrimination, is wrong—morally and otherwise. It can harm an organization and its workers in many ways, including decreasing production and triggering acts of violence, especially in the form of sabotage.

Managers need additional skills beyond merely assigning and overseeing tasks and measuring productivity. Typically, at the lower ranks where violence is most often seen, managers may be more focused on production and product than on the interactions of workers. Supervisors may lack the skills to deal with the personal element, visiting among the workers and interacting with them. They must be trained also to watch for signs of stress or dissatisfaction. Different people react to different stimuli or stressors, and they also exhibit that stress in different ways. Some cultures react negatively to receiving public compliments, for example, while others react negatively if they do not receive thanks for every task they complete. Some workers enjoy competing; others cannot tolerate competition.

Managers must understand that workers are not rigid, inflexible objects but developing, changeable adult human beings. Employees who are problems in one situation could be changed and be productive in other situations, such as another company, another time, different coworkers or supervisors, with the help of others in the organization, or with professional help.

Managers also need to know what procedures to follow when they see potential problems and what penalties are authorized by their company. They need to build skill in intervening before a dispute, a disagreement, or anger progresses to an act of violence. As mentioned above, not all people react the same to a particular type of discipline. As a starter, managers should always treat all employees with respect and dignity, apply disciplinary actions consistently, and absolutely refuse to tolerate certain behaviors. Furthermore, it is also important to treat problems confidentially and to be honest about the reason for a termination or layoff. Business reasons, not personal accusations, should be given as the reason for management's concern about behavior. While totally rational behavior cannot always be expected from employees when they are laid off or discharged, extreme adverse reactions can often be avoided by simply not giving bad news to an employee during critical times such as pregnancy, divorce proceedings, critical illness, or a death in the family.

Summary

Those who are on the "front-line"—managers and supervisors—have important roles in reducing the extent to which external stresses impact the workplace and in identifying those workers who may be escalating toward a violent eruption because of environmentally-influenced problems. But other pressures can arise from the workplace itself. Those are covered in the next chapter.

PART III

The Workplace

6

How the Workplace Affects Behavior

As you will recall, our broad definition of workplace violence includes any substantial threat, injury, or attack on an organization's physical, human, informational, or intangible assets. As such, our discussion includes some guidelines to provide security and safety in the workplace through a consideration of the workplace itself. Safer workplaces are less likely to experience violence in any form. Currently, organizational security and safety in a particular workplace may range from nonexistent to adequate to overwhelming to prison-like, whereas we want it to be professional, with reassurance as well as protection.

Individual employees, customers, or other outsiders may engage in acts that are unsafe or that can or will lead to unsafe conditions; and an awareness of this possibility creates stress for our workers even if nothing ever happens. But it is the ultimate legal and moral responsibility of managers and owners to do everything reasonably prudent to provide for, secure, correct, and defend the workplace and the organization. Understanding how the workplace affects behavior can aid managers in redesigning workplaces to reduce not just safety and security risks as they are ordinarily defined but also the risks associated with various forms of workplace violence.

Nevertheless, there are risks associated with any organization and there are risks associated with certain types of jobs and occupations and industries. Some jobs and occupations are just inherently less safe than others. This part of the book focuses on workplace safety as a technique to reduce the risk of workplace violence and, to the contrary, how unsafe workplaces create additional stress that can lead to eruption of the Violence Volcano.

Occupations Traditionally Considered Hazardous

Many of us generally seem to feel that workers in hazardous occupations are paid to accept their high level of risk whereas the prudent practices by most organizations and the presence of governmental regulation make our own workplaces safe. But the rising incidents of workplace violence—including terrorism, stalking, negligence, sexual harassment, and abusive and bullying bosses—is convincing others that all organizations are vulnerable to some form of workplace violence. Nevertheless, some occupations do seem more hazardous than others, largely as a result of accidents alone.

Because it is well established that the unsafe acts of people are the primary cause of accidents, engineers, psychologists, sociologists, and others have studied accidents quite extensively. Among the concepts that have come from this work is the suggestion that some people behave in ways that cause or lead to more accidents—they are accident prone. In addition, some researchers have felt that people have accidents as a subconscious way of withdrawing or avoiding work, although more recent research does not support that view.

From both an individual and an organizational point of view, the root causes of accidents clearly have been attributed to people. The so-called "four horsemen of safety" reflect this view: **Apathy**, lack of concern or indifference; **Complacency**, contentment or lack of vigilance; **Distraction**, inattention or absent-mindedness; and **Deviation**, taking shortcuts or willfulness. Despite the fact that individuals engage in activities that result in accidents, most experts agree that the final responsibility for workplace health and safety lies with management. Indeed, the basis of federal regulation in the area of health and safety is voluntary compliance by the management of organizations.

Vulnerable Organizations Not Traditionally Considered Hazardous

When the general public thinks about workplace violence, the U.S. Post Office and convenience stores immediately come to mind. Yet, more taxi drivers, law enforcement officers, and security personnel were slain in 1993 than U.S. Post Office deaths from 1986 through 1993. Victims who are shot, knifed, or strangled during a robbery attempt typically work for the service sector (e.g., taxi drivers, food-service workers, convenience stores, gasoline stations). Those who handle cash are most vulnerable, as are women, older workers, and teenagers.

No business is immune, however. Traditionally dangerous types of work such as police work, bar tending, social work, firefighting, bank tellers, and others are not the only work groups at risk. Organizations inside buildings that are easy to enter and exit by automobile are more likely to experience violence, as are those that have high turnover and low employee loyalty. Clearly, some organizations are more vulnerable than others; for example, those that are located in high crime areas, do a lot of business at night, are poorly lighted or poorly visible, involve valuable property or possessions, employ only a small number of workers on a shift, or employ a relatively large number of "more vulnerable" persons such as minorities, females, or relatively young or old workers.

Schools, colleges, and universities have also become targets of violence. In some cases student protest movements or even celebrations after athletic victories have gotten out of hand. In other cases, students have lashed out against other students or student organizations—jocks against nerds, "haves" against "have nots," or some other form of "class struggle." And in some instances students have sought violent redress against teachers or administrators whom those students felt had wrongfully treated them. For example, in 2000 a Florida Middle School teacher was shot to death by a seventh grade student. In 2002 a nursing student at the University of Arizona, despondent over flunking out, killed three professors and then committed suicide.

The attitude of management is important as well. Organizations that treat their employees, customers, or suppliers poorly or indifferently are more likely to have potentially violent reactions from those individuals than are organizations that treat them otherwise. Negligent attitudes on the part of managers and supervisors toward the safety and health of personnel are also more likely to lead to retaliatory behavior from those personnel. Unethical behavior on the part of managerial personnel also tends to engender similar responses from employees. Research is increasingly demonstrating that workplace anger and aggression frequently arise from feelings of unfair treatment. Under conditions of undue stress or abusive supervision, that anger, and aggression can readily boil over into violent behavior.

In other cases, organizations may knowingly or unknowingly create abusive work environments that cause negative reaction to build, thus leading toward workplace violence. Abusive work environments are those in which employees are subjected to conduct that is severe enough to cause physical or psychological harm. Abusive conduct is a broad concept that includes verbal abuse, such as the use of derogatory remarks, insults, and epithets; verbal or physical conduct that a reasonable person would find painful, threatening, intimidating, or humiliating; or the gratuitous sabotage or undermining of a person's work performance.

Abusive, bullying bosses tend to be highly autocratic; they have high power and control needs. They dictate how and what decisions are made, allowing little debate or participation in decision-making. It is not uncommon for bosses who make tons of mistakes themselves to show no tolerance for errors, making employees live under the constant threat of "one strike, you're out." Subordinates who question them or raise concerns about the managers' behavior are regarded as having a negative attitude, being paranoid, or engaging in whistle blowing. Bullying bosses exaggerate their own contributions and are reluctant to acknowledge the contributions of others; they frequently micromanage day-to-day operations; have difficulty communicating in an open and healthy manner, and often feel threatened by competent employees.

An abusive or bullying manager's aggressive behavior occasionally involves screaming and shouting but more often manifests itself in criticism, insulting comments, asking others to "look into" reports of improper behavior or poor performance, and other more sinister behavior. The effect of this more sinister behavior is humiliation and intimidation. These latter forms of aggression can often be found in gestures, tones, facial expressions and other non-verbal messages. However, the victims are left in no doubt about their demeaning content. The coercion may be subtle, but nonetheless the effect is achieved and the victim feels varying degrees of fear and terror.

From a legal standpoint, most states would not regard a single such act as constituting abusive conduct, unless it were particularly severe and offensive. However, a pattern of such behavior on the part of one or more managers should never be tolerated as it is not only bad management but could also lead to violent consequences. Indeed, any form of poor or bad management could eventually lead to workplace violence although that which directly impacts human assets is likely to do so more quickly than that which impacts them less directly.

In the late 1990s about two-thirds of all workplace victimizations occurred in private companies with the remainder in federal, state, or local government offices. More precisely, the locations included restaurants, bars, nightclubs, offices, factories, warehouses, or other commercial establishments, as well as on school property, in parking lots and garages, and on public property (streets and parks). The occupational group with the highest number of work-related homicides was sales workers, with service occupation workers next, followed by executives, administrators, and managers. Organizations and employees who have never before been concerned about workplace violence now have reason to become concerned.

Organizations that handle cash are far more likely to experience violence than those that deal only in credit or don't handle financial transactions at all. Fast food restaurants, taxis, financial institutions and similar businesses have higher robbery rates. In addition, robberies that occur at closing time for these organizations are more likely to involve violence since they are frequently committed by someone known to the victim and because no customers are present to serve as witnesses. Nevertheless, while workplace violence is most likely to occur in the evening or at night and especially in those organizations that operate around the clock, it can happen at any time. Employees who handle cash understandably live under the stress of knowing that they could be looking down the barrel of a gun at any moment.

Healthcare organizations or health clinics that have drugs on their premises may be targeted by those seeking access to those drugs. Organizations that are frequented by mentally unstable individuals, such as certain types of health care facilities, may have higher risks of violence than other organizations. These organizations may be particularly targeted by aptly-named insane terrorists, who are individuals suffering from psychological and sometimes physical disorders. These violent individuals are frequently "copy cats" desiring attention more than making a point or seeking money. Acting irrationally, they use violent tactics such as shooting, bombing, or kidnapping; and their goals may be only remotely or strangely related to the targets they choose (or to the people who become the inadvertent victims). In many ways this is the most difficult type of terrorism to prevent since there is virtually no way to predict what mentally disturbed individuals are likely to do. One of the more recent and best-known examples of a mentally unstable terrorist was the Unabomber of the 1980s–1990s. Again, it is easy to see why employees in these organizations live in constant, although maybe silent, fear for their own safety.

Clients or patients of some healthcare organizations have also been victims of violence. Nursing and retirement home abuse and neglect have become increasingly widespread and seem to be growing. It is clearly a serious problem affecting thousands who are dependent on the services provided by these organizations for their care and well-being. Abuse and neglect can be difficult to recognize and are often covered up by staff members for a variety of reasons.

These are just a few examples of some organizations that readily come to mind when thinking about violence in organizations, but *all* organizations are vulnerable in today's society. For example, the U.S. Department of Labor reports that about two-thirds of all workplace violence occurs in the healthcare and social-services industries and includes doctors, nurses, pharmacists, home health-care workers, nurses' aides, and welfare workers. The rate of workplace violence in that industry can run as high as 47 cases per 10,000 workers, as compared to 3 cases per 10,000 in private industry as a whole.

Organizations Disliked By Fanatics

Note: In the following discussion, we are not referring to groups that engage in reasoned discourse with the missions of organizations. We are referring instead to those who resort to the use of violence to attempt to achieve illegal objectives—terrorists—and we repeatedly identify them as such.

Even those organizations with healthy internal environments can still be targets of violence. The nature of the organization itself can be a major cause of workplace violence. Clearly, some organizations are more vulnerable than others. Organizations that are perceived to be wealthy are more likely to be targets for thieves. Schools, universities, and hospitals—which at one time would have been considered safe havens—are today in danger of becoming high-priority targets because of the research or work that they do.

Accessibility alone has become one of the most recent causes of vulnerability, especially to political terrorists. Common organizations like shopping malls, movie theaters, and churches that are "open to the public" are easier to gain entrance than other so-called "high-priority targets" such as nuclear plants, airplanes, courthouses and other government buildings that are given extra protection. Until recent fortifications and lock-down measures, schools and hospitals were also in this group of "convenient" organizations; some still are.

Organizations that are perceived to damage the environment are more likely to be targets for environmental or ecological terrorists. The memberships of these terrorist groups frequently overlap those of the animal rights and bio-terrorist groups. Such groups violently destroy property in the name of saving the environment from further human encroachment and destruction. So-called "animal rights" groups of bio-terrorists have targeted food processing firms and universities. These groups have vandalized or fire-bombed meat companies, fur stores, fast-food restaurants, leather shops, medical research laboratories, and even the Gillette Razor Company for testing its products on animals. They stalk and even attack high-profile women who dare to wear furs.

Certain other types of organizations—abortion clinics, bars, X-rated movie theaters, for example—are more likely to be targeted by religious fanatics. In these instances, the groups are imposing their religious views upon everyone else. If their religion opposes abortion, then they feel that they have a moral right to bomb abortion clinics and murder the workers at that location and the physicians who perform abortions. If their religion opposes the consumption of alcohol, they feel that they have a moral right to close bars. And so on.

Law enforcement agencies are likely targets for those who feel our criminal justice system is failing. Those who oppose strong governments will seek to assault government organizations. Organizations with operations in third-world countries may be attacked more frequently than those that are strictly domestic in operations.

Organizations that represent something important in society are frequently targets for political terrorists. Indeed, the very basis of capitalism poses a threat to some and is a target for others. Political terrorists are among the oldest type of terrorist. Recently, most political terrorists have been Marxists who generally have specific demands to make and who believe that American companies are the root of all evil. A variant of this type, religious fanatics, will readily give their lives because they feel God will reward them for killing His enemies. The individual martyr may not even articulate any demands. Some writers have even suggested that the term "fundamentalist" and to a lesser extent "orthodox" almost imply individuals and/or organizations that are or could easily resort to terrorism (Bowman, 1994, p. 54).

While sometimes propounding political views, criminal bandits create fear and intimidation through their terrorist acts for the purpose of obtaining large sums of money quickly. In other words, these are criminals who use political excuses to hide their real motivations. Many cases of international kidnapping are carried out by this type of terrorist. In the United States, criminal-bandit terrorism has been largely confined to what we call Organized Crime and, to a lesser extent, organized gangs. More recently, however, other copycat criminals appear to be emerging, including international pirates that attack major shipping vessels on neutral waters.

In other words, if perceived negatively by some group, an organization and its employees are more likely to be targeted for violence by that group. Hence, it is important for organizations to understand how they are perceived by others in society and to plan accordingly to minimize their risks by protecting their assets.

Any Organization

As already indicated, anything in the workplace that unduly increases stress could also increase the risk of workplace violence. That stressor could be the physical environment (crowding, noise, air quality, ambient temperature, exposure to excessive heat or excessive cold, or high levels of noise and vibration) or it could be the work station design. Heavy manual labor or rotating shift work may place the body under physical stress because the body's natural circadian rhythm cycles are thrown out of adjustment.

In additional to physical stress, people experience stress when they face anxiety or frustration from aspects of their work that they cannot control. Employees may not be able to fully utilize their skills and knowledge. They may face conflicting demands. They may not receive the respect or recognition they expect for their accomplishments, or they may perceive that one or more other workers are treated better, paid more, or allowed to slide by while others pick up the slack . They may be bullied or humiliated by a supervisor.

Employees may become frustrated from overly repetitive work. Excessive work demands may be distressful and potentially lead to emotional stress when they exceed an individual's capabilities. Excessive work without appropriate breaks may also be distressful. Unclear or conflicting job responsibilities lead to confusion, frustration, and stress.

Jobs which involve the care and welfare of others can be emotionally draining. The distress that results can eventually lead to a condition known as burnout, which means that the person is emotionally and physically exhausted. Individuals in these situations frequently end up blaming themselves when things go wrong for the people in their care. Health care, custodial and social workers are particularly vulnerable to these problems and can sometimes "snap" and become violent towards the organization and those in it.

Those who must work in isolation also frequently suffer from undue stress. Some work processes separate people and create feelings of isolation, which may in turn cause distress. Interestingly, this seems similar to those who receive little feedback and have little job satisfaction. The lack of job satisfaction and uncertainty about job performance also seem to be contributing factors to work stress. Related to these is a concern for job security. A feeling of insecurity can come from several sources. The lack of feedback, poor economic conditions, downsizing within the organization, and possible discrimination are all examples of stressful situations that employees can experience.

Summary

Clearly all the various characteristics of an organization or the organization's workplace may influence the risks of workplace violence. As we have seen, the type of industry, the nature of the work itself, the location of the organization, the physical plant, lighting, location, the way the organization is perceived by others, and even the very assets of the organization could draw perpetrators of violence to the organization. The stress created by this vulnerability can move workers one more step toward displaying violent behavior or erupting as soon as they encounter "the last straw." How to reduce the influence of the organization's environment is what we shall discuss in the next chapter.

7

Dealing with Workplace Influences

It is not naïve to expect organizations to examine workplace influences and to make changes when necessary in an effort to reduce the potential for violence. We assert that effectively addressing "violence triggers" within the organization itself requires infusing democratic values into management practices. Only when the organization develops a culture that truly values human assets within both society in general and the organization in particular will the risks of workplace violence be substantially reduced.

Developing such a culture means that owners and managers must first demonstrate true concern for the health and safety of organizational stakeholders. Secondly, they must be vigilant so they are not distracted from paying attention to those concerns or lured into taking shortcuts. OSHA regulations require organizations to furnish a place of employment "free from recognized hazards" that may cause death or serious physical harm to employees. Workers who feel that their organizations are not striving to meet these regulations may be more prone toward violence than are others. Individual factors (e.g., alcohol consumption, hostile attributional bias) and organizational factors (e.g., over-controlling supervision, perceived injustice) help in predicting who is most likely to engage in aggression. Owners and managers must accept that they have the final responsibility for workplace health and safety. They must not only voluntarily comply with governmental regulations but also go beyond to demonstrate genuine commitment to all stakeholders of their organizations. It is this commitment that is so vital at preventing eruptions of the Violence Volcano.

Recognize Potential Problems

In order to be able to prevent such eruptions, individuals in organizations must first be able to see them coming; that is, to recognize potential problems before they become actual problems.

In Occupations Traditionally Considered as Hazardous

Organizations in the United States have grown safer and safer over the years, thanks to the efforts of the National Safety Council, the Occupational Safety and Health Administration, the National Institutes of Health, the American Public Health Organization, and other safety and health organizations too numerous to name. While admirable, this does not mean that everything that can be done has been done. Nor does it mean that every organization is safe from workplace violence or that every manager cares about the safety, health, and well-being of his or her subordinates. Construction jobs, driving taxicabs, being a clerk in an all-night convenience store, serving in the police, fire, or similar jobs are all still generally considered at least potentially hazardous.

In general, the industries that involve substantial physical activity by workers have come under considerable scrutiny and have invested relatively large amounts of resources in efforts to provide safer work environments outside the realm of workplace violence. For the most part, their efforts have been successful. More recently, even those industries that primarily involve office work have begun to recognize that they, too, most pay more attention to health and safety issues. In other words, all organizations must now give adequate attention to workplace violence as a threat to employee safety.

But industry classification is not always an indicator of potential workplace violence. Economic pressure may cause some organizations and managers to be less diligent or to take one too many shortcuts. One organization may be less concerned about health and safety issues, thus making it more vulnerable than another. One may be less vigilant and hence incur greater risks. Owners and top-level managers must carefully examine the practices of their organizations to make certain that health and safety are primary concerns of their organizations, whatever the source of the problem.

In addition, the activities of all managers should be examined to be sure that none of them is succumbing to pressures to meet objectives that have resulted in shortcuts to safety considerations or to paying less attention to safety. Managerial attitudes need to be assessed to be certain that these company leaders genuinely believe that safety matters. Those who don't may be dangerous, jeopardizing not only the health and safety of their workers but also the fiscal well-being of the organization.

In Vulnerable Organizations Not Traditionally Considered Hazardous

As noted in the previous chapter, not all "hazards" faced by organizations are as obvious as those that might result from "the usual" accidents and injuries. Yet organizations usually not considered to be hazardous still must address these different types of "hazards" that arise from environmental pressures, poor management, individual stresses of the job, and the like. Those "non-hazardous" organizations include almost all office work—law, engineering, real estate, and insurance, for example—because even in those organizations care must be take if cash, securities, or other liquid assets are present.

Robberies or attempted robberies are a major source of workplace violence, so organizations need to take all reasonable precautions to prevent them. Personnel in organizations who handle cash are especially vulnerable, as are women, older workers, and teenagers. Physical facilities should be designed to provide as much security for these individuals as possible. Install security alarms and cameras. To permit a clear view from both the outside and the inside, avoid cluttering windows and doors with signs and posters. Make sure that the facilities are well lighted both inside and out. Train your personnel to watch for suspicious customers who seem to be browsing a long time without demonstrating real interest or buying anything. Have them watch for persons loitering around outside especially in parked cars.

Be very careful with all cash operations. The cash register area should be monitored by a security camera and should be visible to outside observers. Post highly visible signs (in as many languages as needed) indicating that you do not accept large bills and that only a certain minimum amount of cash is in the register at any given time. Have a safe that requires two keys and post a notice to that effect on the safe. Vary the manner in which cash is transported to the bank (avoid the obvious money bags), and vary the times and routes used.

Always have at least two people working at night. Always have two people on hand at opening and closing times, one of whom should check for signs of disturbance while the other waits near a phone in case of trouble. Keep side and rear doors locked and, if they must be used, employ some form of security to assure that only authorized personnel use them. Install height markers at doorways to assist personnel in estimating the height of suspects involved in any robbery attempts.

In the event of a robbery, all personnel should be instructed to take no action that would jeopardize the personal safety of themselves or anyone else. They should be told to follow instructions given to them by the robbers and to assume that any firearms are loaded and that the perpetrator will use them. They should try to remember as much as possible about a robber and his get-away vehicle. While they should be alert to opportunities to escape, they should avoid any action that might cause a robber to become agitated or violent.

Schools, colleges, and universities in some instances have had to follow the lead of organizations protecting themselves against aggression. Metal detectors, security cameras, increased lighting, and other security measures have been installed around laboratories and other facilities deemed high risk. For certain events, increased security including visible identification tags and careful monitoring are used on a more routine basis. Dress codes and "zero tolerance" policies are being implemented more frequently in K–12 school systems in an effort to reduce the risks of violence in schools. And virtually all school now have carefully articulated and highly publicized anti-violence policies.

Educational institutions need to develop strategies that carefully involve all major stakeholders—employees, students, parents, community leaders (business, government, law enforcement, and so on). Each of these groups should be asked to prepare materials supporting anti-violence and possibly conduct some sort of workshops, seminars, or discussion group meetings to raise the awareness of the community about violence. Students should be encouraged to report potential violence problems to their parents or to school or law enforcement officials. In addition, students, faculty, and other employees should have more specific information about what to do in case a violent event were to occur—who to contact, where to go, what actions to take, and so on. Follow-up interviews after many school violence incidents have revealed that perpetrators often give hints or tip-offs but these signals are often not recognized soon enough to allow intervention.

Increasingly, research shows that negligent attitudes on the part of managers and supervisors toward the safety and health of personnel are likely to increase the risks of workplace violence of one form or another. Thus, it is extremely important to ensure that your organization has a climate that affords proper treatment for employees, customers, suppliers and, indeed, all stakeholders. Unethical managers breed unethical employees. Abusive supervisors can cause employees to snap and burst into violent behavior.

Due diligence requires that any reports of abusive, bullying behavior be carefully investigated. An ombudsperson should be in place to provide anonymity for those reporting such behavior. The ombudsperson should have full investigative power from the very highest level of the organization. A zero tolerance policy should be in force for such behavior, including verbal abuse such as derogatory remarks, insults, and epithets; verbal or physical conduct that a reasonable person would find threatening, intimidating, or humiliating; or the gratuitous sabotage or undermining of a person's work performance.

Managers should be trained to keep their power and control needs within reasonable bounds. They should not be allowed to become autocratic. Instead, they should be encouraged to use participative decision-making and be open to suggestions and concerns from subordinates. Managers should be instructed to praise in public and criticize in private and to provide criticism in constructive, developmental ways. They should readily acknowledge the contributions of others and avoid micromanaging day-to-day operations. They should communicate in an open, friendly, and professional manner, always focusing on helping subordinates accomplish their goals.

In Organizations Disliked by Fanatics

Note: Just as in the previous chapter, in the following discussion we are not referring to groups that engage in reasoned discourse with the missions of organizations. We are referring to those that instead resort to the use of violence to attempt to achieve illegal objectives—terrorists—and we repeatedly identify them as such.

As mentioned earlier, managers need to be aware of how their organizations are perceived. If the organization is perceived negatively by some group, it is more likely to be targeted for violence by that group, so management will need to plan accordingly. In the previous chapter, numerous examples were provided of organizations that are the targets for such fanatics. Organizations that are perceived to damage the environment are more likely to be targets for environmental or ecological terrorists. Abortion clinics, bars, X-rated movie theaters, and similar organizations are likely to be targeted by religious fanatics. Law enforcement agencies will be targets for those who feel our criminal justice system is failing. Government organizations will be targets for those who oppose government or its policies. Organizations with operations in third-world countries are more likely to be targets than those that are strictly domestic in nature. Organizations that are perceived to be wealthy are more likely to be targets for thieves. Those that represent something important in society are more likely to be targets for political terrorists.

Once managers understand how their organizations are perceived, they can take steps necessary to protect their assets. Safety equipment and programs are necessary in every organization, of course. Standard protection against robbery and theft should also be employed. The design of the physical facility should be examined to assure that there are no obvious weaknesses that could either endanger the safety of employees or make it easy for outsiders to commit violence. Lighting, security alarms and cameras, and other physical security systems should be evaluated for their potential use. Just as with other organizations, if money is involved, extra security precautions should be taken because the availability of money is a powerful attraction to criminals.

All personnel should be trained to deal with emergencies, including violence and terrorism. Plans should be in place for handling emergencies before, during, and after violent events. Policies should be in place to inform everyone that violence of any kind, including managerial abuse and bullying, is not tolerated. Procedures for reporting concerns should be established and clearly communicated. With proper policies, procedures, and training, an organizational culture of non-violence is more likely to evolve, and managers and all personnel are more likely to conduct themselves in a manner to reduce the risks of workplace violence.

In addition, these organizations need to take actions to offset negative perceptions through education and public relations efforts. Educational efforts should include developing employee awareness of what the organization does and why as well as striving to have that same awareness in the general public. The media should be used through both advertising and public relations (press releases). In addition, executives and managers should be available to appear before student groups, on Chamber of Commerce programs, and in other ways to educate and project a more positive image to the general public.

In Any and All Organizations

Since stress is so clearly associated with workplace aggression and violence, organizations should carefully assess the levels of stress in their workplaces and take the necessary steps to minimize undue stress. The nature of supervision should be evaluated to assure that employees are not being subjected to undue stress as a result of abusive or bullying managers. The physical environment should be analyzed and modified as necessary to prevent stressors such as crowding, excessive noise or vibration, poor air quality, and unsatisfactory ambient temperature; and the design of the workplace itself should also be evaluated and redesigned as necessary.

Workplace redesign efforts should be studied to assure that the nature of the work provides individuals with the ability to control their own performance. Jobs should require a sufficient variety of skills to prevent boredom and preferably to provide a challenge to employees. Ideally, every job should have an identifiable aspect to the work being performed, and every member of the organization should understand and appreciate the significance of their work both to the organization and to society. Performance feedback is also critical. Each individual should receive, either from the work itself or from carefully developed performance appraisal systems, knowledge of how well he or she is performing. If all jobs within the organization possess these characteristics, dysfunctional stress will decrease and motivation and commitment will increase. In addition, combining tasks can improve the nature of work by giving those with more tasks greater control over their own work as well as increasing the variety of tasks performed. Forming natural work units among jobs can help accomplish the same objectives.

Open, organic organizational arrangements will tend to optimize the levels of stress encountered by those in the organization. Those arrangements include making tasks more interdependent and more clearly linked to organizational objectives, having upward and downward communication that is honest and receptive to criticism, and managers who see themselves not as all-powerful bosses but rather as leaders, facilitators, and developers of people.

In addition, time management techniques can be used to minimize stress and thereby decrease the probability of workplace violence. These techniques involve the following.

Plan Goals:

- Keep long-term goals in mind even when doing small tasks and unpleasant activities.
- Review and revise your longer-term goals periodically—don't worry if they change.
- Review your shorter-term goals frequently and identify daily activities to accomplish those goals.

Prioritize:

- Priority refers to importance in accomplishing longer-term goals. Just because something is due "tomorrow" doesn't mean that it is a priority item.
- Use a daily "TO DO" list, with specific items to be done each day.
- Arrange them in priority order [A = highest priority—the ones that are most likely to move you toward achieving your goals; B = intermediate priority; C = lowest priority].
- Try to complete the "A's", not "B's" or "C's."
- Have a so-called "C drawer" to store those items that you don't throw away immediately (or a personal folder in your e-mail for e-mails that you don't delete).
- Use the "80–20" rule or Pareto's Law to remind you to keep focused on those things which are highest priority [80% of your goal accomplishment will come from 20% of your activities (the "A" items)]
- Do not skip items on the daily "TO DO" list just because they are difficult or unpleasant.
- Use your workplace for work, not storage. Put the most important thing in the center of the work area.

Analyze:

- Examine old habits for possible elimination or streamlining.
- Keep a diary or time log to help you identify your major problems and opportunities.
- Identify that portion of the day when you are most creative or productive, and try to schedule routine meetings and administrative duties at other times.
- Use the power of your computer (if you have one) to make your job more efficient.

Use Time-Management Techniques:

- Give up waiting time. Use it instead as a gift of time to relax, plan, or do something that you would otherwise not have done.
- Carry blank 3 × 5 cards or a small notebook to jot down ideas and notes
- Concentrate on only one thing at a time.
- Set deadlines for yourself and others.
- Delegate where feasible and practicable, given the time demands on others.

- Screen visitors, mail, and phone calls as much as possible.
- Write replies directly on the original memo or letter (keep a copy for yourself or keep the original and send the copy).
- Be considerate of others' time as you want them to be considerate of yours. Generate as little paperwork as possible, and throw away as much as possible.
- Do something with each piece of paper you handle: respond, route it to someone else, request other information before completion if possible, etc. (this is sometimes referred to as "handling each piece of paper only once")
- Respond to e-mail only at certain times of the day (have "office hours").

Have a Time Management Philosophy:

- Take time to relax and do non-work activities, especially at night and on weekends.
- Remember the importance of interpersonal networks—don't cut off your friends.
- Always keep in mind that it is time quality, not quantity, that matters.

These time management concepts can be applied by anyone in the organization regardless of level or function. Employing these basic concepts can do wonders for reducing undue stress at the personal level.

Identify, Prioritize, and Protect Organizational Assets

In addition to these stress reduction strategies, organizations need to determine exactly which assets are most in need of protection from workplace violence.

Define and Prioritize Organizational Assets

Assets in need of protection include those that are personal, personnel, physical, and fiscal, not just the latter two. These assets would include employees who are most likely to be targeted by angry employees or outsiders, and critical facilities and equipment such as the company power plant, generators, telephone switchboard, computers, and so on.

Since not all assets can be secured immediately, the next step is to establish priorities for providing protection. The primary human targets (senior management, supervisors, and Human Resource personnel) should be given a protected place and also a secondary exit for escaping from the facility. Since receptionists are often the first to encounter violent individuals, they should be protected, trained to spot potential problems, and also given detailed instructions as to the actions they should take when they observe a potential problem.

Perform a Needs Assessment

Problem areas should be identified in a formal "needs assessment" of the employer's unique requirements. Such assessments are best performed with assistance from an outside, independent consultant. The outsider should be aggressively managed by the company, however. Fully protecting all of the assets may be too great, but some steps can be taken: e.g., a silent alarm button at receptionist's desk, a bullet-proof glass partition and locked door for the receptionist, or double doors with a security guard at each building entrance to check badges for access. The outside consultant should also perform attitude/climate surveys and meet with employees and others in focus groups to identify problems and issues that may need to be addressed. Finally, existing programs, policies, and personnel should be evaluated to determine whether they promote a positive, non-violent atmosphere.

One of the industries most vulnerable to acts of terrorism and workplace violence, the commercial airlines, provides a good example of the reason for conducting needs assessments periodically and for using outside consultants. Years ago, needs assessments resulted in various security measures to which the traveling public has become accustomed, such as x-raying baggage and using metal detectors to screen boarding passengers. More recently, needs assessments that were prompted by a new round of terrorism have identified the tarmac, not the boarding area, as perhaps the most vulnerable point. The simplest way to slip an explosive device on board is to get a job refueling the plane, cleaning the interior, or loading the baggage and the food. Pre-employment screening of such workers can never be 100 percent sure. Hence, the toughest challenge today may be the plugging of this hole in security before another plane goes down.

Correct Security Problem Areas

In a free society the rights of the organization and the rights of individuals must be balanced. These individual rights unquestionably make a company's anti-violence task more difficult. For that reason, many organizations are aware that they need to respond to violence in advance. Most major corporations conduct building security checks, employ burglar alarms, and monitor their premises via closed-circuit TV. Many others also have installed electronic card ID systems and employ armed guards. Executive protection and other internal security programs that help to ward against kidnapping, are fairly new but growing, particularly for overseas assignments. Even with such protective measures, many organizations are still quite vulnerable and therefore need to assess their situation and take preventive action.

As discussed earlier, the physical plant should be as secure as possible. All areas, both inside and out, should be well lighted with no shadow areas in which someone can hide. Coupled with the lights, landscaping should be arranged so that no one can hide behind shrubs or trees near walkways, parking lots, and buildings. Modern closed-circuit television with high-quality images should monitor interior corridors and stairwells as well as outside walkways and parking lots. Locks and sensors need to be controlled carefully to ensure limited access. Barriers such as concrete benches, sculpture, and trees should be used to prevent vehicles from delivering bombs within striking distance of the buildings. Similarly, to the extent possible, parking should be located far enough away from buildings to prevent the placement of an automobile that is carrying explosive devices that can be detonated remotely.

Establish Necessary Administrative Controls

Physical security measures alone are not enough. Regardless of how "safe" the company makes its security system, over-reliance on physical security measures is a mistake that must not be made. The most sophisticated cameras, alarms, and key-card access systems can be thwarted by a determined, violent person. More importantly, companies that rely heavily on physical measures often resort to sub-standard security personnel or ignore the internal environment. In addition to physical measures, some administrative controls may also be necessary. For example, the company may be justified in requiring that employees not work alone, that a guard be called to escort employees to their cars after hours, that passwords be changed often, that employees wear specially coded ID badges, and so on.

The company may also elect to use Post Employment Behavioral Observation Programs (BOPs), which are designed so that supervisors can note job-related behavioral changes. The forms generated in this program by managers or supervisors should then be sent to an independent agency. BOPs work well because they reduce confrontations between supervisors and employees, leading to more effective referrals for counseling.

Develop an Early Warning System

Surprise attack, possession of reliable information, and predictability of the victim's movements are major components of terrorists' operations as well as some other forms of workplace violence. Reducing the element of surprise, then, can provide some limited protection. One method of accomplishing this is to establish a prevention team to develop a surveillance awareness plan so outsiders are not able to conduct surveillance. No one can easily surprise a potential victim who constantly watches for and notes the make, model, year, color, license number, general condition, and the number of people in a vehicle that may be following him or her. Individuals should make notes on what they observe in their surroundings; a pocket tape recorder is excellent for this purpose, particularly because observers may assume that the individual is in two-way communication with someone.

To make the perpetrator's information less reliable and the victim's movements less predictable, top managers should become unpredictable in terms of their schedules—not arriving and leaving work at the same time, for instance. They should examine driving and walking routes to determine which are the most vulnerable and then alternate the routes used to the extent possible. Maintaining high levels of alertness at all times is probably impossible for many organizations, particularly "open to the public" facilities such as malls and hospitals; nevertheless, plans should be prepared.

Train and Familiarize All Employees with Security Procedures

Security procedures should be in writing, and everyone in the organization should be trained to be familiar with them. Those procedures should indicate who would be in charge during a crisis and others who would be likely to play important roles. A confidential list of potentially violent persons should be kept and periodically updated. This list should have names, descriptions and other details (such as automobile descriptions) and should be made available not only to security personnel but also to others (receptionists, clerks, and so on) who are likely to encounter the potentially violent individuals. These members of the organization should be given previously agreed-upon conditions and procedures for informing others in the organization when a potentially violent person is around. The procedures should establish the types of behavior that must be reported and the covert signal or alarm procedures for calling security, medical emergency teams, police, and/or other individuals or groups.

The organization should also provide some sort of trauma training before a violent event occurs and then be prepared to provide trauma relief counseling after any violent event. Training programs might be conducted by the organization's human resource department, an Employee Assistance Program unit, or by appropriate outside consultants. In all likelihood, trauma relief counseling will be conducted by outside consultants who have extensive experience rather than by individuals within the organization, who are less likely to have very much experience.

Summary

All organizations should strive to provide safe and secure workplaces for all personnel not just because it is legally or morally required, but also because it helps to prevent eruptions of the Violence Volcano. The nature of the work, the location of the organization, the assets of the organization, and, most importantly, the behavior of managers will dictate many of the approaches or techniques that will be employed for that purpose. However, the culture of the organization is critical to genuinely achieving that purpose.

Developing a culture that minimizes the risks of workplace violence, means that owners and managers, must first demonstrate true concern for the health and safety of all organizational stakeholders. They must be vigilant in that concern and not be distracted or lured into taking shortcuts. They must accept that theirs is the final responsibility for workplace health and safety. They must not only voluntarily comply with governmental regulations but also must go beyond to demonstrate genuine commitment to all stakeholders of their organizations especially in assuring that the treatment of all personnel is professional, ethical, and humane. This responsibility includes identifying and prioritizing assets, correcting security problem areas, establishing administrative controls, developing an early-warning system, and training and familiarizing all members of the organization with the security procedures.

PART IV
Employees

8

Employee Factors That Influence Violent Behavior

As we all know, workers differ greatly from one another as to the problems they experience both at work and outside of work. They also differ greatly as to the manner in which they respond to stimuli and are, in turn, influenced by the different reactions or responses of the people around them. Thus, just as the environment and workplace play an important role in shaping behavior, so do the individual's own job expectations, problems, motivations, attitudes, and personality traits. When these clash with the realities of the workplace, workers may reject their situation and begin to express their stress and frustration in the form of unacceptable behavior and even violence.

In other words, various expectations and motivations that are strong enough to entice or oblige workers to keep their jobs can just as easily drive them to behave inappropriately if those motivations are unfulfilled. The methods used include sabotage, subversion, threats, and revenge as well as more extreme actions such as bodily injury or murder.

Financial Factors

The struggle to meet financial obligations is one of the most familiar causes of stress and workplace violence. Sometimes that stress results in negative behavior directed toward coworkers or supervisors, especially if the overly stressed person fears losing a job or being passed over by a coworker. We are all familiar with highly-publicized cases where the employee is provoked to kill his supervisor because he lost his job and hence could not support himself or his family. As might be expected, termination is the last straw for a person who has a family to feed and other financial needs, especially under tight economic conditions with high unemployment. And if the reason for termination is tied to the worker's performance or behavior, as through firing, the negative influence on the employee may be substantially greater than if the employee were terminated because of downsizing. He may exhibit violent behavior not only because he feels desperate but also because he has little or nothing to lose.

Even when not faced with a high probability of termination, a worker can feel intolerable stress when his take-home pay is inadequate to meet his needs. He may feel trapped because he is unable to find a higher-paying job, especially during bad economic times or in small towns, or if his own job skills do not measure up to competitors in the job market. The situation is worsened considerably when that worker is also experiencing additional problems in his personal life or a stressful situation at work (e.g., a bully boss or coworker, productivity standards he cannot meet). The feeling of hopelessness will be exhibited in some manner, either internally or externally. It can lead to unacceptable treatment of coworkers, especially those who seem content, happy, and/or highly competent—or coworkers who do not show any understanding of this worker's plight.

Workers who direly need to earn more money may take additional jobs to supplement their incomes. This "moonlighting" takes away their personal and "winding down" time and increases their fatigue. A tired or stressed worker can easily become a disgruntled worker or a "free rider" (one who contributes less than his fair share) who is resented by coworkers; and that rejection can create additional pressures that could in turn lead to violent behavior.

Personal Motivations

People have different reasons for choosing a particular career and a particular employer. They have different reasons for choosing the amount of energy they will put into work—or whether to work at all, period. Coupled with personality traits, the intensity of these motivations influence employee behavior on a day-to-day basis and affect the manner in which individuals approach adversity, personal interactions, communication, problem-solving, decision-making, etc. The important element here is the manner in which each person attempts to pursue his or her objectives within an organization. Those methods can range from positive to dubious, belligerent, aggressive, offensive, combative, malicious, or hostile.

Those motivations lead some workers or their bosses to become organizational terrorists (Kinney, 1995; McCurley & Vineyard, 1998; Van Fleet & Van Fleet, 1998; Van Fleet & Van Fleet, 2006), choosing to achieve their objectives by creating fear through gossip, political tactics, harassment, intimidation, or threats. The key word here is fear. The objective of organizational terrorists is to get what they want by creating fear, not simply lashing out at or sabotaging someone in an act of anger. For example, they prey upon the fears of others who are trying to cope with the unknown and with a maze of legal constraints. Most often, organizational terrorists are intelligent and creative individuals who understand better than their targets the line between behavior that is legally permissible and that which is not. They may try to get others to speak up while they remain quietly behind the scenes, thus minimizing their risk. They may use anonymous letters, notes, and/or memos to lend credence to their ideas or to discredit others. In like manner, they may simply spread malicious gossip to discredit ideas or people. In any event, their goal is to terrorize the organization in a relatively low-key manner, without bringing undue legal attention upon themselves (Kinney, 1995, p. 96).

One example of the organizational terrorist is a minority employee who uses the fear of threatened legal action when his or her requests are turned down, whether they be relatively simple requests (e.g., a modification of policies, a change in procedure, time off for personal business) or larger demands such as a change in assignment, promotion, or salary increase that would most likely constitute favoritism or reverse discrimination. Similarly, an organizational terrorist may also be an individual who is confident that he has power or influence because he possesses vital information or company secrets which, if divulged, would significantly harm the company or individuals within the company. Organizational terrorists may also be employees in powerful positions within the organization or "bullies" who are accustomed to using threatening tactics in all of their interpersonal interactions.

Job and Work Expectations

The differences in what employees expect and what employers provide have contributed to the growing violence at work. Through the years, for example, American businesses have given employees more and more benefit packages: pay increases, health insurance, vacations, pension plans, etc. Employees have come to view these fringes and perks as workers' "rights." Now, however, employers are increasingly saying that skyrocketing insurance costs make it impossible for the company to bear the burden of health insurance. And just as the nation questions whether Social Security will be available in the future for today's taxpayers, employees are being told that their company will either cut back contributions to pension plans or has already made reckless decisions with the long-standing company pension plan. Now workers feel stressed not only about today and tomorrow but also about the years after they leave the workforce. And the workplace may well become a target for violence by older, retired workers who had counted on the company's pension plan providing them with income for the remainder of their lives.

There are other conflicts between what workers desire and what they get. Most people want to work, but they may no longer be willing to work at jobs that fall short of their expectations for enjoyment, pay, self-satisfaction, or fair treatment. Theoretically at least, satisfying jobs pay workers for doing what they enjoy doing and allow them to do what they believe they are capable of doing. Having to find, or being transferred to, a job with equal pay but tedious, unfulfilling work can damage self-esteem and job satisfaction. On the other hand, the work may be fulfilling whereas the pay may not. In such cases, the worker directs the blame toward the supervisor and/or the company. When expectations are not met regarding workplace conditions, relationships, or pay, blame may be directed toward coworkers as well as the company or its supervisors.

Employees also expect a safe workplace and may feel that management is not doing everything it can and should to provide such an environment. As society has demanded more around-the-clock convenience and unemployed workers have become increasingly desperate, workers in some jobs are more vulnerable. Also, people in those lower-paying jobs feel helpless to persuade management to provide more protection. Most certainly the management who cannot or will not pay its employees a decent salary is in neither a position nor the right mindset to spend additional dollars to protect those employees. The already stressed employee knows that the only solution is to quit the job (which can add even more stress) or to get even with the supervisor or the company.

Overtime is another area where the expectations of employees and management may differ greatly. More and more employees are placing a higher value on family time and personal time. Especially when both husband and wife are employed, overtime work can be very inconvenient and stressful. In some cases, workers complain that the organization is ruining their lives in order to save labor cost by avoiding the hiring of more full-time employees. Some people simply do not function well when their schedule is changed, even if they are paid overtime. Their coworkers and managers, in turn, bear the brunt of the unhappiness or stress felt by such workers.

Manager and Supervisor Expectations

Some employees react negatively to a supervisor's management style. Most employees today insist that management treat them respectfully, not as robots, cogs in a wheel, or inferior beings. Many supervisors have neither the time nor the qualifications to deal with the increasingly complex personal problems of their subordinates, especially the younger generations whose work ethic and style differ considerably from the older generations.

In addition, as layers of management have been abolished, spans increased, and budgets tightened, the increased stress on supervisors carries over to their subordinates. Furthermore, in a tight job market managers may take unfair advantage of the fact that an employee simply cannot afford to walk off the job. The frustration and anger that builds when an employee feels trapped in a job can lead to violence if something is not done to alleviate the problem.

Job Security

The fact that workers by the thousands are being displaced has been shocking to Americans, who had heretofore expected to stay employed for life unless their performance was extremely poor. "Job tenure" had come to be viewed as a "social contract." Many workers have parents who had a single employer for life. Starting in the 1980s, everything changed—no more guaranteed employment, no more job security. Change is now the word that is central to all our lives, and Americans find themselves needing to change jobs many times. Loyalty, diligence, and hard work are no longer rewarded with job stability and security. Worse still, finding a new job takes months or even years. Employees are seriously stressed by this instability and insecurity. How can they buy a home or even plan to support a family if they may be unemployed next week and facing relocation or perhaps unemployment for months or even years? In such a stressful time of uncertainty, where do they direct the blame? Toward the government, another country, the company, the boss, or competing coworkers?

Americans understand why layoffs must happen when a company is in financial trouble. But they do not understand why it happens when the business is not in trouble, when it is enjoying record earnings, or when executives are being given big bonuses or golden parachutes. They are angered when they learn that their jobs are being moved to another country—and even more so when that country is not particularly a friend of the United States. And they certainly don't understand it when they see the corporate officers take home millions of dollars in salaries and perks. Nor do they understand why, under those conditions, the employees who remain are expected to continually submit to an accelerated pace and an increased workload, perhaps resulting in conflicts between family and job time demands (role conflict). Such stress and resentment interfere with relationships between coworkers, and what the employee sees as disloyalty and/or greed from the employer can lead to retaliatory acts against the supervisor or against the company as a whole.

Personal Identity

For many people work has value infinitely beyond that of being a mere source of income. It also provides identity and friendships. Personal identity is tied to the individual's work. We tend to be defined and to achieve our place in society in terms of our job or career. Workers who measure the success of an individual by the dollars they earn will suffer psychologically if their pay is reduced; those who measure by their power will feel animosity when someone is promoted over them. Those who use work to provide their primary source of friendship and approval may feel helpless or anxiety-ridden when separated from their job. Such changes in friendship or identity can trigger the worst kind of fears and reactions, including violence.

Dysfunctional Behavior of Bosses and Coworkers

Some of the worst problems experienced by employees are caused by coworkers or bosses who use dysfunctional and unacceptable behavior to achieve their goals at the expense of another worker. They use techniques that are closely associated with the organizational terrorist. If the objective is to create fear, the act is clearly organizational terrorism; if not, it is "only" yet another form of workplace violence, sabotage, or dysfunctional behavior in organizations.

A common form of dysfunctional behavior by bosses is the abuse of power, in particular the use of coercive techniques such as threatening, becoming heavy-handed, or harassing workers. Other behaviors may involve the failure to control anger, being rude to employees, yelling and demeaning them, some even having explosive temper tantrums. Crudeness is also generally dysfunctional. Micromanagers are not only annoying but also they can lower a worker's productivity and increase dissatisfaction. On the other hand, the inability to accept criticism by bosses indicates that the employee is insecure or incompetent and can lead to dysfunctional responses.

Co-workers can be just as much of a problem. For example, a coworker may attempt to sabotage or subvert another person's work in a vengeful effort to create problems for that coworker, a boss, or the organization. Or a boss can undermine a subordinate's efforts to achieve a raise or promotion by withholding important work assignments, showing favoritism by giving or withholding sales leads, giving undeservedly bad performance reviews, or denying bonuses. Workers who would never think of stealing from a coworker or the company or bringing a gun to work will nevertheless engage in dysfunctional behavior such as sabotaging a project, withholding information, or discrediting someone by intentionally spreading false or misleading information.

The use of slander and misinformation campaigns, especially through the use of computers, is increasing (Naylis, 1996). For example, a disgruntled or former employee may engage in Internet revenge whereby he or she attempts to discredit his company in the eyes of customers so they will not buy the company's product or service.

Workers who manipulate, threaten, harass, bully, or engage in sabotage clearly are dysfunctional. Those who don't carry their own weight on the job or who in other ways are selfish, unfair, or disinterested are also dysfunctional. This group also includes those who lack interpersonal skills, whether they are inconsiderate, have attitude problems, or don't practice good hygiene and good taste in work attire.

Personal and Personality Factors

When an incident of workplace violence makes the news, we naturally question what would prompt the perpetrator to respond violently. Was he fired or living in fear of being fired? Could it be that this person was understandably upset by a supervisor or a coworker but lacked the skills to discuss the problem amicably? For whatever the reason, did he feel isolated from other workers? Many people are upset by a coworker or boss, feel isolated, or lose their jobs but don't react violently. Individuals respond differently to stimuli, so the question should revolve around what personality factor caused the violent response.

Some workers and supervisors have poor self-esteem and maintain a defensive posture. With no outlet for anger and no opportunity to develop a positive self-image, they are plagued by anger and frustration. Work offers the only opportunity to prove that their lives do matter, that they are indeed somebody. So if work turns out to be just another confirmation of failure, the lack of esteem may be too great to enable them to tolerate frustration, criticism, or negative messages. They receive suggestions negatively and may feel picked on or used.

The lack of anchors or family support is another situation that sometimes triggers violence. Socially isolated individuals, or "loaners," have little or nothing in their life except work. So when work is not fulfilling or is "not going right," they feel completely alone. More than just shy, they may lack social skills to interact, which may cause others to avoid them because they are "out of step."

For an individual who has been emotionally unstable, a violent response is easily triggered by something minor or major. He may have no way to express rage, anger, or frustration except through hitting, throwing, breaking, stealing, and/or substance abuse. He may be a "blamer," whose primary defense mechanism is the projection of blame onto other individuals such as a supervisor or even the entire organization. Feeling persecuted, he obviously is not at fault and is therefore helpless to correct the problem. Ultimately, his only defense would be to get even with, punish, or even eliminate the person who is causing the problem and the unhappiness. He may be suffering from anxiety, wherein anything even remotely negative may push him over the brink to his maximum level of toleration. Indeed, he may be suffering from some form of psychosis, such as paranoia, schizophrenia, or erotomania. A psychotic person will resent the person or group that has slighted him (a phenomenon that he exaggerates) and may attempt to make things right from his point of view by harassing or taking legal action.

Finally, employees who perpetrate workplace violence have access to their weapon of choice and the skill to use it, whether it be a gun, a chemical, a homemade bomb, strong computer skills, or the ability to lie convincingly. And the violent reaction may be caused by alcohol, drugs, or other substances that result in agitation, paranoia, and aggressive behavior. Some substances interfere with reasoning ability, social inhibition, and the ability to distinguish right from wrong, consequently pushing a marginally violent individual over the edge.

True personality disorders (e.g., Antisocial Personality, Borderline Personality, and Benign Personality) are beyond the scope of this material, and individuals with such disorders should be referred to medical professionals. We will note, however, that John Taylor, perpetrator of the violence at the Orange Glen, CA Post Office, was considered a "benign personality." This type of personality, with its all-encompassing desire for harmony at any cost, lets the pressure build inside rather than expressing it. As a result, resentment builds until it reaches the explosion point, where it cannot be vented in any way short of extreme violence.

Personal and personality factors are covered in greater detail in the next chapter, in discussing the training of management and employees to recognize and cope with these factors.

Summary

Just as with the environment and workplace, the influences discussed in this chapter, also can lead to violence. Those who encounter these sorts of situations will react, and if the situation continues, they will reject their situation and begin to express their stress and frustration. By then others, particularly managers, should be aware of the potential for violence; but if nothing significant is done in the eyes of the person or persons involved, their feelings and behavior escalate and intensify and the potential for violence grows quickly. If it is not quelled, eruption will be the result. The next chapter discusses possible ways to deal with these influences.

9

Dealing with Employee Factors Related to Violence

We have seen in the preceding chapter that workplace violence is not always caused by the environment or the workplace but rather by an employee's own personality, problems, or job expectations. As we all know, workers differ greatly from one another as to the problems or difficulties they experience both at work and outside of work. They also differ greatly as to the manner in which they respond to stimuli and are, in turn, influenced by the different reactions or responses of the people around them.

Clearly, the best way to handle workplace violence problems is to have an early detection system, including pre-employment psychological screening, to enable the organization to avoid hiring potentially violent employees in the first place. If potentially violent employees already work at the company, the second best solution is to identify them before it is too late.

Train to Recognize Personal Characteristics and Personal History

Based on available information, several characteristics have been identified that the company should consider when deciding whether to offer or renew an employment contract. Remember, though, that any itemization of personal characteristics, while useful in focusing attention on the early detection and prevention of workplace violence, must also be used very carefully since such lists contain only very general guidance and the lists also change over time as new information is obtained. The presence of one or more of these factors does not guarantee that a person will commit an act of violence in the future.

Was Recently Disciplined

Discipline is often the trigger that precedes violence. Since discipline is a necessary part of work life in order to avoid chaos, it should be handled sensibly (more on this later), and afterwards the individual being disciplined should be observed discreetly by management and workers for negative signs of behavior. Some companies maintain a discipline-based culture where even minor indiscretions are penalized; others have a laissez-faire attitude, giving the employees enough rope to hang themselves. The ideal is probably a balance between too lax and too heavy-handed.

History of Violence

Violence breeds violence. With each criminal act, the probability of future crime increases. Thus, a history of violence is the single best predictor of violence. Care must be exercised in investigating people's backgrounds, however. Asking about convictions is legal, as criminal convictions are public records; asking about arrests is not permissible.

Suspicious Job History

Further scrutiny is in order when an employee or applicant's job history shows unverifiable dates or jobs, unexplained gaps in dates, or hints of troubled relationships. A migratory job history may indicate that the individual cannot hold a job because of outbursts, confrontations, or other anti-social behavior. Do not jump to conclusions, however, as omitting dates from resumes has become common practice to avoid age discrimination. Also, periods of unemployment and job changes have become somewhat common due to the nation's recent economy. When in doubt, ask the individual for an explanation.

Unfavorable Military Record

Disciplinary problems in the military almost always foretell problems in the workplace. While problems can sometimes be explained by the individual's inability to operate effectively in a highly structured setting, such problems should nevertheless be investigated further to see if deeper problems exist. Another potential problem area is fanatical behavior in the military, which is discussed in greater detail below.

Fascination with Guns and Weapons

Ownership of guns or gun collections combined with a fascination with weapons and shooting skills are significant indicators to worry about. As a general rule, it is time to do more than observe when an employee shows a fascination with the military and talks more than normal about owning guns, particularly if that employee is also under stress and fits other aspects of the violence profile.

Certainly not all soldiers, not all Vietnam veterans, are violent. But it has been noted that many people who eventually become violent *do* dress in military camouflage and *do* act like they're about to engage in combat or show some other obsession with the military. According to Bruce Blythe, President and CEO of Crisis Management International in Atlanta: "those with access to guns and those who have killed before may find it easier to use that gun and kill again" (Blythe, 2002). Again, care must be taken not to over-generalize; many of these same people are outspoken against violence. Nevertheless, perpetrators of violence in the workplace seem to have an undue availability of weapons, particularly handguns but also semiautomatic and fully automatic assault weapons. Of course, employees should be advised never to bring a weapon onto company property and always to inform management of any weapon they observe someone else bring to the workplace.

Fanatical Behavior or Extremist Views

Fanatics are extremists on some issue. Usually they focus on political or religious issues but in all cases tend to be intolerant of individuals whose views are different from theirs. Fanatical behavior also extends to excessive interest in media reports of violence, especially workplace violence. Extremists may use a violent act either to capture the attention of the Press, to force their beliefs on others, to rid the world of the "nonbelievers," or to carry out what their Supreme Being or God has supposedly told them to do. Another potential problem is "copycat" actions—which may explain some of the incidents that have occurred in the U.S. Postal Service. The potential copycat may talk repeatedly about the incident but the ultimate warning signal would be a statement like "It could happen here, too," or "I sometimes feel like doing the same thing."

Substance Abuse

Work behavior changes resulting from the abuse of alcohol, drugs, and other substances are almost always in a negative direction. Such abuse results in agitation, paranoia, or aggressive behavior as it interferes with reasoning ability, social inhibition, and the ability to distinguish right from wrong. Consequently, a marginally violent individual can be pushed over the edge.

Some substance abusers are relatively easy to spot from their physical signs—an odor of alcohol, flushed face, disheveled appearance, slurred speech, difficulty walking, and so on. Others may be more difficult to spot, but substance abuse may be suspected when an employee exhibits secretive-type behavior around his/her locker, meets other employees or visitors in remote areas, takes excessively long lunch breaks, has chronic absences, or has a strong pattern of missing work on Mondays.

Emotional Instability

Emotional instability is often the reason that coworkers give for another's violent behavior while at the same time saying things like "We never saw this coming" or "He never gave any indication he had problems." Laymen are not equipped to diagnose emotional instability, but personality tests are available to measure the characteristics that suggest violent tendencies. On *people-relations scales*, for example, low scorers have five times more arguments with customers, arguments with co-workers, and customer complaints. High scorers are more dependable, follow company policies better, and follow work schedules. Low scorers on **workplace safety scales** are more accident prone, having five times as many on-the-job injuries; high scorers rated better on safety by supervisors. Low scorers on **dependability scales** have been shown to be more likely to use alcohol or drugs and miss ten times as much work. These tests should be administered only by a qualified person, however.

Blaming Others

When some workers experience problems or unhappiness, their primary defense mechanism is the projection of blame onto other individuals, such as a supervisor or even the entire organization. They are argumentative and feel persecuted. Obviously, if they are not at fault, they are helpless to correct the problem. If they carry this assessment to its ultimate conclusion, they will have to get even with, punish, or even eliminate the person who is causing the problem and the unhappiness.

No Healthy Way to Express Rage

Violent acts are committed by people who have learned no healthy way to express rage, anger, or frustration. They have grown accustomed to venting their feelings through temper tantrums, hitting, throwing, breaking, stealing, and/or substance abuse.

Heightened Anxiety

Anxiety at work may stem from work-related factors or from frustration with the outside environment. Outside variables can trigger violent behavior at the worksite when the individual reaches his maximum level of toleration. Before it escalates into violent behavior, anxiety may manifest itself in increased aches and pains plus changes in sleep, eating or sex patterns, blood pressure, and muscle tension, as well as causing other behavioral changes such as a flaring temper or drug abuse.

Psychosis

Some violence perpetrators have been clinically diagnosed as suffering from sort of psychosis, such as paranoia, schizophrenia, and erotomania. In addition to being concerned about the safety of employees who work with individuals suffering from psychosis disorders, management must also recognize that the way employees perceive they are treated by management is the way they tend to treat the customers; thus, customer satisfaction is a function of employee satisfaction. A worker may indeed be paranoid or schizophrenic, but the layman is in no position to diagnose such problems. Keep in mind that it is the degree of maladjustment that separates the "normal" from the "psychotic." Having said that, however, for everyone's safety, supervisors and management should be alert to the symptoms listed below that suggest some form or some degree of psychosis:

- Constantly anxious, irritable, angry, annoyed, mad, or disgruntled about some injustice that they perceive at work.
- Feel that supervisors don't take them seriously; feel exploited or slighted.
- Believe that everyone is out to get them.
- Believe they possess insight that no others have (a la Rev. Jim Jones and David Koresh).

- Highly suspicious, which creates anger, hostility, and violence; but may be excellent workers and have good attendance, performance, and conduct.
- Engage in disjointed conversations and may express bizarre delusions about such things as being a revolutionary or anarchist, or being approached by a UFO.
- Depressed, withdrawn, and may talk of suicide.

A psychotic person will resent the person or group that he perceives as having slighted him (a phenomenon that he exaggerates) and may attempt to make things right by harassing or taking legal action. "The persecutory type must be taken seriously because they have the ability for violence" (Baron, 1993, pp. 24–25).

In the erotomania (Romance Obsession) disorder, the individual will stalk, spy on, telephone, and send gifts and love letters to "the fixated object" of his or her attraction. This is not a sexual attraction. Your employee may be the "fixated object," not the person suffering from erotomania; and most likely the only way the company will know about the problem is for the "fixated object" to report the problem—or to become the victim of violence while at the workplace.

Personality Magnification

Employees who tend to be assertive and aggressive may become more demanding and confrontational; those who tend to avoid problems withdraw further even though their resentment increases. While neither aggressiveness nor the desire for solitude is abnormal at some level, either extreme should be closely observed.

Personality Disorders or Lack of Social/Family Support

Personality disorders (e.g., Antisocial Personality, Borderline Personality, and Benign Personality) are beyond the scope of this material and are disorders that should be referred to medical professionals by managers and supervisors. We will note, however, that John Taylor, perpetrator of the violence at the Orange Glen, CA Post Office, was considered a "benign personality." This type of personality, with its all-encompassing desire for harmony at any cost, lets the pressure build inside rather than expressing it. As a result, they build resentment until it reaches the explosion point, where it cannot be vented in any way short of extreme violence.

Perpetrators of workplace violence are often socially isolated—they are loners. Since they have little or nothing in their life except work, when it is not fulfilling or not going right, they feel completely alone. These individuals avoid socializing at lunch, coffee breaks, or other social activities. They seem more than just shy—they may lack social skills to interact, which may cause others to avoid them because they are "out of step." Others may be the product of a chaotic family life, and perhaps perpetuate this in their lives. They either talk about unhappiness at home or exhibit the other extreme: the omission of any mention of home life.

Poor Self-Esteem and a Defensive Posture

With no outlet for anger and no opportunity to develop a positive self-image, workers with poor self-esteem are plagued by anger and frustration. Work offers the only opportunity to prove that their lives do matter, that they are indeed somebody. If work turns out to be just another confirmation of failure, the lack of esteem may be too great to enable them to tolerate frustration, criticism, or negative messages. They receive suggestions negatively and may feel picked on or used.

Problems in Credit and Driving Records

The employee's credit history can help you decide whether the person can be relied on, which may be vitally important if he is to be given responsibility for money, equipment, or inventory. An individual's driving record is of obvious importance if that employee will be driving a company vehicle. It may also help identify an individual who pushes the limits or generally has disrespect for the law.

Train to Recognize Work Behaviors and Relationships

Persons who work together eight hours a day are frequently in a good position to observe behaviors and characteristics that may indicate that something is wrong. These signs and symptoms are signals that the Violence Volcano is rumbling and a person may be capable of being triggered toward violence.

Trained observers see signals that would otherwise be overlooked or ignored, so they can protect themselves and also report any threatening remarks or situations to alert others. Training can help supervisors identify potentially violent employees through post-employment behavioral observation or dangerousness assessments. Such training, along with training employees to recognize danger signs and symptoms, will help create a safe environment, give employees security, and show them that the organization cares about them. In addition, it helps individuals tolerate the additional costs, potential delays, and extra rules that are necessary to prevent violence. At the same time, everyone needs to understand that a person's behavior results from who they are and the situation in which they find themselves. It is important to recognize the interaction between the person and the situation.

Prediction training, then, should focus on behavioral indicators or warning signs, not personality. It should stress tolerance for others regardless of race, age, gender, religion, national origin, or position. Some of the more specific signs and symptoms to look for include the following:

Loss of Interest in Work

In addition to some of the personal characteristics discussed earlier, potentially violent employees frequently lose interest in work and can be expected to portray that attitude in their behaviors and relationships at the workplace; e.g., absenteeism, tardiness, turnover, lowered levels of productivity, a reduction in the work quality, complaining, taking long breaks repeatedly, making excessive personal calls on the phone, or just wasting time in some other way.

Threatening Behavior or Words

An employee who has been pushed to the edge of his tolerance will often become belligerent and overreact to criticism, even to the point of making threats toward another employee or supervisor. He or she may display sudden mood swings or sexual or some other form of harassment toward others. Anyone can overreact to criticism occasionally and everyone experiences changes in mood; the frequency and degree are the important difference with which to be concerned.

Malicious Gossip

A variation of this is when the individual initiates, perpetuates, and/or participates in the spread of malicious gossip and rumors about co-workers or the organization. This is just another way of trying to retaliate against or get even with the individual or company.

Disgruntled Complaints

Surely every worker is sometimes critical of his company or his working conditions. Simply complaining is not so bad, but *overreacting* to a change in corporate procedure or policy is indicative of a deeper problem. Complaints of heightened stress at work (or any kind of chronic complaints, for that matter) are attempts to communicate that the worker feels overburdened. These complaints may not even be originating from work, but if ignored they may give way to rage, anxiety, or lack of control through some other means.

Attendance Problems

As indicated earlier, an employee who has excessive absences or tardiness may be exhibiting a lack of interest in his work or signs of substance abuse. He may also be venting his anger toward the supervisor, co-workers, or the company; or his negative feelings may make it difficult for him to come to work in a timely manner and stay on the job for the entire shift. It is also possible that the individual could be having personal difficulties that could lead to more serious problems unless addressed soon.

Property Destruction or Theft

Individuals who destroy, sabotage, or steal property clearly have the potential for greater violence and should be dealt with quickly. In some cases, the behavior is an immediate, observable reaction from anger; in other cases, it is more devious. In either case, the question is where and how will it end.

Labor–Management Disputes

Most people who have the previous characteristics also have many unresolved labor/management disputes or physical or emotional injury claims. They become so frustrated that they explode when these elements are not taken care of promptly or properly. Numerous unresolved physical or emotional injury claims suggest that a deeper problem is bothering the employee. This behavior may be a psychosomatic or stress-laden indicator of physical or mental health problems; but it may also represent genuine anger toward the company. Either way, the behavior must not be ignored.

Uncontrollable Temper and Outbursts

Anytime a loss of temper-control culminates in a threat, it is time to take preventive, intervention-based action, as little time may remain to correct the problem before it escalates into a violent action. Also of concern anytime are emotional outbursts, physical violence, unpredictable behavior, inappropriate remarks, including vague or blatant threats; or statements which might be interpreted as delusional, such as referencing UFOs, the end of the world, being spied on, seeing elves, and secretive behavior (Baron, 1993, p. 51).

Concentration Problems

If any employee suddenly starts becoming easily distracted and forgetful and is obviously preoccupied with outside concerns, he or she may be displaying the first step towards potential violence. On the other hand, sometimes it may also signal physical problems, depression, or family worries that are carrying over to the workplace and could or could not result in violence.

Requires Much Supervision

If an employee requires an inordinate amount of time from managers coaching or counseling him concerning personal problems or having to redo his work, it is a signal that the employee is in need of additional assistance outside the supervisor's expertise. The role of the supervisor is to develop skills and increase productivity, not to be a counselor. If after working with an employee the supervisor does not observe changes in performance, other steps such as referring the employee to professional care should be taken.

Change in Behavior or Personal Appearance

Supervisors and workers should be alert for significant changes in another employee's behavior or personality. Many workplace murderers change from quiet, silent employees who have a lot on their minds to deranged killers who come full circle. They need help quickly if a behavior change is already apparent. Marked changes in personal grooming habits are important signals to note.

Inconsistent Work Habits

Alternating high and low productivity may indicate substance abuse or signal physical problems or depression. Closer observation should be taken to ascertain whether there is a pattern that necessitates action.

Decline in Productivity or Performance

A pronounced deterioration in work performance should always be noted and investigated. There is always a reason for an employee's performance shifting from good to poor, or for high-quality work going to a high level of mistakes. Missing project deadlines and wasting time or materials likewise represent a change in attitude or health that could lead to more serious problems. The deterioration of performance after years of good service is a glaring warning sign of trouble ahead. It could signify illness, drugs, depression, or many other things — but it is a warning sign.

Bullying and Abusive Behavior

Bullying or abusive behavior by workers or managers is another warning sign. Bullies are power or control seekers who are insecure, feel inadequate (without admitting it), or who experienced abusive behavior in their home or work lives. Bullies may act alone or in a group. While most bullies are easy to identify—they shout at co-workers or subordinates, throw things, slam doors, or are insulting and rude—others are more difficult to identify. Remember the kid in first grade who was already an expert in hurting other children but had the face of an angel when the teacher was looking? Managers or coworkers may appear reasonable and courteous but engage in rumor mongering, plotting behind someone's back, sending anonymous memos that attack people's character, and sabotage others' work. Bullying or abusive bosses or co-workers can cause real and serious physical and emotional damage to people in the organization and so should be identified and eliminated from the organization.

Train to Recognize How Violence Builds Through Different Levels

As already indicated, a worker exhibiting the signals discussed above may never resort to violence in any form. And contrary to what many people think, violence does not "just happen;" it is a process. In virtually all instances of workplace violence, the emotionally enraged employee had experienced a build-up of life stresses over time. These problems or stressors simply built to a level that became too much to bear, making the person view violence as the only alternative. It would be helpful, therefore, if supervisors and coworkers could foresee that breaking point.

Baron (1993) believes that violent employees fall within one or more of three groups that he has defined on the basis of the number and type of work characteristics and behaviors.

Level One:

- Refuses to cooperate with supervisors
- Spreads rumors and gossip to harm others
- Argues with co-workers
- Belligerent toward customers/clients
- Swears at others
- Makes unwanted sexual comments

Level Two:

- Argues increasingly with customers, vendors, co-workers, and management
- Refuses to obey company policies and procedures

- Sabotages equipment and steals property for revenge
- Expresses a desire to hurt co-workers and/or management
- Sends sexual or violent notes to others in the organization
- Feels victimized by management

Level Three:
- Frequent displays of intense anger resulting in:
- Recurrent suicidal threats
- Recurrent physical fights
- Destruction of property
- Utilization of weapons to harm others
- Commission of murder, rape, and/or arson

Take Special Precautions with Computers

Companies are beginning to learn that they must monitor the Internet sometimes more zealously than they monitor their physical premises. They must also be careful with their treatment of employees, especially discipline and termination. A more recent tactic, mailbox stuffing, can effectively shut down the company's online operations, costing it dearly in both dollars and goodwill. Unfortunately, the company learns about this only when it attempts to read its e-mail.

Although the Internet is a relative newcomer to the business scene, already it is becoming a powerful tool in the commission of organizational crime and as a means of instilling fear. One simple message or even a question posted Online can cause a public-relations nightmare at best for the unsuspecting company. Because of the speed with which it can spread rumors and innuendo, considerable damage can be done before the company even knows something has been said.

In 1995, for example, a Prodigy member posted a false message online, saying that the public stock offering that had just been made by a certain New York investment bank was a fraud. Without checking the accuracy or authenticity of the message, Internet users assumed that it was an honest statement; and the bank suffered irreparably even though it was entitled to file a libel suit. In other cases, disgruntled individuals simply raise a question or pass along an alleged comment that they know other Internet users will spread (e.g., I've heard that XYZ's new Product is good on Criterion A but is severely lacking on Criterion B. Has anybody tried it?).

In 1995, K-Mart hired Rod Fournier of Detroit to create a Web site for them. Using what Fournier now recognizes as poor judgment, he created a link from that page to his own personal Web site, which included some adult material that caused a customer to complain to K-Mart. K-Mart fired Fournier, and he decided to get even with the large Troy, MI merchandising giant. The disgruntled former employee went straight home and in three hours created what is now referred to as "the world's first K-Mart Sucks home page." Fournier used the page to give his own version of the firing, to show reprints of articles condemning K-Mart's action, and to post e-mail messages from hundreds of other people who thought he was right and K-Mart was wrong. Fournier was able to create much ill will for K-mart while escaping the possibility of being held libelous, as he carefully chose his words.

Before the Internet became commercialized, Phoenix, AZ attorneys Lawrence Cantor and Martha Siegel posted an ad for their services on the net. Angry Internet veterans who opposed commercials on their communication highway flooded the attorneys' e-mail boxes with hate letters and forced them off the Internet temporarily. By mid-1996, flooding e-mail boxes seemed to be one of the most common forms of Internet revenge.

The Internet has also become the medium of choice for social networking, e.g. Facebook and Twitter. Social networking sites are increasingly being linked to efforts to reduce workplace, domestic, and other forms of violence, but there are legitimate concerns about their being used to post or twitter comments that result in incidents of violence. The open communication of social networking can shed light on incidents, provide support groups for victims and potential victims, and bring about political pressure for legislation or reforms to reduce violence. However, sometimes that same open communication can serve to push abusers "over the edge" so that they increase their level of violent behavior or spread harmful and untrue information about products or companies.

Train to Diffuse Potentially Violent Situations

Organizations typically begin their intervention training with first-line supervisors. Yet some problematic employee behaviors are commonly seen, felt, and addressed first by coworkers since most work groups have a rather well-defined social order that serves to mediate a variety of work group ills. Sometimes this backfires; for example, after excessive absences by an employee, others begin "taking their turns" calling in sick to get their share of the time-off pie. Thus, all employees and not just first-line supervisors need training in how to help diffuse a hostile and potentially violent situation. This training should particularly include how to diffuse tension and deal with harassment, diversity, and preventing workplace violence. Managerial and supervisory training programs should include the following topics:

- Stress management
- Communication, including incident reporting
- Conflict resolution
- Dealing with difficult people, particularly customers
- Conducting terminations
- Personal safety
- Liability issues
- Managing change
- Team building
- Cultural diversity

That training must also include recognizing the indicators of potential violence—the early warning signs of emotional upset, not just the final indicators of explosiveness (covered later in this chapter). They must know not to treat disturbed employees like other, more stable employees, as they have special needs and may respond negatively to "normal" behaviors on your part. Such personal knowledge of subordinates requires that supervisory personnel spend adequate time with their subordinates on the job to get to know each one well enough to be able to detect early warning signs of stress, depression, or hostility.

It is always helpful if coworkers and managers know when an employee is undergoing stress from any of the environmental influences discussed in an earlier chapter. While they may be unable to solve another worker's problem by intervening directly, coworkers may be able to alleviate some of the stress simply by showing camaraderie or by being careful not to add to the worker's stress.

Provide an Adequate Support System to Prevent Violence

From a financial point of view, if workers were considered replaceable parts, little or no effort would be justified for helping them solve personal problems. But labor is a variable cost, not a fixed cost, to organizations. As such, labor can be expensive to replace.

Although no plan can actually guarantee freedom from workplace violence, many incidents can be avoided if organizations will take threats seriously. Management should understand that the organization expects loyalty and that employees expect compensation and security. Employees want to think that they will retain their jobs if they do their work well. Also, since identity is tied to work, employees look to their job in time of need. But when personal performance no longer guarantees security and employees can no longer count on their job to fulfill their needs, stress results. That stress is further compounded when family or other forms of social support also cannot be obtained. As we know all too well, workplace violence is frequently committed by *former* employees whose anger has continued to build, often because of perceived mistreatment. So the organization especially needs to have effective programs in place to help employees who are having problems or are facing termination. Some of the more popular programs include the following:

Behavioral Observation Programs (BOPs)

The company may elect to use Post Employment Behavioral Observation Programs (BOP), which are designed so that supervisors can note job-related behavioral changes. The forms generated in this program by managers or supervisors should then be sent to an independent agency. BOPs work well because they reduce confrontations between supervisors and employees, leading to more effective referrals for counseling.

Employee Assistance Programs (EAPs)

As a support system for employees, Employee Assistance Programs (EAPs) generally have four objectives: assisting managers with performance deficits associated with personal problems; offering professional help to employees and their families; educating employees to prevent future problems; and reducing the social stigma often associated with personal problems (Berman, 1986). EAPs can help management and employees both with prevention of incidents and recovery from incidents.

Prevention: Employee Assistance Programs (EAPs) can reduce the likelihood that employees who are highly stressed would engage in various forms of workplace violence. EAPs conduct education and training programs for employees as well as for managers. Those programs contribute to the employee's ability to resist psychological and physical stress. EAPs further assist employees by addressing issues in work flow, scheduling and the use of flextime, lateral transfers, and employee wellness. Many companies already have EAPs to deal with substance abuse, rising health and safety costs, and increased stress in the workplace. EAP services may range from counseling to offering a wide range of employee services including emergency financial aid assistance, wellness programs, legal aid services, car pool assistance, health and wellness equipment and workout gyms, smoking-cessation assistance, and substance-abuse programs (Martin, 1989).

Recovery: Functions of an EAP after a violent incident would include identification of symptoms of employee stress, emotional problems, and substance abuse. Ways to reduce stress caused by an incident of violence could include management development programs to address problematic team work, personality types, decision-making skills, and sociopsychological interaction skills. Most employees may need some form of counseling or support group to cope with the trauma. Counselors specializing in trauma should be brought in to assist with psychological debriefing of personnel. For those who want to be transferred, relocated, or retired, career assessment and development skills would be appropriate. Safety improvement and reduction of ergonomic factors that contribute to an employee's psychological and physical stress would also be covered (Rosen, 1985).

EAPs also help organizations by providing professional help to those affected by workplace violence, stress, emotional problems, and substance abuse. To reduce these problems, the EAPs sponsor management development programs that address problematic team work, personality types, decision-making skills, and socio-psychological interaction skills.

Through education and training as well as counseling, EAPs can assist managers and supervisors in understanding the performance deficits that are the natural result of workplace violence. That understanding helps to prevent adverse negative reactions on the part of management.

Reasons for Using EAPs: There are at least three good reasons for recommending the extension of EAPs to include violence prevention: (a) the involvement of EAPs in worker welfare is familiar to both management and employees, (b) the infrastructure is already in place, and (c) the potential success of EAPs in providing other types of worker assistance has been confirmed. As of the late 1980s, estimates of the number of firms using EAPs varied from 5,000 (Lyons, 1987) to 12,000 (Stackel, 1987) and from approximately 60 percent of all *Fortune* 500 companies (Watts, 1988) to over two-thirds of the first 50 of the 1986 top 500 Canadian companies (Conlon, 1987). Since 80 to 90 percent of all industrial accidents have been attributed to personnel problems, EAPs that are focused on prevention, treatment, and rehabilitation could save an organization a great deal of money (Jansen, 1986). Indeed, the U.S. Bureau of Labor Statistics has estimated that $800 million invested in EAPs each year generates about $4 billion in total savings (Cook, 1991). EAPs have been estimated to cost only $22 to $25 per employee per year (Stackel, 1987). Clearly, extending the mandate of EAPs to include violence prevention should prove beneficial to organizations.

Many EAPs are handled by external vendors to alleviate problems of confidentiality. The availability of professional expertise 24-hours a day and the geographic location also are factors contributing to the success or failure of the programs. Programs developed to deal with employee productivity and substance abuse seem to be regarded as valuable (Neddermeyer, 1986). Most employees are thought to have been helped by early detection and intervention. Once an employee problem is suspected, observation, documentation, confrontation, referral, and follow-up are needed.

Reduce Social Stigma

The social stigma felt by workers when facing personal problems can be reduced by providing wellness programs at the job site, performing health screening, offering employee education, stress management programs, smoking cessation and substance-abuse programs.

Eliminate Bullying

To eliminate bullying and abusive behavior, organizations should establish a zero-tolerance anti-bullying policy. That policy should clearly define bullying and abusive behavior. It should state that the organization supports the right of everyone to a workplace free from such behavior. It should be communicated to all members of the organization. Everyone should be trained to recognize bullying and abusive behavior and to report it immediately. The organization should have a process by which it can investigate charges of such behavior that will assure those who report the behavior that there will be no retaliation against them.

Exhibit Post-Violence Patience

Management must recognize that performance will not return to normal immediately after employees have experienced a violent ordeal. Productivity can be expected to be sub-normal for a period of time. Fatigue, hurt, fear, and anger will initially distract everyone from their jobs. Absenteeism, tardiness, and general productivity declines are likely to continue for a while. Managerial personnel need to be aware of this and not complicate the problem by striving to return to normal performance levels too quickly.

Train for Emergencies When Violence is Not Preventable

Finally, training for workplace violence should include how to cope with emergencies that may result from various types of violent events that could not be prevented, including first aid, CPR, notification of officials and families, reuniting points after the event, and certainly personal safety protection.

Training for emergencies should be conducted in a low-key but intense and thorough manner like safety drills for fire, earthquakes, and similar catastrophic events; and procedures should be similarly posted throughout the workplace. Two of the primary points must be (a) take responsibility for your own safety first, and (b) attempt to assess the acuteness of the situation so you will know how much you can also help others. Foremost among instructions given to employees and also posted in the plant are (a) phone numbers for security, Human Relations, EAP, law enforcement, and/or specific individuals who should be alerted first; (b) evacuation routes and how/where to re-establish contact with the company; and (c) how to render First Aid and CPR. Everyone will benefit from having employees trained to make informed judgments as to when they can and should attempt to intervene and when they should flee the scene.

Based on the findings from the surveys mentioned earlier, employees may also need training in other areas, such as how to enter a potentially risky area, how to travel safely, and how to operate specific pieces of equipment properly.

Summary

A whole host of characteristics have been shown to be related in greater or lesser degrees to and individual's propensity to display violent behavior. They include the following:

- Was recently disciplined
- Has a history of violence
- Has a suspicious job history
- Has an unfavorable military record
- Has a fascination with guns and weapons
- Displays fanatical behavior or has extremists' views
- Shows evidence of substance abuse
- Displays signs of emotional instability
- Tends to blame others for problems
- Does not seem to have a healthy way to express rage
- Seems to be having heightened anxiety
- Shows signs of psychosis
- Displays personality magnification
- Lacks anchors or family support
- Has poor self-esteem and a defensive posture
- Has problems in credit and driving records

In addition to personal factors that may push an employee toward violence, other pressures can arise from the organization itself. Those are covered in the next chapter.

PART V
The Organization

10

Organizational Influences on Workplace Violence

Although individuals cannot be absolved from blame for violence, in some cases it is the organization itself that is "sick" enough to trigger workplace violence. In a "sick" environment, individuals may relieve their stress or vent their negative feelings by engaging in destructive behavior. If the organization does not acknowledge and change its climate, the hostility continues to build and can be expected to erupt in more extreme violent behavior, such as death or other irreparable damage.

A "sick" environment may exist because of mismanagement, including either negligent or intentional practices and behaviors on the part of management. It may result from control mechanisms that are either too tight or too lacking. In the early 1990s for example, the U.S. Postal Service's employee surveys showed that "a significant percentage of the organization's 700,000 employees were unhappy with working conditions and management styles" (Kinney, 1995, p. 37). As a result, those workers became abusive toward their supervisors, company property, customers' mail, and each other.

Symptoms of a "sick" internal environment include higher-than-average levels of turnover, disputes, grievances, injury claims, coercive behavior, sabotage, and other indications of over-stressed personnel. Stress that could lead to workplace violence may be increasing due to inappropriate management behavior, inappropriate organizational policies, a reliance on management fads, or any number of other factors. Other characteristics of an organization's internal environment that could lead to violence include an authoritarian management style, the use of extremely tight control mechanisms, improper treatment of employees, and other working conditions to which employees strongly object. In the following discussion, we address these characteristics of the undesirable internal environment under separate headings, which results in unavoidable overlap of some points. We beg the reader's indulgence for this repetition.

Inappropriate Management Styles/Behaviors

The changing nature of work environments and of the workforce discussed in earlier chapters necessitates different managerial styles than were practiced and accepted fifty years ago. Extreme authoritarianism that once was the mode has long since been shown to be dysfunctional to modern organizations. The same is true of bullying, abusive behavior.

Strained working relationships, rivalries with co-workers, hidden agendas, lack of trust, and bullying and abusive managerial tactics are all examples of inappropriate managerial behavior. Managers whose attitudes and behaviors are intimidating or degrading hinder employees rather than develop them. As a result, these inappropriate managerial behaviors obstruct long-term high performance and lead to harassment, conflict, resistance to change, and only lip service being paid to ethical values.

Abusive Management

Managerial abuse can take a variety of forms. While not intended to be all inclusive, the following list captures some of the more common forms:

Visual Abuse: rolling eyes, obscene gestures, threatening gestures, graffiti

Verbal Abuse: either oral or written insults, swearing, name-calling, gossiping, spreading rumors, taunting

Physical Abuse: hitting, slapping, pushing, kicking, squeezing, shaking, shoving, pinching, misuse of any medication, withholding appropriate health care, undue restraint

Sexual Abuse: inappropriate touching, use of sexual terms, displaying sexually explicit photographs, demanding sexual favors for favorable assignments or personal actions, sexual assault, rape, or other sexual acts
Psychological Abuse: threats of harm; shunning; humiliation; shouting; bullying; name-calling; intimidation; rumoring; harassment; lying to turn employees against one another; undesirable, inappropriate, or impossible work assignments
Financial or Economic Abuse: withholding money or possessions, intentional mismanagement of finances or property, theft, fraud, embezzlement, misappropriation of finances
Discriminatory Abuse: action, decisions, or language that constitutes harassment of or discrimination against individuals because of their race, sex, age, disability, faith, sexual orientation, or age
Abuse of Civil Rights: the denial of or coercive influence on an individual's constitutional or legislated rights

While weak economic conditions and poor job markets may permit brutal treatment of employees in pursuit of short-term goals, a better-educated and more mobile workforce could cause such behavior to be short-lived through collective and/or legal action. The advice to "praise in public but criticize in private" has never been more appropriate. Yet, even that advice does not work well for employees from a few cultures where public praise is considered undesirable. Today's managers need to be sensitive to various cultures and then treat employees accordingly.

Intentional Mismanagement

Some organizations have managers who intentionally mismanage. The most common form is dodging responsibility by making employees scapegoats. Managers have been known to turn off safety devices to save money while endangering the lives of employees. Next might be cooking the books—subtly or not so subtly altering accounting or other records to make the organization's performance appear better than it really was. Even worse is the practice of coercing employees to alter records or perform other illegal or immoral acts, often under overt or implied threat of losing their jobs. In a similar vein, managers have been known to sabotage projects to cover up cost overruns or other signs of incompetence. Intentional mismanagement in recent years by top management at companies like Enron, Adelphia Communications, and WorldCom has demonstrated that workers have reason to be tense about their employment stability and future retirement. There will no doubt be many similar instances when the truth is known about practices leading up to the 2008–2009 crises in the mortgage and banking industries.

Management Fads

Adopting management fads can also lead to a poor work environment. The *One Minute Manager* (Blanchard & Johnson, 1983) leads to the *59 Second Employee* (André & Ward, 1984). In poor economic times popular press books advocating "militaristic" or "police" approaches seem to become popular. However, managers adopting those approaches quickly see them as dysfunctional, leading to legal problems in the longer term.

Inappropriate Management Policies

In addition to inappropriate behavior, many organizations have inappropriate management policies. Among these are policies that are out of place for the local culture, such as a complete prohibition of alcoholic beverages in a country or other area in which wine is the normal drink at lunch or forcing employees to participate in prayer breaks. Attempting to restrict non-work activities of organizational members, or forcing them to "volunteer" for other non-work activities or to contribute involuntarily to political or charitable causes, would be inappropriate as well. Policies that tell employees that they must "buy American" in their household purchases, including automobiles, would be yet another example. Another policy that raises red flags is forbidding employees to discuss their pay with their spouse in an attempt to prevent employees from finding out surreptitiously what their coworkers are paid. Performance appraisal policies and systems that rely heavily on subjective judgments rather than on objective performance can lead to perceived inequity in rewards that in turn creates a climate that can lead to workplace violence. In like manner, poor termination procedures that embarrass or humiliate people can also lead eventually to violent reactions.

Organizations deal with pressures that arise from both internal and external sources. The greater the pressures, the more likely individual managers will feel that their actions are justifiable. For profit-seeking organizations, the external pressures come primarily from the capital markets. Short-term performance indicators such as earnings or revenue growth, financial ratios, or other measures often overwhelm longer term indicators of performance. The practice of motivating management with stock options and other equity instruments that attempt to align management and shareholder interests can further tie the goals of managers to short-term financial targets. Consequently, under these conditions, managers can begin to engage in practices that are detrimental to long-term performance, although the short-term results may look favorable. Examples that we have witnessed in recent years include paying exorbitant salaries and stock options to top management while employees are laid off, assigning excessive overtime, expecting more work over fewer hours for less pay, or rewriting job duties to include tasks that are insultingly below-grade or impossible under existing conditions.

Poor Communication

Effective managers spend most of their time communicating. After all, everything that goes on in an organization involves communication of one sort or another. Without effective communication there can be little or no performance improvement, creativity, understanding of clients, avoidance of personnel problems, and on and on.

Many managers, however, do not communicate well and also may fail to create a climate in which effective communication can occur. Think about it—a manager who communicates ineffectively and does not encourage effective communication is not very likely to ever hear about a problem until things are in extremely poor condition or a violent incident occurs. Poor communication lacks the all-important "feedback loop," making employees reluctant to "communicate" their concerns because they perceive the manager as not being receptive. Problems are less likely to be discovered and solved when managers do not seek input or feedback, or regard employee suggestions or even questions to be fault-finding.

Managers today need to improve their communication skills. In a survey of chief financial officers, 61 percent indicated that the biggest challenge companies face is a lack of communication with staff (RHI Management Resources, 2004). More recently, 48 percent of executives indicated that better communication was the best remedy for low morale (Weiss, 2008). Relying on electronic forms of communication, because of the speed that they provide, can be a costly mistake. Electronic communication cannot replace personal, face-to-face interaction. Face-to-face individual and group interaction needs to occur on a regular basis. Projects that employ several teams are prime candidates for miscommunication and unassigned tasks, making such meetings vital to their success.

Management's Poor Relationship with Employees

The psychological contract discussed in an earlier chapter refers to the perceptions of individuals and their employing organization about what their mutual obligations are towards each other. The contract is informal, imprecise, and inferred from statements, actions, or past events—thus also wide open to misunderstanding. It is based on an employee's sense of fairness and trust as well as a belief that the employer is living up to the "bargain." Where the organizational culture is positive and supportive, the contract leads to employee commitment, satisfaction, and loyalty and thus has a positive impact on performance.

Historically, the psychological contract seemed to suggest that so long as an employee performed well on the job, he or she would have an expectation of continued employment. Economic conditions of the 1990s–2000s and the continuing impact of increased international competition and globalization seem to have diminished that historical expectation. Employers no longer offer security and employees no longer demonstrate loyalty. Under these conditions, the potential for workplace violence increases.

Why? If the employer is offering fair pay and treatment plus opportunities for training and development, shouldn't that be enough? Perhaps it would be IF fair pay and fair treatment were in fact being offered. Fairness is, first of all, a perception. In addition, all too frequently organizations have taken advantage of poor job market conditions (from the employees' standpoint) to hold down wages, salaries, and benefits and to increase autocratic or even abusive managerial practices. This disregard for employees and these types of unacceptable behavior increase the potential for violence.

Disagreeable or Distressful Job Factors

Jobs are changing. More employees work part time or on temporary contracts. Outsourcing has become commonplace. Task variety has been substantially increased for many jobs. Downsizing means that each individual employee is expected to carry more weight in the organization. Groups and teams do more of the work so that complex interpersonal relations have increased. All of this means that stress on the job has increased dramatically.

Many individuals perceive that their control over their own work has diminished. They are in groups where they must depend upon others. They have their performance measured by staff personnel along criteria that they don't fully understand. So they feel a lack of feedback about how they are doing coupled with a lack of control to correct deviations.

More jobs than ever involve the job holders coming into contact with customers, suppliers, or others in the organization. Here, too, the extent and complexity of interpersonal interaction has greatly increased. Those with limited interpersonal skills or who have limited training feel stress from this change as well.

The number of work hours per day and the number of work days per week have also changed for many jobs. As hours and work days have changed, many organizations have been less willing to work with employees in arranging schedules that would recognize family obligations. Equally important, with the increased availability of new technology such as the Internet and cellphones, a great many employees feel that they are never away from their bosses or their work, even at night, on weekends, or on vacations. Those employees, then, feel that their organizations no longer care for them or respect them as individuals who also have non-work obligations.

Pressures from Downsizing/Reorganizing

Most managers, when planning a reorganization or downsizing effort, will spend their time and effort on who should go and who should stay and how necessary tasks will be re-allocated. They will identify those that are to be laid off, schedule the terminations, arrange for security during the period of layoffs, and start the very busy time of rearranging tasks and jobs. The problem is, of course, that those who are being retained will undergo massive job and relationship changes, with little attention paid to them and those changes. Even human resource departments tend to focus more on career development, counseling, and assistance for those who are leaving rather than providing services for those who are staying. All too often the "survivors" are left to work things out on their own. Not infrequently one hears, "The ones who were laid off were the lucky ones."

For these reasons, after downsizing or a major reorganization the workplace frequently is characterized by confusion about goals and tasks and increased workloads. In addition, employees often feel undervalued and unappreciated. They perceive a lack of commitment on the part of the organization, a sense of betrayal by the organization, distrust toward the organization and its managers, and a sense of futility with respect to long-term career planning.

In many cases the distrust and hostility felt by employees toward the organization spills over to their relations with customers and suppliers, further decreasing the performance of the organization. In other cases this results in increased stress and conflict, more competition within the firm for scarce resources, and everyone "looking out for number one"—protecting themselves and their jobs rather than working together for the benefit of all. And in still other cases some employees become listless and do only the bare minimum to keep their jobs. None of these consequences is good for the organization.

Negligent Attitude Toward Safety/Health of Personnel

As noted under the "Intentional Mismanagement" heading earlier, managers have been known to turn off safety devices to save money while endangering the lives of employees. In other cases employees or customers are exposed to risk or danger through negligence rather than intent and that negligence may be through ignorance or inaction. Rather than take the time and incur the expense of careful risk assessment after downsizing or a major reorganization, managers may instead ignore or understate risks in an effort to meet short-term performance or sales goals. They underestimate the likelihood of accidents or regulatory intervention. When a serious incident occurs (fire, explosion, significant employee illness due to toxic exposure, etc), it can jeopardize the operations of the organization. Such incidents can also lead employees to believe that management does not care about them and, from there, to not caring about management, and then to express their feelings in a violent reaction.

While most organizations realize that "slip and fall" accidents will occur and have taken precautions to minimize them and their consequences (including legal action), they frequently overlook security issues. Security includes guard operations, hiring, screening, training needs and supervision; alarm systems and other security methodologies, including lighting, closed-circuit television (CCTV) monitoring; and drug screening. Inadequate security can not only send a message to employees that the organization does not care for them but also give rise to assaults, robbery, sexual assault and homicide. Since any of these can lead to legal action, organizations should have a double motivation to provide for adequate security—to minimize their legal risks and to assure their employees that they do care for their well being.

Negative Organizational Culture

As has been noted throughout this chapter, the organizational culture is a major influence on what happens in an organization. Positive cultures promote success; negative cultures foster failure and potentially workplace violence. But just what is a negative culture? How do you know one when you see one?

An organization's culture can be identified by the manner in which members of the organization are treated by management. In a positive culture, people (members of the organization, suppliers, and customers) are treated as mature adults—with respect and with an eye toward developing their knowledge and skills to benefit both them and the organization. In a negative culture, just the opposite exist—people are treated like children who must be constantly watched and corrected.

An organization's culture can also be identified by the way its managers behave and handle situations. In a positive culture, managers achieve their positions based on their competence, knowledge, attitude, and ethics. In a negative culture, managers may have gotten to where they are through years of service or through some type of "connections," regardless of their competence and knowledge. In addition in a negative culture, managers may act unethically, bullying and abusing their subordinates.

As noted in the preceding section, an organization's culture can be identified by the manner in which management treats the safety and health of employees and customers. In a positive culture, security measures are taken seriously, employee assistance programs are in place, and safety and health programs exist and are taken seriously. In a negative culture, the opposite exists and people tend to feel that they don't really matter to the organization.

Employee relationships are another indication of an organization's culture. To be sure, employee relationships both affect and are affected by the organizational culture. One commonly used technique in some groups for dealing with those who are not liked can lead to violent reactions. Shunning, ostracizing, and banishing employees who do not "fit" in with other employees or who are not wanted by management can send negative signals that tear down a person's's dignity and sense of self-worth. That, in turn, can cause the victim to become potentially violent.

Job Overload and High Turnover

One consequence of downsizing and reorganizing is job overload. It can also occur for particular individuals as a consequence of their attempting to work too many jobs in order to cope with difficult economic conditions. Managers need to be observant and perceptive enough to sense when an employee is beginning to suffer from the distress of job overload for whatever reason. If managers are not sensitive, the resulting stress can lead to a violent incident that should have been preventable.

Similarly, many organizational and economic changes lead to high turnover within organizations. As a consequence, existing employees have increased stress while covering a job that is vacant and while attempting to learn how to interact with a constant stream of new faces in the organization. Again, managers need to be sensitive to these stresses.

Summary

Clearly, there are numerous organizational influences on workplace attitudes and behaviors. Individuals experiencing any of these will react and soon reject their situation, the managers, and the organization. They will express their stress and frustration, and if no improvement in their situation occurs, they will move to the next level of the Violence Volcano. Finally, of course, if things don't get any better, the volcano will erupt. How to minimize the impact of these organizational influences and manage their occurrence and consequences is what we shall discuss next.

11

Dealing with Organizational Influences

Even though violence is recognized as a problem that can often be prevented, the organization itself can instead be a contributing factor unless it maintains a healthy, positive internal environment that balances the rights of problem employees with the rights of all other employees to a safe workplace. Management can no longer hide its head in the sand like the proverbial ostrich, waiting until something happens and hoping it never does. Instead, to minimize the organization's associated risks, senior managers must understand the importance of being proactive in developing and communicating a violence prevention program. Not only does violence prevention enhance organizational effectiveness and profitability but it also satisfies legal, moral, and ethical obligations. Most organizations need to do more, though, than merely accept existing human resource or security policies and programs as sufficient. They need to take a proactive approach.

First, let's remind ourselves that workplace violence, as defined in Chapter 2, refers to more than physical harm to another worker, manager, or company property. It also includes coercive behavior that leads to significant negative results, including psychological trauma or diminished productivity. Thus, the organization must make an effort not only to provide protection for the physical plant but also to provide a positive and hostility-free atmosphere for its people, to balance the rights of all personnel, and to train managers and employees to recognize problems before they result in violent actions or reactions.

Develop and Maintain Security

The organization is responsible for developing and maintaining security, and that means more than just protecting the physical plant. Security means minimizing risks—risks to employees from accidents or from other employees, and also risks to the organization from employees disclosing valuable information to competitors. As noted in the preceding chapter, security includes guard operations, hiring, screening, training needs and supervision, alarm systems and other security methods including lighting and closed-circuit television (CCTV) monitoring and drug screening.

The creation of a positive organizational culture is also part of security. Employees need to feel that the organization and its managers care for them and their well-being. They need to have a complaint/grievance process to use when problems do occur. They need an ombudsperson process to assure them that their issues can be brought to the attention of top management without fear of reprisal. And they need an employee assistance program to help them when such support is needed.

Establish A Positive, Hostility-Free Workplace Environment

Establishing a hostility-free workplace environment entails applying everything in this book, but two major organizational responses constitute the absolute minimum: eliminating both managerial bullying and harassment. Those two things are among the most frequent complaints in organizations that have experienced more than one violent incident. Bullying and abusive behavior on the part of management and harassment of any form must be ferreted out and eliminated as the first step in establishing a positive, hostility-free workplace environment. Such behavior, incidentally, may vary greatly in style, ranging from harsh words and actions to subtle, behind-your-back, deceptive maneuvers.

Organizations that rely on autocratic styles of leadership and punishment-based discipline systems seem to be where many workplace violence incidents have happened. Clearly, then, management should use participatory styles of leadership and base its discipline system on positive reinforcement rather than punishment.

The best way to handle a problem is to have an early detection system that allows you to prevent a problem in the first place. Preferably, pre-employment psychological screening will enable the organization to avoid hiring potentially violent employees in the first place. If potentially violent employees already work at the company, the second best solution is to identify them before it is too late, either by training supervisors to recognize the potential problem or by using post-employment behavioral observation or dangerousness assessments.

Post Employment Behavioral Observation Programs (BOPs) involve the supervisors' notations of job-related behavioral changes. Because the forms are then sent to an independent agency, BOPs help reduce confrontations between supervisors and employees, thus reducing the likelihood of causing a violent reaction and also leading to more effective referrals for counseling. The challenge here, though, is convincing employees that their responses will indeed remain confidential.

Dangerousness assessment (Pinard & Pagani, 2001) should also be considered as a tool to help identify potential problem employees. Dangerousness assessment refers to a formalized psychological evaluation to determine if a person represents a clear and imminent threat to those around him. Where called for, it should be done by a licensed psychologist or psychiatrist trained in assessments. The best system is one in which all employees are given psychological evaluations for "fitness-for-duty" or dangerousness assessment. This precludes a focus on isolated individuals and, in turn, protects privacy.

Employers often hesitate to use Dangerousness Assessment, however, because they are not sure about the legitimacy of referral criteria, because they are afraid that doing such testing may trigger violence by an already unstable person, or because they are afraid that legal restrictions may pose more problems than they are prepared to deal with. As a first step in overcoming this reluctance, state laws should be checked before using any such testing. The legal concerns can be addressed by having carefully defined procedures regarding referral, treatment, and return to work, and by involving a licensed medical practitioner in the process.

Any employee who is having severe domestic problems that could spill over to the workplace should be encouraged to have a dangerousness assessment made of his or her partner. This is particularly valuable for "battered women" as a way of predicting the likelihood that the batterer may escalate the situation and kill the woman. Not surprisingly, many of the indicators of workplace violence are also predictors of such individuals (Campbell, 1995; Goodman, Dutton, & Bennett, 2000).

Balance Rights of Troubled Workers and Other Employees

An organization must do more than prevent a hostile environment, though. It also must provide a positive atmosphere that balances the rights of problem employees with the rights of all other employees to a safe workplace. Laws that protect the privacy of individuals must be respected. Labeling someone can lead to slander suit. An employer could be alleged to breach an employee's rights if harassment results in a hostile work environment. The employer could be found liable for the contractually implied duty to provide a safe and healthy workplace. If all or many employees are threatened, the problem employee's identity may have to be disclosed and the group informed of the problem. The problem employee may need to be suspended (with or without pay), transferred, or asked to resign with a severance package.

In a free society, the rights of the organization and the rights of individuals must be balanced. These individual rights unquestionably make a company's anti-violence task more difficult. Attorneys can be helpful in balancing these rights. Many organizations are aware that they need to respond to violence in advance (Braveman, 1996). In a study of the Fortune 1000 companies, the Figgie Report found that 88% conduct building security checks, 66% employ burglar alarms, 48% monitor the premises via closed-circuit TV, 38% have installed electronic card ID systems, and 24% employ armed guards (Scotti, 1986, 13–14). Executive protection and other internal security programs that help to ward against kidnapping are fairly new but growing, particularly for overseas assignments (Kelly & Cook, 1994; Korsky, 1990; Kelly & Barnathan, 1988). Even with such protective measures many organizations, and hence their employees, are still very vulnerable to violence and need to assess their situation and take preventive action (Barton, 1993a & 1993b; Maddox, 1990).

On the other hand, it should be understood that attempts to balance the rights of victim and perpetrator could instead hasten a violence problem. If there are no witnesses to a reported incident of harassment, for instance, the victim may need to be given an opportunity to confront the perpetrator, thus revealing to him that the worker has filed a report with the company. The victim of threat may be reluctant to file a complaint for fear it will worsen the problem.

Select and Train Positive Managers and Supervisors

Since managers may well be the problem, it is imperative that care must be taken in their selection and training. Managers must unequivocally support organizational policies that promote the creation of a non-hostile environment. They must be trained in the development of positive organizational cultures that strive to achieve the goals of all organizational stakeholders—employees, customers, suppliers, shareholders. They need training in effective communication skills and the professional treatment of personnel. And, as noted earlier, they must be trained in participatory styles of management and leadership.

Managers must also be trained to look for signs of stress or behaviors that could signal the potential for the eruption of violent behavior. When situations arise where potential problems could exist, managers should understand and be capable of carrying out due diligence. Due diligence in this case means taking sufficient time and trouble to show that you care about the individual and the company—about obtaining the truth in contentious situations, about the security of the physical plant, and about protecting your employees. In terms of reports or complaints, due diligence means that managers must hear all sides and assure that unbiased decisions or actions follow the gathering of information. In terms of the physical plant and security, due diligence means that managers must be proactive in identifying potential hazards or security issues and in moving to correct them. Managers must also be trained in the basics of helping employees who are having problems. This means that they must be trained not only to look for signs of stress or behaviors that could signal the potential for a violence incident but also to know the first steps to take to reduce that stress. Their training should include learning where potential problem employees should be directed inside or out of the organization for professional help.

Eliminate Sick Work Environments

From what we know about workplace violence, it is clear that any violence prevention program must immediately strive to help employees deal with their stress and make contingency plans to deal with behavior problems as they arise. To be effective, however, the program must also eliminate sick work environments. Symptoms of a "sick" internal environment include higher than average levels of disputes, grievances, injury claims, and stressed personnel along with an authoritarian management style (Kinney, 1995). Other characteristics of an organization's internal environment that could lead to violence include aversive treatment of employees and the use of extremely tight control mechanisms (O'Leary-Kelly, Griffin, & Glew, 1996). Sick work environments encourage good employees to leave and deter good applicants from applying for jobs; violent work environments harm productivity and damage profitability. It is equally clear that violence prevention entails monitoring the internal and external environments for indicators or warning signs of violence.

Most importantly, the focus should be on improving performance rather than on decreasing the symptoms of sick organizations. In that way, the characteristics of the sick organization will be gradually displaced by characteristics of effective ones. This means focusing on the basic vision, mission, goals, objectives, and strategies of the organization. What is our vision? What is our mission? What are our specific, achievable objectives? Periodically revisiting these questions will help to keep everyone on "the same page" and avoid many of the characteristics of sick organizations. Having a vision, mission, and strategies that are developed through participation and, hence, are widely accepted tends to be a strong unifying and motivating force in organizations.

Careful environmental monitoring and strongly participative approaches to information should be used to assure that rumors and misinformation are kept in check. This will help to assure that members of the organization keep "their eyes on the prize" and focus on the strategic goals of the organizations rather than opportunistic or short-term goals.

Additionally, having an open and participative organization builds trust. Getting managers to interact casually with others in the organization (e.g., joining them for lunch or coffee breaks on occasion) will help to open up lines of communication and establish feelings of trust among everyone in the organization. By opening up communication even about problems, organizations can create efficient, competitive systems that compete more effectively.

Open communication does not, of course, mean that everyone should vent their complaints about the organization. While letting off steam can be useful and even necessary, it needs to be managed and focused. Individuals should always be encouraged to indicate how things could be better and not just what is wrong. Ask for solutions whenever anyone indicates a problem. Shift the focus to what will work instead of why this won't work. Getting everyone to focus on superordinate or long-term goals can defuse conflicts over more immediate, short-term problems.

Participation is also helpful, especially in high-pressure situations. Not only is communication improved and the potential for idea generation increased, but also the social interaction can ease stress and increase cohesion. While the development of a cohesive organization can improve performance, it is unlikely to do so unless members of the organization genuinely desire to perform well. Therefore, efforts should first concentrate on the development and acceptance of high performance expectations for those in the organization. Cohesion generally will occur on its own as members of the organization learn through participation to pull together to accomplish high performance. Buttons, pins, mottoes, and logos based on organizational goals and high performance can be morale boosters. Casual get-togethers to develop camaraderie and events for recognizing and celebrating high performers can all serve to help everyone keep focused on what really matters to the organization.

If a problem seems particularly difficult, moving away from it temporarily can be beneficial. Don't focus on the problem but rather re-examine its origins or history and then the possible future consequences of differing solutions. In other words, place the problem on hold for a while and move to another (hopefully easier) problem. Take a break and exercise or get a snack. Just do something to break the present impasse. This can also be a way of dealing with organizational sickness that has resulted from a major change. Additionally, setting a series of short-term goals that will lead to long-term success can break the lethargy and routineness that frequently results from such major changes.

Summary

Organizations must strive not only to provide protection for the physical plant but also to provide a positive and hostility-free environment for all members. They must balance the rights of all personnel and train both managers and employees to recognize problems before they result in violent actions or reactions. In addition, they must work to eliminate sick work environments.

PART VI
General Approaches to Workplace Violence

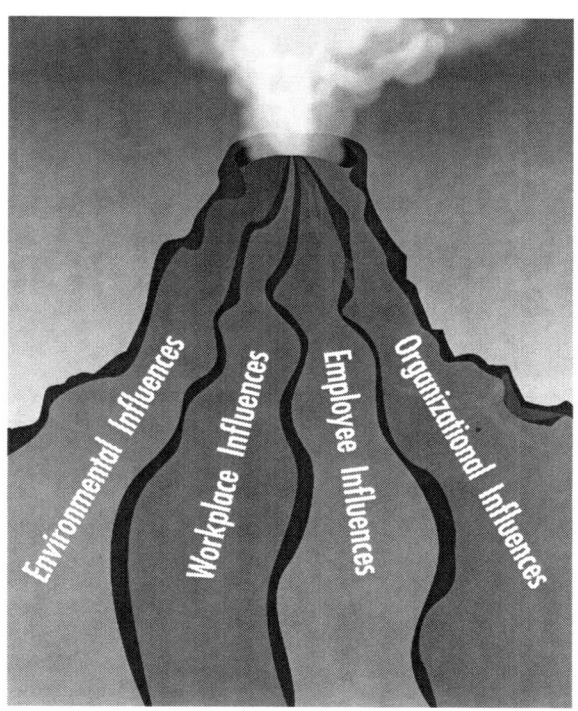

12

Administrative Ways of Reducing Risks

People and organizations make all kinds of predictions to exploit good outcomes or to avoid bad outcomes, but trying to predict violent behavior without planning for the predicted outcomes is foolish. Organizations that plan for expected crisis events (e.g., snow days, strikes, product failures and recalls, and even natural disasters) and rely on insurance and risk management processes to deal with those events are known as crisis-prone organizations. Organizations that go beyond that and prepare for the unexpected (e.g., workplace violence and terrorism) are referred to as crisis-prepared organizations (Pauchant & Mitroff, 1992). All organizations should be crisis-prepared.

It should be clear by now that, in order to stave off eruptions of the Violence Volcano, organizations must create cultures that minimize the risks of violence. Those cultures don't tolerate abusive, bullying, or harassing managers or employees. Those cultures support due diligence in investigating claims against employees. Those cultures carefully screen applicants prior to employment, properly induct and orient them as they join the organization, and continuously train and develop them after they join the organization. And, of course, those cultures maintain a positive and close working relationship with law enforcement and public safety agencies in their efforts to control workplace violence.

Establish Anti-Violence Policies

Organizational cultures are made visible through the policies and procedures of the organization; so as a first step management must have a clear policy that shows a commitment against violence. That policy must be repeated in company documents and communicated to all employees and outsiders who deal regularly with the company. And, of course, it must be enforced. Such a policy may say nothing more than, "This company will not tolerate violence and aggression," or "This organization will not tolerate abuse, violence, aggression, bullying, or any other practice that abuses the dignity of our stakeholders, including our employees."

Better still is a more comprehensive policy that also specifically mentions behaviors that are not to be tolerated, such as threats and verbal abuse from within the organization plus abuse from outside the organization (stalkers, customers, etc.). It should indicate examples of unacceptable behaviors and the sanctions to be applied when they occur. Bullying and sexual harassment, in particular, should be specifically condemned, perhaps in separate policies. Further, the policy should indicate that all jokes about violence, all remarks about violence, and all incidents involving shouting matches, vandalism, sabotage, or anonymous threats are to be reported and will be investigated immediately. An example of a good anti-violence policy followed by one company is reproduced below:

> This organization is committed to providing a hostility-free workplace for its employees. All acts and/or threats of violence against the life, health, well-being, family or property of individuals in the workplace or in connection with an employee's conduct of the organization's business will not be tolerated. Any such acts or threats by employees may be grounds for immediate dismissal whether or not the employee making the threat intended to carry it out. Additionally bullying, abusive or derogatory statements and behavior, sexual harassment, and all other forms of treatment by managerial personnel toward employees will not be tolerated and shall subject said personnel to immediate disciplinary action that may include dismissal.

Any and all anti-violence policies should be publicized through posters, newsletters, and talks by senior management. The message should be conveyed to all workers, including part-time and contract workers, not just the full-time company employees, but at the same time care should be taken not to unnecessarily alarm employees. Having an anti-violence policy is not a confession that there is a problem, nor is the failure to express such a policy an indication that the organization has nothing to fear.

Many organizations have "zero tolerance" policies regarding threats of violence or actual violent behavior. "Zero tolerance" can mean immediate termination but, more commonly, it means immediate action to deal with the situation. Along with the anti-violence policy many organizations establish codes and prohibitions. Codes of conduct to establish standards of acceptable and unacceptable behavior as well as codes of sanctions proscribing the result of noncompliance help clarify and amplify the message. Virtually all organizations prohibit weapons, drugs, alcohol, and sexual harassment to further provide safe working environments.

Improve Asset Security

In addition to establishing anti-violence policies, organizations should take care to secure their assets—human, physical, and fiscal. The security problem may come from inside or outside, an employee or manager, a business associate (customer, supplier, regulator), someone associated with an employee (a spouse, relative, friend, former lover), or even a terrorist. The problem may involve computer sabotage, data destruction, theft, arson, burglary, vandalism, threats, kidnapping, or murder.

While organizations are clearly responsible for the protection of their assets, they need to avoid overly complex or restrictive systems that could do more harm than good. Articulated anti-violence policies coupled with training serve as the first step in raising the awareness of members of the organization about security concerns. Classes, seminars, and briefings further assist in establishing a climate of protection and prevention.

Conduct Security Needs Assessment

Security, however, is more than merely policy and awareness. A formal Security Needs Assessment or Hazards Assessment of the company should be conducted to identify problem areas. A Threat Assessment Team could be established to conduct such an assessment, or it could be handled by the Crisis Management Team or outside consultants. These assessments are best performed with assistance from an outside, independent consultant, who should be aggressively managed by the company.

Such an assessment should include a careful inspection of the external environment to identify areas where potential perpetrators could hide (shadows from bushes, trees, shrubs, building corners; poorly lighted parking lots; drainage ditches; unlighted stairwells; etc.). But assessments should not be limited to physical aspects of the organization. Reviews of security policies and procedures, personnel needs, and equipment needs should be included. The organization's culture should be assessed to determine if it is exacerbating potential violence. Finally, assessments should include estimates of risks for both personnel and facilities. Readiness can also be assessed and tested through regular drills or simulations.

Consider Facility Design and Provide Security Devices

Fully protecting all of the assets may be too great, but some steps can be taken; e.g., a silent alarm button at the receptionist's desk, a shatterproof glass partition and locked door for the receptionist, or double doors with a security guard at the building entrance where badges and bags are checked before access is permitted. At the very least there should be guidelines to control non-member access to the organization's facilities.

The basic design or layout of the organization's facility or facilities also must be considered. Executive offices should have limited access, preferably on the highest floor or the furthest location. In addition, they should be accessed only through a reception lobby. Human Resources people must be accessible to job applicants, but their security is important. If possible, they should be located in a separate building or a separate wing so that unauthorized people can't say they're there for job-hunting as an excuse to gain entry to others in the organization.

Depending upon the nature of the organization and the results of the Security Needs Assessment, parking may need to be restricted and barriers may need to be erected to limit access to facilities as a means of making it difficult to get within close range of buildings, thereby thwarting car/truck bombs or suicide bombs. All openings (windows, doors, gates, roofs, walls) may need to be monitored. Shrubbery, chain-link fences, or other types of fences may need to be installed at outer perimeters. Back-up auxiliary power generators may need to be provided.

Numerous other security devices may be necessary, depending upon the nature of the organization and the results of the Security Needs Assessment. One of those would be the locking of interior office doors (to corridors and from corridors to private offices) so that an intruder cannot go through. Other devices could include an intrusion detection system, especially on the ground floor and openings to critical areas; silent duress alarm switches for receptionists and executives and their secretaries; closed circuit television cameras at doorways, stairwells, and hallways either monitored constantly or activated by silent alarms; and metal detectors at the entrance to rooms where discipline/termination hearings take place.

Address Security Personnel Needs

Who will handle security? Will it be handled internally or contracted out? Once again the nature of the organization and the results of the Security Needs Assessment will help determine the answer to these questions. No matter which alternative is selected, it is extremely important that security personnel dress and behave in a highly professional manner. Sloppy, casual and seeming physically unfit appearances detract from a culture that is trying to say that security and anti-violence are important.

A specialty firm that contracts to provide protection to many organizations can better take advantage of economies of scale and scope than an in-house department that services only its own needs. Therefore, contract security firms usually cost considerably less than do in-house security organizations. However, there are transactions costs associated with using outside firms. Transactions costs generally refer to the cost of organizing and transacting exchanges between arms-length partners in the market. An important element of transactions costs is the cost of negotiating, writing, and enforcing contracts. In addition, of course, there is the problem of leakage of private information. Dealing with independent market specialists may require divulging proprietary product information. Clearly risks are involved, and while those risks may be lessened through insurance and penalty clauses, they are nevertheless real and must be considered.

Consider the activities that your security force may be called upon to perform. It may assist your human resource personnel in screening applicants through background investigations. It may assist your managerial personnel in disciplinary and termination procedures, including either covert or overt investigations. It may need to be trained and equipped to provide guard coverage for the physical plant and personnel. It may need to monitor closed circuit televisions and perform electronic sweeps of facilities. It may be expected to provide training programs and videotapes for all levels of personnel. It may need to qualify for and carry insurance (hostage, kidnap, ransom, etc.). Most likely it will need to provide computer and information security. It may do internal security consulting and prepare a variety of manuals for its own personnel and others to use.

The more activities that your organizations needs, the more likely you may need to seriously consider a contract security company. Before you contact prospective companies, identify as clearly and precisely as you can what assets you want to protect and what activities you want the company to perform. Contact your local law enforcement agency, attorney, or a security advisor for a list of firms with experience in providing security services. Then ask those potential contract security firms for a list of information. That list should include the following:

- Insurance coverage and A.M. Best Company rating (www.ambest.com/)
- Client retention rate
- References (check carefully by comparing their needs with yours; make an unscheduled visit to one facility to see how things look)
- Professional certification courses it requires for its technicians
- Licenses it holds
- In-house training it requires of its employees
- Security clearances held by the firm
- Workers' compensation interstate EMF (Experience Modification Factor) rate (10 yrs.)
- Previous major litigation with clients
- Statement about how it screens its own employees
- Statement about how it supervises its own employees

In evaluating the information from the above list, consider the following. The insurance rating should be "A" or higher. The higher the client retention rate, the better. Checking the references is subjective but should give you a good "feel" for how the firm operates. A security firm that requires professional certification courses for its technicians is likely to be more serious about keeping up to date and providing higher quality service; the same is true for licensing. Certification and licensing are not legally required or enforced in all states so using in-house training as a "standard of excellence" is a proxy of quality of service. Since the terrorist attack on September 11, 2001, many government agencies have ordered security firms to meet increased levels of security-clearance requirements, so you may be able to secure the services of one of those firms to obtain even more assurance of high quality performance.

Finally, insist on a written proposal that outlines all details of the security plan and the costs as well as any major contingencies. Develop a contract that incorporates responsibilities, costs, and a schedule for payments and activities. And last but not least, insist on frequent progress reports.

In addition to security measures, some administrative policies and controls may also be necessary. For example, the company may be justified in requiring that employees not work alone, that a guard be called to escort employees to their cars after hours; that passwords consist of numbers, letters, and special characters and be changed often; and that employees wear specially coded ID badges with photographs and embedded computer chips.

Provide Access Control

One very important part of security is access control—controlling who can enter parts of your organization's premises. All employees should have identification that allows entry, and they may be required to wear that identification as a badge. The identification should be encased in plastic so that it cannot be altered, and there should be strict rules regarding those who forget or lose their identification. Unless doors are locked and require electronic identification to enter, entry points should be attended by a security officer or receptionist. When employees terminate employment for any reason (retire, quit, fired, etc.), they must surrender their identification. If a terminated employee has made threats or given warnings, every employee (not just security) should be instructed to contact managerial or security personnel if that person is seen on or near the premises again.

Visitors should be subjected to polite but strict access control. They should be screened at a reception point to verify the legitimacy of their visit and that they are expected. Depending upon the nature of the organization visitors may be limited to certain areas within the facility and may even have their belongings inspected. Visitors should be issued badges clearly indicating that they are visitors and the area(s) of the facility to which they have been granted access. They may need to be provided escorts as well. Vendors and solicitors should be treated the same as visitors with the additional proviso that it may be necessary to advise employees or departments that these people may pass through so that proprietary materials and assets may need to be hidden or protected in some way.

Also, it is absolutely critical that employees be screened extremely carefully when they have access to valuable data or restricted data that they could erase, destroy, or misappropriate.. In one act of sabotage or vandalism involving only a few keystrokes, they could ruin the organization. Relatively low-level employees, not just high-level employees, can be vitally important or risky to organizations in the information age. Strict security precautions must be taken to protect the organization and its computers and information.

In order to respond quickly, organizations should periodically evaluate physical security systems and access authorization programs. Regardless of how "safe" the company has made the security system, over-reliance on physical security measures is a mistake that must not be made. The most sophisticated cameras, alarms, and key-card access systems can be thwarted by a determined, violent person. But more importantly, companies that rely heavily on physical measures often end up resorting to sub-standard security personnel and/or ignoring "sick" internal environments. Policies, procedures, and security personnel cannot substitute for assuring that the organization is free from bullying, abusive, harassing managers who create hostile, unduly stressful work environments. That can be done only by creating organizational cultures that are hostility- free and foster open communication.

Improve Communication

A key element in dealing with any potential workplace violence situation is communication. A major objective of effective communication is to hear about and resolve problems before stressors build to the point that violent behavior erupts. Organizations should use as many forms of communication as possible and assure that all communication is two-way. Some form of complaint or grievance process with appeal and review procedures is an absolute necessity. If an act of violence does occur, though, people need to be kept informed. Questions should be answered quickly and honestly. As events unfold, designated individuals should issue frequent communications with everyone in the organization as well as law enforcement officials and the media.

An important part of the communication regarding workplace violence is to provide organization members with information indicating that the Violence Volcano is building. Training is obviously vital in this regard, but providing brief summaries of indicators through tip sheets in pay envelopes, newsletters, bulletins, and e-mail can also be used.

One of the most important communication policies concerns the procedures that managers and employees should follow for reporting threats.

Establish Procedure for Reporting Behaviors and Threats

Coworkers are most often the ones who first hear an enraged worker complain, threaten, or compare the worksite with one where a major act of violence has taken place. For that reason, all workers should know how to react to angry fellow employees, including knowing when to report a remark to someone higher up in the chain of command. Companies need a clear, written policy for employees and managers as to how to communicate all threats of violence including an assurance of confidentiality for the person making the report. Workers often will not report threatening behavior because they don't want to be thought of as being a snitch, because they are not comfortable crossing the line from labor to management, or because it is socially acceptable to give people the benefit of a doubt by attributing the remark to letting off steam or just having a bad day.

The organization should have a place and a procedure for reporting threats and all incidents, and everyone in the organization should be trained in making such reports. All incidents should be reported and records maintained about them, perhaps in a computerized database. A special telephone number (preferably a 24-hour "hotline") may need to be installed to ensure confidentiality, thus making it more likely that individuals will report problems. To assure that security personnel are able to communicate in emergencies, they should be provided with equipment such as pagers, cell phones, or two-way radios. And, of course, if an employee is actually threatened, the organization must provide personal protection for that person.

Organizations may also require that its psychiatrists/psychologists inform the company when a person is likely to commit a violent act. Recent court cases have held that medical professionals are liable for acts committed by their patients if they do nothing to try to stop them. Similar cases have extended that same responsibility to Employee Assistance Plans and mental health clinics, with "reasonable care" being used as the key. In other words, giving unnecessary warnings is considered "a reasonable price to pay" to save the lives of possible victims. The key element here is that disclosure is made in good faith.

Follow Established Disciplinary Procedures

Knowing who is in control, and when, is important to both management and employees, thus making those items an important part of the company's policies regarding discipline. Direct supervisors may ordinarily handle discipline, but company procedure may dictate otherwise, especially if there is potential for personality conflicts. If unions exist, their representatives must be involved.

Since it is virtually impossible to put aside differences when a supervisor views an employee as a troublemaker or a problem employee, an unbiased person should be used instead and every effort must be made to assure that due diligence is performed. If the supervisor is afraid of the employee or if the supervisor is perceived as "out to get the employee," it is best to err on the side of caution. Use someone from human resources or a higher level superior who both sides can agree is unbiased.

The most commonly recommended disciplinary procedure involves a four-step process with due diligence and appeals provided. The first step is for the immediate supervisor to discuss the matter with the employee and issue an oral warning to the employee. While this is oral, a written record is made in a file or an e-mail or memo sent to verify that the oral warning was made and on what day the warning was made. The next violation of the same offense escalates the process to a formal written notice of the offense detailing the circumstances and making reference to the earlier discussion and warning. A copy of the formal written notice is placed in the employee's personnel file and the employee is provided with instructions as to how and when the employee may appeal the notice. A third infraction of the same matter leads again to a written notice accompanied by some form of disciplinary action—a letter of concern, a formal reprimand, suspension, or discharge—depending upon the severity of the matter. Again, the notice is placed in the employee's personnel file and the employee is provided with instructions as to how and when the employee may appeal the notice. A fourth infraction, then, results in discharge.

If the organization has information that strongly suggests that the individual concerned is a potentially violent employee, the organization need not follow this four-step disciplinary process but may terminate the individual immediately. For instance, if an employee intentionally injures another employee, that first employee may be discharged immediately without an oral reprimand.

Practice Non-Exacerbating Termination Procedures

Discharging an employee may trigger physical violence sooner or later, so it is vitally important that procedures related to discharging an employee should be in writing and carefully considered to weigh individual employee rights against the rights of other workers. The termination policies that management makes should recognize that employees get more upset at how they were terminated than why. In may be necessary to have security personnel on the alert when terminating a potentially violent employee. Sometimes relocating a perpetrator or restructuring that particular job may be better than firing the worker. Protecting other workers normally requires that the company repossesses the discharged worker's badge, keys, and other items; change locks and security codes; and even contact law enforcement if necessary. In addition, potential victims may need to be transferred to a different site, undisclosed to the perpetrator.

Some commonly accepted guidelines for minimizing negative aspects of terminations are as follows. Have the meeting in a confidential location away from the individual's normal work area so that his or her colleagues don't easily become aware of what is happening. Hold the meeting either at the beginning or the end of the workday, and immediately after the meeting have all of the person's personal belongings retrieved from the work area and have the person leave the premises. Unless the person has a history of violence or is judged to be a security risk, do not have him or her escorted from the premises. Have at least one other member of management attend the meeting as a witness.

Have in hand all forms that need to be signed, along with the final paycheck that includes all outstanding vacation, sick time, and so on. Keep the meeting as short as possible and do not get into a discussion as to why the termination is necessary. The purpose of the meeting is to finalize the employment, not to discuss the reasons for the action. If the employee persists, indicate to him or her that there are legal rights available after termination that may be pursued, then conclude the meeting and escort the employee from the premises.

Prepare for Bomb Threats

Bomb threats are a specific form of workplace violence that, thankfully, doesn't pertain to most organizations. However, given the increasing frequency of these, it was deemed important to discuss them here. All bomb threats should be taken seriously, and all employees should be trained to react as steadfastly as they do for fire alarms. Only one person should be authorized to order an evacuation for a bomb threat, and everyone should know who that person is. Each telephone should have emergency numbers nearby to facilitate quick action, in this case a call to Security and perhaps to the individual authorized to order an evacuation.

Since switchboard operators are usually the first to receive a bomb threat, they should be thoroughly trained in requesting information from the caller, listening for background noises, activating a recording and call-tracing system, sounding appropriate alarms, and notifying appropriate personnel. All employees should know exactly where and how to evacuate their buildings, where to meet outside the premises, and how and when to return to their workplaces. They should also be trained not to touch any suspicious-looking devices or packages and not to tamper with debris after an explosion. With the assistance of police, fire, and security personnel, management should establish plans not only for evacuation routes but also for cutting off electric, gas, and fuel lines and for assisting emergency personnel in their search of the premises.

The company should, of course, make every possible effort to prevent the planting of a bomb on company premises. Police and fire department personnel can help the company identify potential hiding places for explosives. Security can conduct routine inspections of areas where explosives could be hidden, particularly trash cans and stair wells. Surveillance can be vastly improved by installing closed-circuit TV cameras and inspecting all packages going into and out of the premises. Employees, particularly in the mailroom, should be taught to watch for suspicious-looking mail.

Minimize Negative Effects of Reorganization

All re-organizational efforts—layoffs, downsizing, restructuring, re-engineering, and the like—should be handled in an open, honest, and careful manner. Communication at this time is crucial to preventing misinformation, rumors, and increased stress that could cause an individual to commit a violent act ranging anywhere from, say, sabotage to murder. If employees are to be laid off or otherwise negatively impacted, they should be notified in a straightforward, caring way. Universal severance packages along with career and psychological counseling could be provided as could outplacement services.

Notify employees sufficiently far in advance of changes so that they can make plans. They may need to organize finances, job searches, make new domestic arrangements, and so forth. Communicate about the reorganization and do so frequently, truthfully, and directly. Explain the reasons and how it will take place. Offer support to your employees during the reorganization and encourage your employees to express their emotions and reaction about it. They should be able to acknowledge their fears, resistance, and concerns, but you should help them focus on coping and offer empathy soliciting input on how to cope with the reality of the situation. Present yourself as a leader who understands people's feelings and responds kindly but maintains a focus on getting the mission accomplished.

Involve your employees as much as possible in the reorganization process. Ask for and listen to their views and request feedback as the process goes forward. Understand affected attitudes and behaviors so that, as the "new" organization emerges, employees will be motivated to help it succeed. You want to be viewed as a successful leader in the new organization.

Provide Outplacement Services

Effective outplacement services can be established for those affected by the change in job status, using either internal human resources personnel or independent consultants. Providing outplacement services demonstrates to both terminated and remaining employees that the organization cares. It is a reassuring safety net to individuals in cases of termination or downsizing. Outplacement services can be a strong factor in reducing stress and the possibility of a violent reaction from an employee.

High-risk individuals, in particular, need effective outplacement to reduce their potentially violent reactions. This group may include not just those who fit the profile for potentially violent people but also those who have difficulty adjusting to change, who have been laid off previously, who have other family members experiencing job loss, or who are emotionally fragile. These people should be identified as early as possible and referred to Employee Assistance Programs for outplacement.

Terminations create enormous stress. Sometimes angry, resentful employees will attempt to seek revenge or to sabotage the employer. Now is the time for security personnel to be high-profile. Although state and federal regulations must be met regarding advance notification, notifying employees too far in advance can increase the probability of sabotage, theft, and declining productivity. Potentially violent employees who are affected by the reorganizing effort should be identified and referred for help. A 24-hour rumor and assistance hotline should be established. For the protection of others the organization must repossess badges, keys, and other items from workers who are being terminated; locks and security codes must be changed. In addition, it is vitally important for receptionists and security to be notified and provided with descriptions of persons and automobiles to be on the alert for.

Finally, Employee Assistance Programs (EAPs) should be provided to all personnel who are impacted by reorganization. EAPs can provide stress management programs for your organization and greatly aid your employees' adaptation to the new arrangements.

Assist with Stress Management

Few stresses are more dramatic than those encountered through workplace violence. Employees may have been threatened, the security of their normal workaday world turned upside down, and their very lives seriously thrown off balance. Often after violence occurs it takes more time than employees and employers anticipate to restore productivity and a culture of well-being in their unit. This is true when violence occurs directly in the unit's workspace, when a member of the unit is a victim of violence outside the workplace, or when a member of the unit commits suicide. It is important to understand that recovering from such an incident varies from person to person and from one workplace to another.

After a workplace violence incident, employees need to be given time to heal. This will be a difficult time for them and they will need support from those in the organization. They should be encouraged to communicate their experiences with family or friends or even to keep a diary. The organization should help in identifying local support groups or professional consulting groups that could assist employees in recovering from the violent event. Employees should be instructed that this is not a time to make major life decisions such as changing jobs or careers because that would just add stress to an already stressful situation.

In addition employees should follow more usual stress management activities such as avoiding alcohol and drugs, eating well and at regular times, having an exercise program, and getting plenty of rest. They should set up "to do" lists, prioritize their daily activities, and establish long- and short-term goals for themselves. Having plans, establishing structure, and getting focused are among the best things that employees can do to help overcome the anxiety and stress that follow violent events. Management should help them do these things so that they and the organization can recover as quickly as possible.

Establish a Crisis Management Team

Even with effective procedures and policies, every organization remains somewhat vulnerable to violence. Management therefore needs more formal methods of control to assure that its administrative policies and procedures are working to reduce the risks of violent behavior. The organization needs to establish a Crisis Management Team that will be responsible for developing written plans and procedures for the entire organization to follow when an emergency erupts.

Crisis Management Team members should come from several areas of the organization including human resources, legal, security, employee assistance, labor relations, and facility management. Having a senior management person on the team lends it greater credibility and, where applicable, union representatives should be included. The use of outside consultants to assist the team should certainly be considered. Every manager should have phone numbers for the Crisis Management Team members as well as for security and police. Trauma Training Programs will be conducted for the Crisis Management Team by HR, EAP, and appropriate outside consultants; and the Team will develop for management a full-scale Trauma Plan upon completion of appropriate assessments of the workplace, including current personnel. Training was discussed in Chapter 9.

The Crisis Management Team should develop tactical plans to minimize the risks associated with workplace violence. These plans should include an Organizational Crisis Plan dealing with (a) what to do when violence is only a threat (threat intervention or de-escalation) and (b) what to do when a problem has escalated to the point where traumatic violence seems eminent (trauma intervention or trauma prevention) and (c) a Post-Violence Trauma Plan dealing with what to do after a Level 3 incident (highest level, see Chapter 2) of violence erupts.

Among the other responsibilities of the Crisis Management Team are the following:

- Establish a Telephone Team to call family members and notify employees when to return to work, where they can receive help, and so on.
- Establish a secondary communication system and operation site in case the company phone lines are destroyed.
- Identify a Media Relations person (preferably a high official in the company) who will be kept informed and will manage the release of sensitive information to outsiders.
- Determine the role of Security—when and by whom they are to be notified, what their immediate and longer-range actions will be, who will be in charge, etc.
- Identify and stock a Support Center that will be equipped with whatever the Trauma Team needs and that will serve as a place for traumatized workers to get immediate assistance.
- Select a trauma counselor(s), who will be called by the Telephone Team immediately to come on-site to provide assistance.
- Assign responsibility for instituting an emergency triage process that identifies those individuals who should receive intensive treatment and monitoring, those who will need only limited counseling, and those who will recover quickly.
- Have the Trauma Team and EAP personnel work together to keep employees informed of what is going on, when they can return to work, where they and their families can go for help, etc. Prepare to debrief employees within 24 hours so they can begin the healing process.
- Devise a method to keep open the channels of communication and attempt to control rumors. A Hot-Line is usually an effective way to accomplish these purposes.

- Decide who will convey the bad news to the victims' families (see note below).
- Assign responsibility for notifying customers and suppliers about changes in orders and other business operations.
- Conduct a full-scale post-incident investigation to help the Company learn how to prevent a recurrence of violence.
- Support the prosecution of offenders by cooperating with law enforcement authorities and accommodating employees in making court appearances.
- Continue to be sensitive to employee needs and to show concern for their well-being.
- Have a post-trauma team debrief and counsel the workers periodically, and continue to inform other workers of the status of those employees who were more seriously injured.

Establish an Organizational Crisis Plan

To be fully protected from workplace violence, potential victims must give up some of the freedoms to which they have grown accustomed and instead subject themselves to some degree of control. Since it is difficult to prevent all acts of violence in a society that is accustomed to such freedom as exists in the United States, every organization should have a crisis plan ready for immediate implementation when the inevitable happens.

Establish Distress Signals and Procedures

To ensure that appropriate actions are taken quickly and decisively, an organizational crisis plan should have numerous elements, starting with a pre-arranged distress signal or code words. Every employee from the receptionist in the lobby to the employee on the shop floor should know what number to dial and what to say when workplace violence is suspected or observed in progress. The role model here could be the airlines, whose pilots and attendants know to report a hijacking quickly and in a low-key style by saying something like, "We have a passenger who wishes to go to Country X..."

Also, the company should have a list of telephone numbers and addresses of every employee's family and associates in case contact needs to be made. For an employee who may be holding other employees hostage, these contacts can provide valuable information such as potentially effective negotiating points or medications being taken by the hostage-taker.

In addition, conditions and procedures for calling security, emergency teams, and/or law enforcement agencies should be clearly identified. Those external agencies should be aware of the organization's facilities and work locations. Locations should be identified where people will report immediately and where they will actually perform their work in the event of an emergency. Likewise, in the event of an emergency, employees need to know and understand the pay and benefit policies that are in force. The company should plan to use a variety of communication media, and employees need to know what those are. An employee assistance program (EAP) should be established to help people cope with trauma (see also Chapter 9). After an emergency it is important to get key people back into facilities to assure others that it is safe (obviously the structural integrity of the facility must first be assured).

Set Up Early-Detection System

The organizational crisis plan should identify actions for the Crisis Management Team, one of which is to set up an early-detection system. Thus, one of the first things that the Crisis Management Team should do is examine the organization and its physical facilities so that ways can be put into place to detect possible violence early. As noted earlier in discussing access control, driving and walking routes should be examined to determine which are the most vulnerable. Walking routes should be examined for lighting at night and the placement of shrubbery and other items that could shield potential attackers. Entry ways and access points and methods should be examined as well. How could a potential perpetrator gain access to the physical facility other than the normal entryways? Are those entry points also secured? Maintaining high levels of alertness at all times is probably impossible for many organizations; nevertheless, plans should be as well prepared as possible.

Identify and Communicate Who Handles Problems

The plan should clearly identify individuals who are designated to handle problems for different units within the organization and assure that this information is well known to everyone in the organization. Their locations and phone numbers should be posted and readily available to all personnel when needed. Physical locations for emergencies should also be noted so that everyone knows where to go in case of a violent incident that leads to an evacuation of their workplaces. If the organization has an Emergency Operations Center (EOC) for handling natural disaster, fires, or law enforcement situations, it could be used as a Crisis Communication Center

(CCC). If not, then the organization should form a CCC perhaps using key executives and public information or public relations personnel.

Train Personnel in Well-Defined Procedures

Everyone in the organization should receive training in utilizing defensive strategies and coping with emergencies. Such training should help all employees recognize warning signs and encourage them to avert violence by reporting any threatening remarks or situations. People who are trained can see signals that would otherwise be overlooked or ignored, so they can alert others and be on the alert themselves. First aid, CPR, safety awareness, personal safety, and recognizing potentially violent situations in the workplace should all be covered. Training of this nature should help create a safe environment, give employees security, and show them that the organization cares about them.

The organization's procedures should clearly spell out that supervisors act quickly when dealing with potentially violent employees, and supervisors should be trained how to respond if one of their subordinates appears ready to lose control. The many cases of workplace violence in the past prove that a potentially hazardous or outright dangerous person can cause damage and/or get the organization in legal trouble. So, too, can an upset but competent computer user, a top-notch account manager, a quality-control operator, a competent accountant, as well as assembly-line workers. Role playing, case discussion, and other participative training approaches should be used to help supervisors gain confidence in handling crisis situations.

Prepare a Post-Violence Trauma Plan

Once a Level 3, high-magnitude (highest level, see Chapter 2) violent incident has occurred, supervisors should act quickly to report it through the proper channels, insure the safety of others in the area, secure the area until an investigation has been made, and debrief the victims, witnesses, and anyone else who might have pertinent information. A Post-Violence Trauma Plan ensures that all of this happens in an organized and timely manner.

A Post-Violence Trauma Plan can be of tremendous value to an organization in resuming normal operations, retaining valuable personnel, and decreasing the number and severity of civil suits. It helps to restore confidence in the organization. Employees feel more confident that "things are under control," and customers and suppliers are more confident that business will return to normal quickly. Indeed, that very confidence will help to assure that the organization will successfully recover from the violent event.

Like all effective plans, a Post-Violence Trauma Plan should be in writing, and copies should be readily available at all times to those employees who will be playing a key role in the operations. Copies should be kept at selected locations in the organization. Among the topics that should be address by a Post-Violence Trauma Plan are the following:

- Company policies that impact the proposed plan
- Evacuating premises
- Emergency medical actions
- Calming and interviewing witnesses
- Arranging transportation for evacuated personnel
- Repairing inoperable phones
- Securing and searching the premises
- Cleaning up property or grounds
- Managing the release of sensitive information to outsiders
- Taking care of essential details so grieving employees can heal
- Planning how to handle disruptions of routine (delayed orders, changed schedules, etc.)
- Restoring damaged or destroyed payroll and personnel information
- Returning the organization and its personnel to normal productivity
- Notifying victims' families

As most people know, the U.S. Armed Forces notifies families in person, day or night, in all kinds of weather, when a relative is gone. They do it this way because to do otherwise is impersonal and fails to reflect true, sad feelings. It lacks a sense of caring and a sense of how important this event is. Many other organizations, on the other hand, are cold and cruel by comparison. All business and government organizations should deliver bad-news messages personally by one of its own to next of kin. Usually the best individual for this task is the first-level supervisor, or the one who has the best relationship with the employee. In some situations, however, a high-ranking official should be sent to convey a sense of genuine concern to those receiving the message.

Summary

So let's summarize what organizations should be doing to prevent and cope with the Violence Volcano. The organization's culture is the key to minimizing the risks of violent behavior associated with the workplace. A culture that does not tolerate abusing, bullying, or harassing managers or employees will go a long way toward preventing an eruption of the Violence Volcano.

This culture can be developed through administrative ways. The organization should establish anti-violence policies and improve asset security while working closely with law enforcement and public safety organizations. When hiring, background checks should be conducted, focusing on the individual's employment and criminal history. For higher level and/or particularly sensitive positions, psychological testing should also be done. Due diligence in investigating claims against employees, carefully screen applicants prior to employment, properly induct and orient them as they join the organization, and continuously train and develop them after they join the organization.

Organizations will review their physical security, evaluate current personnel, screen new personnel, and develop plans for dealing with potential and actual violence as a means of minimizing the risks associated with this perplexing problem.

Effective communication, including procedures for reporting behaviors and threats, can help in identifying and resolving problems before stressors build to the point that violent behavior erupts. All managerial personnel should also be trained in the use of termination guidelines, particularly for individuals who may be prone to violence or for whom termination is the result of gross misconduct.

The organization should have a violence prevention plan developed with senior management participation. That plan should include periodic briefings for senior management and immediate briefings if a serious incident occurs. The organization should have an EAP that also provides for outplacement services for terminated employees. Following any serious incident there should be a review to learn from the incident and to correct any deficiencies encountered. Company officials will conduct risk analyses, develop profiles of potential perpetrators, make emergency plans, train managers and personnel, and take other similar steps to reduce risks. In this way, then, hopefully the Violence Volcano will not erupt.

13

Legal Issues and Law Enforcement

The very nature of workplace violence makes clear that many or most incidents involve the law, even though specific legislation mandating that organizations have a duty to prevent workplace violence is nonexistent or rare, but more and more administrative regulations and case law are establishing the organization's responsibility for protecting workers. Also, the organization's general duty to provide safe workplaces was clearly indicated in the Occupational Safety and Health Act of 1970 (OSHA, 2006). The growing efforts by legislatures and courts to more specifically deal with forms of workplace violence suggests that everyone in organizations needs to have at least a general understanding of the legal issues surrounding workplace violence.

Legal Issues

Legal issues pertaining to workplace violence vary from state to state and are constantly changing. Nevertheless, there are some basic aspects that seem to hold at least in broad, general terms. This chapter discusses some of the more relevant ones of those.

Responsibility and Liability

Two broad legal issues to consider are responsibility and liability. One is the responsibility and the corresponding liability of organizations to provide safe workplaces, the "Duty of Care" standard (Witting, 2005). The other is the responsibility and the corresponding liability of organizations to provide for employee rights before and after an incident (behaviors, threats, etc., and investigation, discipline, etc.). In general terms, then, organizations could be found liable for failure related to one or the other of these responsibilities if such failure leads to personal or property damage or harm. The liability could result from the organization's or management's failure to properly or adequately protect, train, supervise, investigate, do due diligence, or discipline individuals in the organization.

Legal liability is often considered both as a strategy for attempting to motivate organizations to act in such a way as to prevent workplace violence and as a compensatory mechanism for individuals impacted by such violence. Legal theories abound to address the problem: negligence (tort), agency, contract, civil rights, and regulatory law to name a few (Brakel, 1998). Traditional legal approaches to deterring workplace violence (e.g., laws dealing with assault, battery, homicide, terrorism) seem to have been insufficient, thus resulting in the development of legislation, administrative regulations, and case law to focus more specifically on particular types of workplace violence or specific occupations (Barish, 2001).

Much of the legal attention surrounding workplace violence has centered on negligence in one form or another. Those include (a) negligent employment in hiring, retention, supervision, or assignment; (b) negligent training; (c) negligent entrustment or respondeat superior; and (d) negligent recommendation.

Negligent employment may exist in the form of negligent hiring if the employer knew or should have known of problems in advance, negligent retention if the employer becomes aware or should have been aware of problems after hiring, negligent supervision if the employer fails to provide adequate supervision or to discipline violators of anti-violence policies including the failure to protect one employee from another, or negligent assignment if the employer knew or should have known that an employee had a particular problem that could lead to violence (Davies & Hertig, 2007; Kaufer, 2001; Paetzold, 1998; Howie & Shapero, 2002; White, 2002).

Negligent training exists when an employee's action results in injury or harm to someone else as a consequence of the employee not having been properly trained (Thibodeau, 2007).

Negligent entrustment or respondeat superior could also come into play. Negligent entrustment typically involves weapons and, as the name implies, exists if an employer knows or should have known that an employee entrusted with a weapon does not know how to properly use it and someone is harmed by that weapon (Holzer, 1978; Kaufer, 2001). Respondeat superior involves the employer's liability resulting from the actions of an employee who is an agent of the employer and acting within the scope of his or her employment (Davant, 2002; Kaufer, 2001), whether on company premises or not and whether actually performing duties at the time (e.g., attending a company party that the employee is expected to attend).

Negligent recommendation or misrepresentation is most closely associated with instances in which an organization provides a favorable recommendation for, or fails to disclose complete and accurate information about, an individual that it knows is a problem employee. While organizations should be very cautious as to the information they provide in references, they should never suppress the truth. On the other hand, the organization must never misrepresent the truth by providing negative, unproven information that constitutes defamation of a current or former employee.

In addition, organizations have a duty to warn an employee if those in the organization know or have reason to suspect that the employee may be the target for potential violence. This may be particularly important where domestic violence is involved.

Vicarious liability is yet another concept of liability that could be involved. It suggests that an organization may be liable for the actions of its members even if the organization did nothing wrong. While seldom employed in criminal law, its use may be attempted in civil actions especially in medical and healthcare organizations (Chaney, 1987; Gabel, 1987) and cases of product liability (Stapleton, 1994).

Harassment

One particular form of behavior that can lead to legal problems for organizations is harassment (Fitzgerald, 1993; O'Leary-Kelly, Bowes-Sperry, Bates, & Lean, 2009; O'Leary-Kelly, Paetzold & Griffin, 2000). Different forms of harassment (sexual, sexual orientation, race, religion, age, or disability) can lead to liability actions under a variety of state and/or federal statutes. The situation can be quite complex as not only must there be clear evidence that harassment occurred but also it must be clear that the organization was aware of it and did not take action to stop it. Preventing harassment, of course, necessarily involves training all members of the organization as well as maintaining an organizational culture that in no way supports or condones it. An important first step in that direction is the formation, dissemination, and posting of a policy statement that indicates zero tolerance of harassment.

Stalking

Closely related to harassment is stalking. Employees who are being stalked don't leave the problem when they arrive at work. Receptionists, supervisors, and coworkers should be aware of the problem so that they don't inadvertently expose the victim to danger. Victims should provide a description (a photo, if possible) of the stalker to those in the organization so that they may help protect him or her. Stalking can be even more of a problem if the perpetrator is a supervisor, coworker, or customer (Mullen, Pathé, & Purcell, 2000). Victims, and in many cases their employer, can usually obtain a temporary restraining order (TRO) to help in controlling the stalker. Expert opinion differs, however, as to whether TROs may instead serve as catalysts to push stalkers over the edge (de Becker, 1997; Lardner, 1995; Wallace & Kelty, 1995). Also, state laws on restraining orders are extremely varied and so must be consulted for the particular state at issue.

Domestic Violence

Another problem organizations may face that can involve legal issues is that of domestic violence (Buzawa & Buzawa, 2002). While case law varies and is changing, many states have enacted statutes related to domestic violence and its relation to work. In particular, many states provide that victims of domestic abuse or violence are entitled to leaves of absence to obtain medical or legal services (American Bar Association, 1999; Gedman, 1998).

Mental Disabilities and the ADA

The Americans with Disabilities Act (ADA) can complicate organizational responses to reduce the likelihood of workplace violence. The reasonable accommodation requirement of ADA may seem to limit an organization's actions at least to the extent that employees with disabilities, particularly mental disabilities, are involved. However, as Paetzold, O'Leary-Kelly, & Griffin (2007) point out, that is not the case for several reasons. Many mentally impaired employees are not disabled under the ADA and, even if they are, if their problems can be handled through medication and they fail to take their medicines, they would no longer be covered by the ADA. Organizations need to work with law enforcement and other public safety agencies to assure that they are in compliance with ADA but not overreacting to it.

Approaches to Reduce Liability

While all litigation cannot be avoided, organizations can reduce their liability by the use of corporate compliance programs (Stokols, McMahan, Clitheroe, & Wells, 2001; Walsh & Pyrich, 1995) that involve carefully monitoring and verifying behaviors in and policies of the organization. In addition, the approaches suggested elsewhere in this book should be used. Those include the following:

1. Establish, maintain, and adhere to a workplace violence policy
2. Communicate and coordinate with law enforcement and public safety agencies
3. Take steps to assure asset security:
    3.1 Conduct a work site analysis
    3.2 Act to prevent and control hazards
    3.3 Conduct safety training
4. Perform due diligence during hiring:
    4.1 Conduct adequate background checks
    4.2 Ask probing questions in the interview process
    4.3 Check public sex-offender registries
    4.4 Conduct thorough reference checks
    4.5 Use references in addition to those provided by the applicant
    4.6 Where appropriate, obtain releases from applicants and obtain copies of personnel files
5. Develop plans and teams to deal with situations expeditiously:
    5.1 Establish a crisis/threat management team
    5.2 Establish an organizational crisis plan
    5.3 Prepare a post-violence trauma plan
    5.4 Prepare for bomb threats
6. Treat all threats of violence seriously
7. Train all employees in the Violence Volcano warning signs
8. Establish clear procedures for reporting behaviors and threats
9. Keep careful, accurate records and documentation
10. Improve communication within the organization and with public safety and law enforcement
11. Practice non-exacerbating termination procedures
12. Provide outplacement services
13. Assist with stress management

In addition to these general guidelines that pertain to all organizations, OSHA has suggestions for many specific types of organizations that are especially vulnerable to violence, e.g., late-night retail establishments, healthcare and social service workers, and the like. OSHA's guidelines provide very detailed recommendations for those particular situations.

Law Enforcement

In spite of an organization's best efforts, violent incidents may still occur. Some such incidents will necessitate involving public safety organizations or law enforcement. Thus, it behooves managers and business owners to establish and maintain good working relationships with those agencies. Not only will they be needed in case of a violent incident, but also they can provide invaluable assistance in making plans, evaluating the physical facilities, and generally helping the organization to prepare for eventualities.

Jurisdictional and Other Limitations

Just as legal issues vary from state to state, so, too, do law enforcement jurisdictions, funding, manpower, and experience. Some agencies are quite active in working with organizations to prevent and respond to workplace violence while others do so only in emergency situations. In either case, it is in the organization's best interest to develop open channels of communication with law enforcement before an incident occurs. Both sides need to understand the limits and capabilities of the other. Organization officials need to understand the local procedures and processes, including contact information, so that they can build that information into their plans and internal communications. And they need to be sure that law enforcement agencies have accurate information about the organization, too (contact information, access points, emergency exits, and so on).

Pre-Incident Happenings

One element that needs careful consideration is when to notify law enforcement of behaviors or threats that appear to be very serious but have not yet resulted in physical harm or the level of a criminal violation. Bringing in law enforcement may prevent an eruption of the Violence Volcano—or it may trigger it. Crisis/threat management teams must conduct very careful analyses of these situations to try to make correct decisions. Having good, cooperative relations with law enforcement can be beneficial in assessing the pros and cons in these situations. If both the organization and local law enforcement are concerned, the FBI's National Center for the Analysis of Violent Crime (NCAVC) could be asked by the police to perform a risk assessment and provide advice on how to handle the situation. The NCAVC is part of the FBI's Critical Incident Response Group (CIRG) and provides investigative support to law enforcement agencies around the world for crimes such as terrorism, bombings, arson, threats, serial rapes, or extortion.

When Violence Occurs

Among the incidents that should be reported to the proper law and safety agencies are those that involve the use of weapons or serious threats, those that result in physical assault or significant property damage, and, of course, those that involve criminal conduct. Obviously a violence incident that becomes an emergency should always result in a 911 call by someone (anyone) in the organization. In these circumstances, the first responders (law enforcement or other emergency personnel) assume the responsibility for the situation and take action to manage events. In the case of law enforcement, they may make arrests, conduct interviews, and gather evidence concerning the incident.

Employee Rights

Employee rights constitute an important legal issue and one that can involve law enforcement. As noted in Chapter 11, organizations must balance the rights of problem employees with the right of all other employees to a safe workplace. In many instances, actions that seem appropriate for maintaining security also seem to infringe upon employee rights. One important element in this seemingly catch-22 situation is that all members of the organization must understand that information systems used by the organization belong to the organization. This means, in particular, that e-mail, voicemail, and computer files can be reviewed by the organization and that employees have no rights to privacy while using the organization's system and/or equipment.

In addition to the right to a safe work environment that is free from discrimination and harassment, one of the more important rights involved in safety and security issues, is the right to privacy. In particular, when domestic violence may or does spill over to the workplace, balancing employee privacy with employee security is a difficult task. It should be clear, however, that workplace safety must never be compromised since it involves more than a single individual. Nevertheless, actions in such cases should be taken as unobtrusively as possible and with great sensitivity for individual privacy and security.

Employee rights are generally covered in employment law. Employment law, however, is quite varied covering such issues as discrimination, wrongful termination, wages, taxes, and safety, and security. Generally, employment relationships are based on contracts, so state contract law may be the primary concern. However, federal and state law statutes dealing with specific elements of employee rights have also been enacted. While government employees generally have greater rights than do those in the private sector (Cohen & Cohen, 2007), four privacy rights are frequently identified for all employees. They are:

> Intrusion—There should be no unwanted or unreasonable intrusion into one's personal workspace.
> Personal Information—There should be no unwanted or unreasonable disclosure of one's personal information, particularly medical.
> Character—There should be no public release of information that would malign or vilify anyone.
> ID—An individual's name or identification should not be used without his or her consent.

It is important to note, though, that some states have explicitly rejected one or more of these privacy rights so that an understanding of the specific laws in a given state is important. As technology develops, issues concerning employee's computer use, particularly for e-mail and Internet access, become more important. Other related technologies such as the use of GPS (Global Positioning System) devices, radar/laser detectors, and the like also come under scrutiny. Dress codes, weight restrictions, and policies dealing with general appearance and demeanor can also be involved in issues of employee rights.

Care must be taken not only to protect the rights of victims but also to safeguard the rights of alleged perpetrators. Allegations are not proof. Singling out an individual and either terminating that individual or warning others about him or her could lead to charges of libel or slander or a wrongful termination civil suit. Again, working with law enforcement and other public safety agencies should mitigate the possibility of such actions.

Summary

Although laws relating to workplace violence vary from state to state and are constantly changing, the basic principles that underlie those laws are responsibility and liability. Organizations are responsible for hiring, protecting, training, supervising, investigating, doing due diligence, and disciplining their members. A failure to do so could make the organization liable under the law.

Organizations should establish and maintain good working relationships with law enforcement and public safety agencies. Not only may those agencies be needed if violence occurs, but they also can provide assistance in planning, evaluating the physical facilities, and helping the organization to prepare for possible violence.

An important legal issue is employee rights. Organizations must balance the rights of problem employees with those of others in a dynamic legal environment. Privacy requires a particularly difficult balance, especially as technology changes.

APPENDICES

A

Organizations That Assist in Learning About Workplace Violence

American Medical Association
515 N. State St
Chicago IL 60654
(800) 621-8335
www.ama-assn.org/ama/home/index.shtml

American Society for Industrial Security
1625 Prince St
Alexandria VA 22314-2818
703-519-6200
www.asisonline.org

American Psychological Association
750 1st St NE
Washington DC 20002-4242
800-374-2721
www.apa.org/

Centers for Disease Control
1600 Clifton Rd NE
Atlanta GA 30333
404-639-3311
www.cdc.gov/

Center for Crisis Management
Graduate School of Business
Bridge Hall 200
University of Southern California
Los Angeles CA 90084-1421
213-740-8504

Center for the Study and Prevention of Violence
Institute of Behavioral Science
Campus Box 442
University of Colorado at Boulder
Boulder CO 80309-0442
303-492-8465
www.colorado.edu/cspv

Crisis Management International, Inc.
8 Piedmont Ctr Ste 420
Atlanta GA 30305
800-274-7470
www.cmiatl.com/

Crisis Prevention Institute, Inc.
3315 K, N 124th St
Brookfield WI 53005
800-558-8976
www.crisisprevention.com/

Federal Bureau of Investigation
J. Edgar Hoover Building
935 Pennsylvania Ave NW
Washington DC 20535-0001
202-324-3000
www.fbi.gov/contactus.htm

International Association of Chiefs of Police (IACP)
515 N Washington St
Alexandria VA 22314-2357
703-836-6767 or 800-THE-IACP
Fax: 703.836.4543
www.theiacp.org/pubinfo/pubs/pslc/svindex.htm

National Center for Victims of Crime
2000 M St NW Ste 480
Washington DC 20036
202-467-8700
www.ncvc.org/

National Crime Prevention Council
1000 Connecticut Ave NW
Washington DC 20036
202-466-6272
www.ncpc.org/

National Crime Victims Research and Treatment Center
Medical University of South Carolina
165 Cannon St
PO Box 250852
Charleston SC 29425
843-792-2945
www.musc.edu/cvc/

National Criminal Justice Reference Service
PO Box 6000
Rockville MD 20850
800-851-3420
ncjrs.gov

National Health Resource Center on Domestic Violence
The Family Violence Prevention Fund
383 Rhode Island St Ste 304
San Francisco CA 94103-5133
415-252-8900 or 1-888-RX-ABUSE
Fax: 415-252-8991
www.fvpf.org/health

National Institute for Mental Health
Room 8184, MSC 9663
6001 Executive Blvd
Bethesda MD 20892-9663
866-615-6464
www.nimh.nih.gov/

National Institute for the Prevention of Workplace Violence
22701 Woodlake Ln
Lake Forest CA
949-770-5264
www.Workplaceviolence911.com

National School Safety Center
141 Duesenberg Dr Ste 11
Westlake Village CA 91362
Phone 805-373-9977
Fax 805-373-9277
www.schoolsafety.us

National Sexual Violence Resource Center
123 North Enola Dr
Enola PA 17025-2521
Phone: 1-877-739-3895 or 717-909-0710
TTY: 717-909-0715
Fax: 717-909-0714
www.nsvrc.org

NIOSH, New England Field Office
PO Box 87040
South Dartmouth MA 07248-0701
508-997-6126

NIOSH, Atlanta Field Office
Mailstop E-74
1600 Clifton Rd NE
Atlanta GA 30333
404-498-2550

NIOSH, Denver Field Office
PO Box 25226
Denver CO 80225-0226
303-236-6032

Occupational Safety and Health Administration
200 Constitution Ave NW
Washington DC 20210
800-321-6742
www.osha.gov/

Post Trauma Resources
1811 Bull St
Columbia SC 29201
800-459-6780
www.posttrauma.com/

Society of Human Resources Management
1800 Duke St
Alexandria VA 22314
800-283-SHRM
www.shrm.org/

United States Department of Labor
200 Constitution Ave NW
Washington DC 20210
866-4-USA-DOL
www.dol.gov/

Workplace Violence Research Institute
1281 Gene Autry Trail, Suite K
Palm Springs CA 92262
800-230-7302
www.workviolence.com/

B

Example Documents

Incident Self-Report

Date Filed _____ Employee Name _____

Date & Time of Incident _____

Title/Department _____

Where did the incident occur? _____

What were you doing just prior to the incident?

_____
_____
_____
_____

Describe what happened (include names of everyone involved, the extent of any injuries, and the names of witnesses):

_____
_____
_____
_____
_____

What weapons were involved, if any?

_____
_____

Signature of Employee _____

Department _____

The employer is responsible for maintaining copies of reports, which shall be used when the program is reviewed and updated.

More detailed examples may be found at: www.osha.gov/SLTC/etools/hospital/hazards/workplaceviolence/confidentialreportform.html

Violence Prevention Checklist

Please CIRCLE your Yes or No responses.

Violence Prevention Plan

Yes No   Is there a Violence Prevention Plan that includes policy, training, and response plans?

Yes No   Does it include evacuation plans and alternative work locations in the event of an extreme emergency?

Policy Statement

Yes No   Is the Workplace Violence Policy statement available and understandable to everyone?

Controls

Yes No   Have appropriate physical/structural controls been implemented? (These might include door controls, panic buttons, closed circuit monitoring, metal detectors, safety glass, well lighted parking and stairwells or similar controls.)

Yes No   Have appropriate process controls been implemented? (These might include a separate and secure reception area, sign in/sign out procedures, visitor escorts, ID badges, emergency numbers and contacts posted by every phone and computer, security guards, and similar controls.)

Training

Yes No   Is there a training program for all members of the organization?

Yes No   Are employees required to repeat it as a "refresher" periodically?

Yes No   Does that training include (1) understanding and use of physical/structural and process controls, and (2) understanding of both organizational and individual conditions that may lead to violence?

An Evaluative Instrument

Identifying Your Organization's Propensity to Elicit Violence

Which of the following are true for your organization?

This list of indicators is by no means inclusive but rather is suggestive of the kind of organizational environments that are conducive to workplace violence. The higher the number, the greater the propensity for violence.

USE THIS SCALE — The higher the number, the greater the propensity for violence.

1 = not true at all
2 = rarely or hardly ever true
3 = sometimes true, sometimes not
4 = mostly true
5 = completely or always true.

☐ 1 ☐ 2 ☐ 3 ☐ 4 ☐ 5   Managers do not control their anger.
☐ 1 ☐ 2 ☐ 3 ☐ 4 ☐ 5   Managers yell at employees.
☐ 1 ☐ 2 ☐ 3 ☐ 4 ☐ 5   Managers use offensive language.

☐ 1 ☐ 2 ☐ 3 ☐ 4 ☐ 5 Managers belittle, demean, or degrade employees.

☐ 1 ☐ 2 ☐ 3 ☐ 4 ☐ 5 Managers display angry outbursts and tantrums.

☐ 1 ☐ 2 ☐ 3 ☐ 4 ☐ 5 Managers abuse their power.

☐ 1 ☐ 2 ☐ 3 ☐ 4 ☐ 5 Managers threaten employees.

☐ 1 ☐ 2 ☐ 3 ☐ 4 ☐ 5 Managers take undue or unfair advantage of their employees.

☐ 1 ☐ 2 ☐ 3 ☐ 4 ☐ 5 Managers are heavy handed in the treatment of employees.

☐ 1 ☐ 2 ☐ 3 ☐ 4 ☐ 5 Violence/threats are accepted or overlooked as "part of the job" by managers and others in the organization.

☐ 1 ☐ 2 ☐ 3 ☐ 4 ☐ 5 Managers exhibit poor management skills.

☐ 1 ☐ 2 ☐ 3 ☐ 4 ☐ 5 Managers micromanage.

☐ 1 ☐ 2 ☐ 3 ☐ 4 ☐ 5 Managers perform performance appraisal poorly or not at all.

☐ 1 ☐ 2 ☐ 3 ☐ 4 ☐ 5 Managers show favoritism.

☐ 1 ☐ 2 ☐ 3 ☐ 4 ☐ 5 Managers do not do real "due diligence" in investigating complaints against other managers.

☐ 1 ☐ 2 ☐ 3 ☐ 4 ☐ 5 Managers use meetings inappropriately.

☐ 1 ☐ 2 ☐ 3 ☐ 4 ☐ 5 Managers are insecure and/or incompetent.

☐ 1 ☐ 2 ☐ 3 ☐ 4 ☐ 5 Managers try to cover up insecurity or incompetence.

☐ 1 ☐ 2 ☐ 3 ☐ 4 ☐ 5 Managers avoid making decisions.

☐ 1 ☐ 2 ☐ 3 ☐ 4 ☐ 5 Managers cannot accept criticism.

☐ 1 ☐ 2 ☐ 3 ☐ 4 ☐ 5 Many managers use authoritarian styles of management.

☐ 1 ☐ 2 ☐ 3 ☐ 4 ☐ 5 Coworkers lack interpersonal skills.

☐ 1 ☐ 2 ☐ 3 ☐ 4 ☐ 5 Coworkers are inconsiderate.

☐ 1 ☐ 2 ☐ 3 ☐ 4 ☐ 5 Coworkers have attitude problems.

☐ 1 ☐ 2 ☐ 3 ☐ 4 ☐ 5 Coworkers disregard appearance and/or hygiene.

☐ 1 ☐ 2 ☐ 3 ☐ 4 ☐ 5   Coworkers lie and manipulate.
☐ 1 ☐ 2 ☐ 3 ☐ 4 ☐ 5   Coworkers threaten.
☐ 1 ☐ 2 ☐ 3 ☐ 4 ☐ 5   Coworkers harass.
☐ 1 ☐ 2 ☐ 3 ☐ 4 ☐ 5   Coworkers bully.
☐ 1 ☐ 2 ☐ 3 ☐ 4 ☐ 5   Coworkers engage in theft or sabotage.
☐ 1 ☐ 2 ☐ 3 ☐ 4 ☐ 5   Coworkers take or subject others to unnecessary risks.
☐ 1 ☐ 2 ☐ 3 ☐ 4 ☐ 5   Coworkers engage in behavior that is potentially harmful to others or organizational assets.
☐ 1 ☐ 2 ☐ 3 ☐ 4 ☐ 5   Coworkers engage in behavior that is potentially harmful to themselves.
☐ 1 ☐ 2 ☐ 3 ☐ 4 ☐ 5   Coworkers don't carry their own weight.
☐ 1 ☐ 2 ☐ 3 ☐ 4 ☐ 5   Coworkers have poor or inefficient work habits.
☐ 1 ☐ 2 ☐ 3 ☐ 4 ☐ 5   Coworkers don't carry out instructions.
☐ 1 ☐ 2 ☐ 3 ☐ 4 ☐ 5   Coworkers are absent from work.
☐ 1 ☐ 2 ☐ 3 ☐ 4 ☐ 5   Coworkers are absent on the job.
☐ 1 ☐ 2 ☐ 3 ☐ 4 ☐ 5   Numerous workers have poor credit records.
☐ 1 ☐ 2 ☐ 3 ☐ 4 ☐ 5   Numerous workers have poor driving records.
☐ 1 ☐ 2 ☐ 3 ☐ 4 ☐ 5   Numerous members of the organization have extreme political views.
☐ 1 ☐ 2 ☐ 3 ☐ 4 ☐ 5   Numerous members of the organization have extreme religious views.
☐ 1 ☐ 2 ☐ 3 ☐ 4 ☐ 5   Reported incidents or violence are not carefully investigated.
☐ 1 ☐ 2 ☐ 3 ☐ 4 ☐ 5   Members of the organization file frequent complaints or grievances.
☐ 1 ☐ 2 ☐ 3 ☐ 4 ☐ 5   Members of the organization have experienced domestic violence issues.
☐ 1 ☐ 2 ☐ 3 ☐ 4 ☐ 5   Members of the organization are not required to report incidents or threats of violence.
☐ 1 ☐ 2 ☐ 3 ☐ 4 ☐ 5   Members of the organization do not feel that they are treated with dignity and respect by others in the organization.

☐ 1 ☐ 2 ☐ 3 ☐ 4 ☐ 5 Members of the organization generally do not feel "safe" when they are at work.

☐ 1 ☐ 2 ☐ 3 ☐ 4 ☐ 5 Members of the organization frequently feel unnecessarily stressed.

☐ 1 ☐ 2 ☐ 3 ☐ 4 ☐ 5 Members of the organization are not encouraged to communicate information about potentially threatening clients or visitors.

☐ 1 ☐ 2 ☐ 3 ☐ 4 ☐ 5 Managers do not inform members of the organization about violent incidents.

☐ 1 ☐ 2 ☐ 3 ☐ 4 ☐ 5 Members of the organization are not very satisfied with their jobs.

☐ 1 ☐ 2 ☐ 3 ☐ 4 ☐ 5 Members of the organization are not very satisfied with management.

☐ 1 ☐ 2 ☐ 3 ☐ 4 ☐ 5 Members of the organization don't understand or accept the organization's mission.

☐ 1 ☐ 2 ☐ 3 ☐ 4 ☐ 5 Members of the organization work in high-crime areas.

☐ 1 ☐ 2 ☐ 3 ☐ 4 ☐ 5 Members of the organization work with drugs.

☐ 1 ☐ 2 ☐ 3 ☐ 4 ☐ 5 Members of the organization work with cash.

☐ 1 ☐ 2 ☐ 3 ☐ 4 ☐ 5 Members of the organization work with patients or clients who have a history of violent behavior or behavior disorders.

☐ 1 ☐ 2 ☐ 3 ☐ 4 ☐ 5 Members of the organization work in isolated work areas.

☐ 1 ☐ 2 ☐ 3 ☐ 4 ☐ 5 There is no training about workplace violence prevention.

☐ 1 ☐ 2 ☐ 3 ☐ 4 ☐ 5 Members of the organization are not carefully screened prior to hiring/using them.

☐ 1 ☐ 2 ☐ 3 ☐ 4 ☐ 5 There are a lot of management/labor disputes.

☐ 1 ☐ 2 ☐ 3 ☐ 4 ☐ 5 There are a lot of injury claims.

☐ 1 ☐ 2 ☐ 3 ☐ 4 ☐ 5 There are a lot of occupational stress claims.

☐ 1 ☐ 2 ☐ 3 ☐ 4 ☐ 5 This organization or its members have experienced violent behavior, assaults, or threats from within the organization.

□ 1	□ 2	□ 3	□ 4	□ 5	This organization or its members have experienced violent behavior, assaults, or threats from outside the organization.
□ 1	□ 2	□ 3	□ 4	□ 5	There is a highly diverse workforce.
□ 1	□ 2	□ 3	□ 4	□ 5	Higher level managers ignore poor lower level managers.
□ 1	□ 2	□ 3	□ 4	□ 5	Higher level managers uphold bad or improper decisions of lower level managers.
□ 1	□ 2	□ 3	□ 4	□ 5	Higher level managers set poor examples for lower level managers.
□ 1	□ 2	□ 3	□ 4	□ 5	Jobs are unsafe or too physically demanding.
□ 1	□ 2	□ 3	□ 4	□ 5	Jobs are in inconvenient locations.
□ 1	□ 2	□ 3	□ 4	□ 5	There are many unpleasant or unsafe workplaces.
□ 1	□ 2	□ 3	□ 4	□ 5	Many workplaces are uncomfortable.
□ 1	□ 2	□ 3	□ 4	□ 5	There are numerous bad bosses.
□ 1	□ 2	□ 3	□ 4	□ 5	There are numerous bad coworkers.
□ 1	□ 2	□ 3	□ 4	□ 5	There are numerous bad customers or clients.
□ 1	□ 2	□ 3	□ 4	□ 5	Many jobs are low paying and/or have little by way of fringe benefits.
□ 1	□ 2	□ 3	□ 4	□ 5	There is little job security.
□ 1	□ 2	□ 3	□ 4	□ 5	There is little opportunity for advancement.
□ 1	□ 2	□ 3	□ 4	□ 5	There are many incompetent managers.
□ 1	□ 2	□ 3	□ 4	□ 5	Many managers are dishonest.
□ 1	□ 2	□ 3	□ 4	□ 5	Many managers are unethical.
□ 1	□ 2	□ 3	□ 4	□ 5	The organizational environment is generally threatening.

Derived from Van Fleet, E. W., & Van Fleet, D. D. (2007). *Workplace Survival: Dealing with Bad Bosses, Bad Workers, Bad Jobs.* Frederick, MD: PublishAmerica.

D

A Training Outline Using the Violence Volcano Metaphor

1. Have participants complete (anonymously) the form in Appendix C and give them to an assistant for tabulation.
2. Cover definition framework from Chapter 2 to make certain that everyone understands the following:
   - the three categories of violent behavior
   - the three different results of violence
   - the three levels of violence
   - the many examples associated with each of the 27 combinations of these.

   Have participants suggest additions to the examples based on their personal experiences or observations.
3. Cover the influence model from Chapter 3 to make certain that everyone understands the three major sets of factors that influence violence:
   - the environment
   - the organization
   - the individual

4. Review the Violence Volcano metaphor from Chapter 3 to make certain that everyone understands how violence builds.
5. Examine administrative ways of addressing workplace violence, including policies and plans.
6. Follow #5 with an emphasis on the reporting of incidents. Return to the Violence Volcano metaphor and the three levels of violence to indicate the importance of watching for any build-up in "volcanic pressure."
7. Bring in the results of the Appendix C (An Evaluative Instrument) form and then draw on material from Chapters 4–14 and participants' personal experiences to discuss potential ways of dealing with incidents.
8. Reporting and handling incidents treats only effects, not causes. Only by getting at the root cause can an organization hope to prevent eruptions in the Violence Volcano. Return, therefore, to the influence model from Chapter 3 to emphasize the importance of trying to determine the cause of any incident.
9. Draw on material from Chapters 4–13 and participants' personal experiences to discuss ways with which different types of influences/causes might be dealt with.

Retrain Using the Program Every Few Years.

Bibliography

American Psychiatric Association. (1987). *Diagnostic and statistical manual of mental disorders* (3rd ed., rev.). Arlington, VA.

André, R., & Ward, P. D. (1984). *The 59-second employee.* Boston: Houghton Mifflin.

Bachman, R. (1994, July). *Violence and theft in the workplace. Crime Data Brief: National Crime Victimization Survey.* Washington, DC: U.S. Department of Justice, Bureau of Justice Statistics.

Barish R. C. (2001). Legislation and regulation addressing workplace violence in the United States and British Columbia. *American Journal of Preventive Medicine, 20*(2), 149–154.

Baron, S. A. (1993). *Violence in the workplace.* Ventura, CA: Pathfinder Publishing of California.

Barton, L. (1993). Terrorism as an international business crisis. *Management Decision, 1*(1), 22.

Barton, L. (1993, March 1). Why business must prepare a strategic response to corporate sabotage. *Industrial Management, 35*(2), 16–20.

Berman, D. C. (1986). Putting employees back on track. *Bottomline, 3*(10), 19–22.

Bernstein, R. (1990, October 28). The rising hegemony of the politically correct. *New York Times,* p. 4–1.

Blanchard, K., & Johnson, S. (1983). *The one minute manager.* New York: William.

BLS. (2005). *Census of fatal occupational injuries.* Washington, DC: U.S. Department of Labor, Bureau of Labor Statistics.

Blythe, B. (2002). *Blindsided.* New York: Penguin Books.

Brakel, S. J. (1998). Legal liability and workplace violence. *Journal of American Academy Psychiatry Law, 26*(4), 553–562.

Braveman, D. D. (1996). Introduction: International terrorism: Prevention and remedies. *Syracuse Journal of International Law and Commerce, 22*(Spring), 5.

Bryngelson, J. (2000). *CARE (Courtesy and Respect Empower)*. Billings, MT: J Bryngelson.

Buddy T. (2003). Substance abuse in the workplace: A dangerous and expensive problem. alcoholism.about.com/cs/work/a/aa990120.htm

Buzawa, E. S., & Buzawa, C. G. (2002). *Domestic violence: The criminal justice response* (3rd ed.). Thousand Oaks, CA: Sage.

Campbell, J. C. (Ed.). (1995). *Assessing dangerousness: Violence by sexual offenders, batterers, and child abusers*. Thousand Oaks, CA: Sage.

Chaney, E. A. (1987). Personal and vicarious liability. *Journal of Pediatric Nursing, 2*(2), 132–134.

Cohen, C. F., & Cohen, M. E. (2007). On-duty and off-duty: Employee right to privacy and employer's right to control in the private sector. *Employee Responsibilities and Rights Journal, 19*(4), 235–246.

Coleman, L. (2004). The frequency and cost of corporate crises. *Journal of Contingencies and Crisis Management, 12*(1), 2–13.

Conlon, P. (1987). Show you care. *Canadian Business* (Canada), *60*(4), 108–111.

Cook, M. F. (Ed.) (1991). *The human resources yearbook*. Englewood Cliffs, NJ: Prentice Hall.

Davant, C. (2002). Employer liability for employee fraud: Apparent authority or respondeat superior? *South Dakota Law Review, 47*, 554–582.

Davies, S. J., & Hertig, C. A. (Eds.). (2007). *Security supervision & management* (3rd ed.). Woburn, MA: Butterworth-Heinemann.

de Becker, G. (1997). *The gift of fear: Survival signals that protect us from violence*. New York: Random House.

Denenberg, R., & Braverman, M. (2001). *The violence-prone workplace: A new approach to dealing with hostile, threatening, and uncivil behavior*. Ithaca, NY: Cornell University Press.

Fitzgerald, L. F. (1993). Sexual harassment: Violence against women in the workplace. *American Psychologist, 48*, 1070–1076.

Gabel, W. (1987). Vicarious liability. *Journal of the American Optometric Association, 58*(7), 599–601.

Gedman, C. M. (1998). Workplace violence and domestic violence: A proactive approach. *Journal of Healthcare Protection Management, 14*, 45–54.

Geen, R. G. (1968). Effects of frustration, attack, and prior training in aggressiveness upon aggressive behavior. *Journal of Personality and Social Psychology, 9*, 316–321.

Gelles. R. J. (1991). Physical violence, child abuse, and child homicide: A continuum of violence, or distinct behaviors? *Human Nature, 2*(1), 59–72.

Goodman, L. A., Dutton, M. A., & Bennett, L. (2000). Predicting repeat abuse among arrested batterers. *Journal of Interpersonal Violence, 15*(1), 63–74.

Griffin, R. W., & Lopez, Y. P. (2005). "Bad behavior" in organizations: A review and typology for future research. *Journal of Management, 31*, 988–1005.

Griffin, R. W., & O'Leary-Kelly, A. M. (Eds.) (2004). *The dark side of organizational behavior.* San Francisco: Jossey-Bass.

Health Alliance. (2004). *Employee assistance program and services.* www.healthalliance.com/EAP.

Hipple, S. (1999, July). Worker displacement in the mid-1990's. *Monthly Labor Review. 122*(7), 15–32.

Holzer, R. J. (1978). Liability to the injured third party for negligent entrustment of a firearm. *Chicago Bar Record, 59,* 346–48.

Howie, R. M., & Shapero, H. (2002). Pre-employment criminal background checks: Why employers should look before they leap. *Employee Relations Law Journal, 28,* 63–77.

Inness, M., Barling, J., & Turner, N. (2005). Understanding supervisor-targeted aggression: A within-person, between-jobs design. *Journal of Applied Psychology, 90*(4), 731–739.

Jansen, M. A. (1986). Emotional disorders and the labour force: Prevalence, costs, prevention, and rehabilitation. *International Labour Review* (Switzerland), *125*(5), 605–615.

Kaufer, S. (2001). *Corporate liability: Sharing the blame for workplace violence.* Palm Springs, CA: Workplace Violence Institute.

Kelloway, E. K., Barling, J., & Hurrell, J. J., Jr. (2006). *Handbook of workplace violence.* Thousand Oaks, CA: Sage.

Kelly, R .J., & Barnathan, J. (1988, November). Out on a limb: Executives abroad. *Security Management, 11*(32), 117+.

Kelly, R., & Cook, W. (1994). Experience in international travel and aversion to terrorism. *Journal of Police and Criminal Psychology, 10*(1), 62.

Kinney, J. A. (1995). *Violence at work: A step-by-step program to protect your employees, company and assets.* Englewood Cliffs, NJ: Prentice Hall.

Kinney, J. A., & Johnson, D. L. (1993). *Breaking point.* Chicago: National Safe Workplace Institute.

Korsky, S. (1990). Terrorism: The new corporate threat. *Management Review, 79*(10), 39–43.

Lardner, G., Jr. (1995). *The stalking of Kristin: A father investigates the murder of his daughter.* New York: Onyx.

LeBlanc, M.M., & Barling, J. (2004). Workplace aggression. *Current Directions in Psychological Science, 13*(1), 9–12.

Lyons, P. V. (1987). EAPs: The only real cure for substance abuse. *Management Review, 76*(3), 38–41.

Maddox, R. C. (1990, November 1). Terrorism's hidden threat and the promise for multinational corporations. *Business Horizons, 33*(6), 48–52.

Martin, W. T. (1989). *Problem employees and their personalities.* New York: Quorum Books.

McCurley, S., & Vineyard, S. (1998). *Handling problem volunteers.* Downers Grove, IL, Heritage Arts /VMSystems

McMillan, R. (1999). *The path of dialogue: Why smart people do dumb things and how they can stop.* A presentation at the Executive Forum's Management Forum Series, March 24, 1999. Lake Oswego, OR: Executive Forum.

Moore, M. H., Petrie, C. V., Braga, A. A., & McLaughlin, B. L. (Eds.). (2003). *Deadly lessons: Understanding lethal school violence.* Washington, DC: The National Academies Press.

Morash, M., Vitoratos, B., & O'Connell, T. (2008, July). *Workplace violence programs in leading edge companies.* East Lansing, MI: The School of Criminal Justice, Michigan State University. Available at www1.cj.msu.edu/~outreach/security/violtsum.html.

Mullen, P. E., Pathé, M., & Purcell, R. (2000). *Stalkers and their victims.* Cambridge, UK: Cambridge University Press.

Naisbitt, J. (1984). *Megatrends.* New York: Warner Books.

Naylis, G. J. (1996). Corporate terrorism: Managing the threat. *Risk Management, 43*(6), 24–48.

Neddermeyer, D. M. (1986). Employee assistance programs: Tackling emotional dysfunction in the workplace. *Nonprofit World, 4*(5), 24–27.

Neuman, J., & Baron, R. (1998). Workplace violence and workplace aggression: Evidence concerning specific forms, potential causes, and preferred targets. *Journal of Management, 24*(3), 391–419.

Nixon, W. B. (2009). *Workplace Violence Prevention: Assessing the Risk to your Business.* www.collegerecruiter.com/employersblog/2009/03/assessing_the_risk_of_workplac.php

Northwestern National Life Insurance Company. (1993). *Fear and violence in the workplace.* Minneapolis, MN: Northwestern National Life Insurance.

O'Leary-Kelly, A. M., Bowes-Sperry, L, Bates, C. A., & Lean, E. R. (2009). Sexual harassment at work: A decade (plus) of progress. *Journal of Management, 35*(3), 503–536.

O'Leary-Kelly, A. M., Griffin, R. W., & Glew, D. J. (1996). Organization-motivated aggression: A research framework. *Academy of Management Review, 21,* 225–253.

O'Leary-Kelly, A. M., Paetzold, R. L., & Griffin, R. W. (2000). Sexual harassment as aggressive behavior: An actor-based perspective. *Academy of Management Review, 25,* 372–388.

OSHA. (2006). *OSHA Act of 1970, Sec. 5. Duties.* Washington, DC: U.S. Department of Labor, Occupational Safety & Health Administration.

Paetzold, R. L. (1998). Workplace violence and employer liability: Implications for organizations. In R. W. Griffin, A. O'Leary-Kelly, & J. M. Collins (Eds.), *Dysfunctional behavior in organizations: Violent and deviant behaviors* (pp. 143–164). Stamford, CT: JAI Press.

Paetzold, R. L., O'Leary-Kelly, A., Griffin, R. W. (2007). Workplace violence, employer liability, and implications for organizational research. *Journal of Management Inquiry, 16,* 362–370.

Pauchant, T., & Mitroff, I. I. (1992). *Transforming the crisis-prone organization: Preventing individual, organizational, and environmental tragedies.* San Francisco: Jossey-Bass.

Pinard, G. F., & Pagani, L. (Eds.) (2001). *Clinical assessment of dangerousness.* New York: Cambridge University Press.

RHI Management Resources. (2004). *We need to talk: CFO survey reveals poor communication is most common management mistake.* detroitcareerboard.4jobs.com/articles/details-25-article.html

Rosen, R. H. (1985). What really ails employees? *Training and Development Journal, 39*(12), 54–56.

Scotti, A. J. (1986). *Executive safety and international terrorism: A guide for travelers.* Englewood Cliffs, NJ: Prentice-Hall.

Sommers, J. A., Schell, T. L., & Vodanovich, S. J. (2002). Developing a measure of individual differences in organizational revenge. *Journal of Business and Psychology, 17*(2), 207–222.

Stackel, L. (1987). EAPs in the work place. *Employment Relations Today, 14*(3), 289–294.

Stapleton, J. (1994). *Product liability.* Cambridge, MA: Cambridge University Press.

Steinmetz, S. K., & Straus, M. A. (1974). *Violence in the family.* New York: Harper & Row.

Stokols, D., McMahan, S., Clitheroe, Jr, H. C., & Wells, M. (2001). Enhancing corporate compliance with worksite safety and health legislation. *Journal of Safety Research, 32,* 441–463.

Straus, M. A., Hamby, S. L., Boney-McCoy, S., & Sugarman, D. B. (1996). The revised conflict tactics scales (CTS2): Development and preliminary psychometric data. *Journal of Family Issues, 17*(3), 283–316.

Toscano, G., & Weber, W. (1995). *Violence in the workplace.* Washington, DC: U.S. Department of Labor, Bureau of Labor Statistics.

Toscano, G., & Windau, J. (1996). *Compensation and working conditions: National census of fatal occupational injuries.* Washington, DC: U.S. Department of Labor, Bureau of Labor Statistics.

Van Fleet, D. D., & Van Fleet, E. W. (2006). Internal terrorists: The terrorists inside organizations. *Journal of Managerial Psychology, 21*(8), 763–774.

Van Fleet, D. D., & Van Fleet, E. W. (2007). Preventing workplace violence: The violence volcano metaphor. *Journal of Applied Management and Entrepreneurship, 12*(2), 17–36.

Van Fleet, E. W., & Van Fleet, D. D. (1998). Terrorism and the workplace: Concepts and recommendations. In R. W. Griffin, A. O'Leary-Kelly, & J. Collins (Eds.), *Dysfunctional behavior in organizations: Violent and deviant behavior* (Vol. 23A, pp. 165–201). Greenwich, CT: JAI Press.

Van Fleet, E. W., & Van Fleet, D. D. (2007). *Workplace survival: Dealing with bad bosses, bad workers, and bad jobs.* Frederick, MD: PublishAmerica.

Wallace, H., & Kelty, K. (1995). Stalking and restraining orders: A legal and psychological perspective. *Journal of Crime and Justice, 18*(2), 99–111

Walsh, C. J., & Pyrich, A. 1995. Corporate compliance programs as a defense to criminal liability: Can a corporation save its soul? *Rutgers Law Review, 47*, 605–691.

Watts, P. (1988). Effective employee assistance hinges on trained managers. *Management Review, 77*(1), 11–12.

Weiss, M. (2008). *Lack of communication with staff most damaging to morale, survey finds.* www.reuters.com/article/pressRelease/idUS168686+06-Nov-2008+PRN20081106

White, G. (2002). *Recent developments in the employment torts of hiring, retention, and supervision.* American Bar Association. Available at: www.bnabooks.com/ababna/rnr/2002/hiring.doc.

Witting, C. (2005). Duty of care: An analytical approach. *Oxford Journal of Legal Studies, 25*, 33–63.

Workplace violence: Employees don't recognize warning signs, survey finds. (2004, March). *Professional Safety, 49*(3), 1.

Zimman, R. (1996). *Respect and protect.* Center City, MN: Hazelden Foundation.

Additional References

Adams, J. S. (1965). Inequity in social exchange. In L. Berkowitz (Ed.), *Advances in experimental social psychology* (Vol. 2, pp. 267–299). New York: Academic Press.

Adams, R. D., & Victor, M. (1985). *Principles of neurology* (3rd ed.). New York: McGraw-Hill.

Adorno, T. W., Frenkel-Brunsurk, E., Lewinson, D. J., & Sandford, R. M. (1950). *The authoritarian personality.* New York: Harper.

Albanese, R., & Van Fleet, D. D. (1983). *Organizational behavior: A managerial viewpoint.* Hinsdale, IL: Dryden.

Albrecht, K., & Albrecht, S. (1987). *The creative corporation.* Burr Ridge, IL: Business One Irwin.

Albrecht, S. (1997). *Fear and violence on the job: Prevention solutions for the dangerous workplace.* Durham, NC: Carolina Academic Press.

Aldis, O. (1961, July–August). Of pigeons and men. *Harvard Business Review*, 59–63.

Alexander, Y. (1987). Terrorism: Threats and trends. *Terrorism, 10*(3), 213–215.

Allcorn, S., & Diamond M. (1994). *Anger in the workplace: Understanding the causes of aggression and violence.* Westport, CT: Quorum Books.

Allen, T. D., Herst, D. E. L., Bruck, C. S., & Sutton, M. (2000). Consequences associated with work-to-family conflict: A review and agenda for future research. *Journal of Occupational Health Psychology, 5*, 278–308.

Alspach, G. (1993). Nurses as victims of violence, *Critical Care Nurse, 13*(5), 13–17.

AMA-Young Physician Services. (1995). *Violence in the Medical Workplace.* Chicago: American Medical Association, Department of Young Physician Services.

American Bar Association, Commission on Domestic Violence. (1999). *A guide for employers: Domestic violence in the workplace.* Washington, DC.

An American crisis: Drugs in the workplace. (1987). *Journal of American Insurance, 63,* 9–11.

Anderson, K. R., Tyler, M. P., & Jenkins, E. L. (2004). Preventing workplace violence. *Journal of Employee Assistance, 34*(4), 8–11.

Andersson, L. M., & Pearson, C. M. (1999). Tit for tat? The spiraling effect of incivility in the workplace. *Academy of Management Review, 24*(3), 452–471.

Ansberry, C. (1995, May 18). The ripple effect: Oklahoma City blast hit 1,000 miles away. *Wall Street Journal,* A-1.

Aquino, K., Bies, R., & Tripp, T. (2001). How employees respond to personal offense: The effects of blame attribution, victim status, and offender status on revenge and reconciliation in the workplace. *Journal of Applied Psychology, 86*(1), 52–59.

Aquino, K. (2000). Structural and individual determinants of workplace victimization. *Journal of Management, 26,* 171–193.

Aquino, K., Tripp, T. M., & Bies, R. J. (2001). How employees respond to personal offense: The effects of blame attribution, victim status, and offender status on revenge and reconciliation in the workplace. *Journal of Applied Psychology, 86*(1), 52–59.

Aquino, K., Tripp, T. M., & Bies, R. J. (2006). Getting even or moving on? Power, procedural justice, and types of offense as predictors of revenge, forgiveness, reconciliation and avoidance in organizations. *Journal of Applied Psychology, 91*(3), 653–668.

Arieti. S. (Ed.). (1966). *American handbook of psychiatry* (Vol. 3). New York: Basic Books.

Armstrong, G., & Griffin, M. L. (2007). The effect of local life circumstances on likelihood of victimization. *Justice Quarterly, 24*(1), 80–105.

A safety lesson from Oklahoma City. (1995, June 1). *Progressive Architecture, 76*(6), 65+.

Ashkanasy, N. M., Härtel, C. E. J., & Zerbe, W. J. (2000). *Emotions in the workplace: Research, theory, and practice.* Westport, CT: Quorum Books.

ASIS International. (2005a). *Business continuity guideline: A practical approach for emergency preparedness, crisis management, and disaster recovery.* Alexandria, VA: ASIS International.

ASIS International. (2005b). *Workplace violence prevention and response guideline.* Alexandria, VA: ASIS International.

Ayoob, M. (1980). *In the gravest extreme.* Concord, NH: Massad F. & Dorothy A. Ayoob.

Ayoob, M. (1983). *The truth about self protection.* New York: Bantam Books.

Ayres, R. M. (1990). *Preventing law enforcement stress.* Washington, DC: National Sheriff's Association.

Babiak, P., & Hare, R. D. (2006). *Snakes in suits: When psychopaths go to work.* New York: Regan Books.

Bandura, A. (1973). *Aggression: A social learning analysis.* Englewood Cliffs, NJ: Prentice-Hall.
Bandura, A., & Walters, R. H. (1959). *Adolescent aggression.* New York: Ronald Press.
Barclay, L., Skarlicki, D., & Pugh, D. (2005). Exploring the role of emotions in injustice perceptions and retaliation. *Journal of Applied Psychology, 90*(4), 629–643.
Barling, J. (1990). *Employment, stress, and family functioning.* New York: Wiley.
Barling, J., & Frone, M. R. (Eds.). (2004). *The psychology of workplace safety.* Washington, DC: American Psychological.
Barling, J., Kelloway, E. K., & Frone, M. R. (Eds.). (2005). *Handbook of work stress.* Thousand Oaks, CA: Sage.
Barnes, G. (1979). The alcoholic personality. *Journal of Studies on Alcohol, 40,* 571–634.
Baron, R., Newman, J., & Geddes, D. (1999). Social and personal determinants of workplace aggression: Evidence for the impact of perceived injustice and the Type A behavior pattern. *Aggressive Behavior, 25,* 281–296.
Baron, R. A. (1977). *Human aggression.* New York: Plenum Press.
Baron, R. A., & Neuman, J. H. (1996). Workplace violence and workplace aggression: Evidence on their relative frequency and potential causes. *Aggressive Behavior, 22,* 161–173.
Bell, C. A. (1991, June). Female homicides in US workplaces. *American Journal of Public Health,* 729–732.
Bell, C. A., Stout, N. A., Bender, T. R., Conroy, C. S., Crouse, W. E., & Myers, J. R. (1990, June 13). Fatal occupational injuries in the US. *Journal of the American Medical Association,* 3047–3050.
Bellows, R. (1961). *Psychology of personnel in business and industry.* Englewood Cliffs, NJ: Prentice-Hall.
Bennett, R., & Robinson, S. (2000). Development of a measure of workplace deviance. *Journal of Applied Psychology, 85*(3), 349–360.
Bensimon, H. F. (1994). Crisis and disaster management: Violations in the workplace. *Training and Development, 28,* 27–32.
Berkowitz, L. (1965). Some aspects of observed aggression. *Journal of Personality and Social Psychology, 2,* 359–369.
Berkowitz, L. (1993). *Aggression: Its causes, consequences and control.* New York: McGraw-Hill.
Berkowitz, L., & LePage, A. (1967). Weapons as aggression-eliciting stimuli. *Journal of Personality and Social Psychology, 7,* 202–207.
Bernstein, A. J. (2001). *Emotional vampires: Dealing with people who drain you dry.* New York: McGraw-Hill.
Berry, C. M., Ones, D., & Sackett, P. (2007). Interpersonal deviance, organizational deviance, and their common correlates: A review and meta-analysis. *Journal of Applied Psychology, 92*(2), 410–424.

Biles, P. D. (1997). *Guidelines for protecting health care workers & social service workers from workplace violence.* (OSHA 3148-01R 2004). Washington, DC: US Department of Labor, Occupational Safety and Health Administration, *Joint Commission on Accreditation of Healthcare Organizations: Environment of Care/PTSM Series* 3, 29–35.

Bloom, H., Eisen, R. S., Pollock, N., & Webster, C. D. (2000). *WRA-20 workplace risk assessment: A guide for evaluating violence potential.* Toronto, Ontario: workplace.calm.

BJS. (1994, July). Violence and theft in the workplace. (BJS 202-307-0784). Washington, DC: U.S. Department of Justice, Bureau of Justice Statistics.

BJS. (1995, August). *Violence Against Women: Estimates from the Redesigned National Crime Victimization Survey.* (NCJ 154348). Washington, DC: U.S. Department of Justice, Bureau of Justice Statistics.

BJS. (1998, April). *Students' Report of School Crime: 1989 and 1995.* (NCJ 169607). Washington, DC: U.S. Department of Justice, Bureau of Justice Statistics.

BJS. (1998, July). *Workplace Violence, 1992–96.* (NCJ 168634). Washington, DC: U.S. Department of Justice, Bureau of Justice Statistics.

BJS. (2001, December). *Violence in the Workplace, 1993–99: National Crime Victimization Survey.* (NCJ 190076). Washington, DC: U.S. Department of Justice, Bureau of Justice Statistics.

BJS. (2006). *Crime & Victims Statistics.* Washington, DC: U.S. Department of Justice, Bureau of Justice Statistics.

BLS. (1996). *Characteristics of injuries and illnesses resulting in absences from work, (1994).* Washington, DC: U.S. Department of Labor, Bureau of Labor Statistics.

BLS. (1997, August). *Fatal occupational injuries by event or exposure, 1992–1996.* (USDL-97-266). Washington, DC: U.S. Department of Labor, Bureau of Labor Statistics.

Bonner, D. (1989, Fall). Combating terrorism in the 1990s: The role of the Prevention of Terrorism (Temporary Provisions) Act of 1989. *Public Law*, 440–447.

Boon, J., & Sheridan, L. (2002). *Stalking and psychosexual obsession: Psychological perspectives for prevention, policing, and treatment.* London: John Wiley & Sons.

Bowers, K. S. (1973). Situationism in psychology: An analysis and critique. *Psychological Review*, 80, 307–336.

Bowie, V. (1997). *Coping with violence: A guide for the human services.* London: Whiting & Birch.

Bowman, J. S., & Zigmond, C. J. (1997). State government response to workplace violence. *Public Personnel Management*, 26(2), 289–300.

Bowman, R. J. (1995, March). Are you covered? *World Trade*, 8(2), 4.

Boxer, P. A. (1993, February). Assessment of potential violence in the paranoid worker. *Journal of Occupational Medicine*, 127–131.

Bradford, M., McLeod, D., & Hofmann, M. A. (1995, April 24). Shock waves from bombing losses. *Business Insurance*, 2.
Braham, J. (1986). Cocaine creeps toward the top. *Industry Week*, *23*(2), 34–38.
Bramson, R. M. (1981). *Coping with difficult people*. New York: Ballantine Books.
Braverman, M. (1993, December 12). Violence: The newest worry on the job. *New York Times*, p. F-11.
Braverman, M. (1999). *Preventing workplace violence: A guide for employers and practitioners*. Thousand Oaks, CA: Sage.
Bregar, B. (1988). Helping troubled employees. *Restaurant Management*, *2*(1), 96.
Breiner, S. J. (1992). Observations on the abuse of women and children. *Psychological Reports*, *70*(1), 153–154.
Brenner, J., & Summerfield, B. (1996). Building a workplace violence plan. *VCCA Journal*, *10*(2), 31–35.
Brett, J. M., Goldberg, S. B., & Ury, W. L. (1990). Designing systems for resolving disputes in organizations. *American Psychologist*, *45*, 162–170.
Briggs, K. C., & Briggs-Myers, I. (1976). *Myers-Briggs type indicator*. Palo Alto, CA: Consulting Psychologists Press.
Brinson, J. A., Kottler, J. A., & Fisher, T. A. (2004). Cross cultural conflict resolution in schools: Some practical intervention strategies for counselors. *Journal of Counseling and Development*, *82*(3), 294
Brockner, J., & Greenberg, J. (1990). The impact of layoffs on survivors: An organizational justice perspective. In J. Carroll (Ed.), *Advances in applied social psychology: Business settings* (pp. 45–75). Hillsdale, NJ: Erlbaum.
Broder, J. F. (1984). *Risk analysis and the security survey*. Stoneham, MA: Butterworth.
Buckwalter, A. (1983). *Surveillance and undercover investigation*. Stoneham, MA: Butterworth.
Bureau of Business Practice. (1994). *Preventing violence in the workplace*. Waterford, CT: Bureau of Business Practice (BBP).
Bush, G. W., Sr. (1986, January). *Public Report Of The Vice President's Task Force On Combating Terrorism*. Washington, DC: U.S. Government Printing Office.
Buss, D. (1993). Ways to curtail employee theft. *Nation's Business*, *81*, 36–38.
Byron, K. (2005). A meta-analytic review of work–family conflict and its antecedents. *Journal of Vocational Behavior*, *67*, 169–198.
Calise, A. K. (1994, June 13). AandA survey identifies risk managers' concerns. *National Underwriter*, 2.
Camara, W. J., & Schneider, D. L. (1994). Integrity tests: Facts and unresolved issues. *American Psychologist*, *49*, 112–119.
Cameron, D. (1987). Dealing with unacceptable conduct at work: An integrated approach. *Business Quarterly* [Canada], *5*(4), 60–66.
Capozzoli, T., & McVey, R. S. (1996). *Managing violence in the workplace*. Delray Beach, FL: St. Lucie Press.

Carroll, V. (1999, October). *Disarming the Threat of Workplace Violence.* A presentation at the Colorado Task Force on Workplace Violence sponsored by the Colorado Nurses Association, 1999.

Carson, R. C. (1989). Personality. *Annual Review of Psychology, 40,* 227–248.

Carter, G. L. (2003). *Guns in American society: An encyclopedia of history, politics, culture, and the law.* Santa Barbara, CA: ABC-CLIO.

Carter, G. L,. & Byrnes, J. F. (2006). *How to Manage Conflict in the Organization* (Rev. ed.) Boston: American Management.

Cavanagh. M. E. (1987). Employee problems: Prevention and intervention. *Personnel Journal, 66*(9), 35–40.

CDC. (1990, August 17). *Occupational Homicides among Women.* Atlanta: U.S. Department of Health and Human Services, Centers for Disease Control and Prevention.

CDC. (1994, August 19). *Occupational Injury Deaths of Postal Workers—United States, 1980–1989.* Atlanta: U.S Department of Health and Human Services, Centers for Disease Control and Prevention.

Chen, P. Y., & Spector, P. E. (1992). Relationships of work stressors with aggression, withdrawal, theft and substance abuse: An exploratory study. *Journal of Occupational and Organizational Psychology, 65,* 177–184.

Civil Service Employees Association, Inc. (CSEA). (1993). *Security in the Workplace.* Albany, NY: CSEA.

Clutterbuck, R. 1978. *Kidnap and ransom.* London: Faber & Faber Limited.

Cocozza, J., & Steadman, H. (1976). Some refinements in the measurement and prediction of dangerousness: Clear and convincing evidence. *Rutgers Law Review, 29,* 1084–1101.

Cole, L., Grubb, P., Sauter, S., Swanson, N., & Lawless, P. (1997). Psychosocial correlates of harassment, threats and fear of violence in the workplace. *Scandinavian Journal of Work and Environmental Health, 23,* 450–457.

Colling, R. L. (1997). *Controlling workplace violence: A security management plan approach.* (OSHA 3148-01R 2004). Washington, DC: U. S. Department of Labor, Occupational Safety and Health Administration, Joint Commission on Accreditation of Healthcare Organizations.

Collins, P. (1981). *Living in troubled lands.* Boulder, CO: Paladin Press.

Conway, F., & Siegelman, J. (1995). *Snapping.* New York: Stillpoint Press.

Cooper, C. L., & Cartwright, S. (1994). Healthy mind, healthy organization: A proactive approach to occupational stress. *Human Relations, 47,* 455–471.

Corcoran, M. H., & Cawood, J. S. (2003). *Violence assessment and intervention: The practitioner's handbook.* Boca Raton, FL: CRC Press.

Crawshaw, S. R. A. (1989, March). Anti-terrorism networks: Information and intelligence for fighting international terrorism. *The Futurist, 23*(2), 12–13.

Cropanzano, R., & Randall, M. L. (1993). Injustice and work behavior: A historical review. In R. Cropanzano (Ed.), *Justice in the workplace: Approaching fairness in human resource management* (pp. 3–20). Hillsdale, NJ: Erlbaum.

Crosby, F. (1976). A model of egoistical relative deprivation. *Psychological Review, 83*, 85–113.

Currall, S. C., Friedmann, R. A., Tidd, S. T., & Tsai, J. C. (2000). What goes around comes around: The impact of personal conflict style on work. *International Journal of Conflict Management, 11*(1), 32–55.

D'Addario, E. (1992). The cooperative fight against violent crime. *Security Management, 36*(6), 57–60.

D'Addario, E. (1995). *The manager's violence survival guide.* Chapel Hill, NC: Crime Prevention.

Daly, C. B. (1994, December 31). Two slain at Boston abortion clinics. *The Toronto Star*, p. A-1.

Davidson, L. (1987). An intervention strategy for assisting the impaired employee. *Hospital Material Management Quarterly, 8*(4), 81–84.

Davis, J. A. (Ed.). (2001). *Stalking crimes and victim protection: Prevention, intervention, assessment and case management.* Boca Raton, FL: CRC Press.

Day, R. C., & Hamblin, R. L. (1969). Some effects of close and punitive styles of supervision. *American Journal of Sociology, 69*, 499–510.

Dietz, P. E., & Baker, S. P. (1987). Murder at work. *American Journal of Public Health, 77*(10), 1273–1274.

DiGirolamo, J. (1991). How human resource managers can communicate in troubled times. In M. F. Cook (Ed.), *The human resources yearbook* (pp. 13–14). Englewood Cliffs, NJ: Prentice Hall.

Distasio, C. A. (2002). Protecting yourself from violence in the workplace. *Nursing, 32*(6), 58–63.

Dobson, C., & Payne, R. (1979). *The terrorists.* New York: Facts on File.

Dollard, J., Doob, L. W., Miller, M. F., Mowrer, O. H., & Sears, R. R. (1939). *Frustration and aggression.* New Haven, CT: Yale University Press.

Dollard, M. F., Winefield, A .H., & Winefeld, H. R. (2003). *Occupational stress in the service professions.* London: Taylor & Francis.

Douglas, S., & Martinko, M. (2001). Exploring the role of individual differences in the prediction of workplace aggression. *Journal of Applied Psychology, 86*(4), 547–559.

Duffy, B. (1955, May 1). The end of innocence. *US News and World Report*, 34–50.

Duffy, B. (1955, May 15). Dry holes, dead ends. *US News and World Report*, 36–39.

Duffy, B. (1995, August 14). Where the finger points. *US News and World Report*, 70.

Duhart, D. (2001). *Violence in the Workplace, 1993–1999.* (Special Report, NCJ 190076). Washington, DC: U.S. Department of Justice, Office of Justice Programs, Bureau of Justice Statistics.

Elliott, J. F. (Ed.). (2003). *Workplace violence prevention: A practical guide.* Vancouver, British Columbia (Canada): Specialty Technical.

Engel, F. (2004). *Taming the beast: Getting violence out of the workplace* (2nd ed.). Montreal, Quebec (Canada): Ashwell.

Ennis, B., & Litwack, T. (1974). Psychiatry and the presumption of expertise: Flipping coins in the courtroom. *California Law Review, 62*, 693–752.

Eppler, M. (1997). *Management mess-ups.* Franklin Lakes, NJ: Career Press.
Erickson, E. (1963). *Childhood and society.* New York: Norton.
Esman, A. H. (1986). Dependent and passive-aggressive personality disorders. In A. M. Cooper, A. J. Frances, & M. H. Sacks (Eds.), *Psychiatry (I): The personality disorders and neuroses* (pp. 283–289). Philadelphia: Lippincott.
Everly, G. (2000). Five principles of crisis intervention: Reducing the risk of premature crisis intervention. *International Journal of Emergency Mental Health, 2*(1), 1–4.
Eysenck, H. J. (1967). *The biological basis of personality.* Springfield, IL: Charles C. Thomas.
Farney, D. (1995, April 21). Oklahoma City bombing: The aftermath: Violence no longer a stranger in heartland–if it ever was. *Wall Street Journal,* A-4.
Federal Bureau of Investigation. (1993). Uniform Crime Reports for the United States. Washington, DC: U.S. Department of Justice, Federal Bureau of Investigation.
Felson, R. B., & Massner, S. F. (1996). To kill or not to kill? Lethal outcomes in injurious attacks. *Criminology, 34*(4), 519–545.
Feshbach, S., & Weiner, B. (1986). *Personality* (2nd ed.). Lexington, MA: D. C. Heath.
Festinger, L. (1957). *A theory of cognitive dissonance.* Evanston, IL: Row, Peterson.
Feuer, D. (1987). AIDS at work: Fighting the fear. *Training, 24*(6), 60–71.
Fiesta, J. (1996, April). Corporate liability: Security and violence–Part II. *Nursing Management, 27*(4), 11–14.
Fiesta, J. (1996, September, Rev. 2004, November). Corporate liability: Security and violence–Part I. *Nursing Management, 27*(3), 14–16.
Filipczak, B. (1993, July). Armed and dangerous at work. *Training,* 39–43.
Fisher, C. D. (1986). Organizational socialization: An integrative review. *Research In Personnel and Human Resource Management, 4,* 101–145.
Flannery, R. (1995). *Violence in the workplace.* New York: The Crossroad.
Flynn, J. P. (1967). The neural basis of aggression. In D. C. Glass (Ed.), *Neurophysiology and emotion* (pp. 40–60). New York: Rockefeller University Press and Russell Sage Foundation.
Fogleman, D. B. (2000). Minimizing the risk of violence in the workplace. *Employment Relations Today, 27*(1), 83.
Folger, R. (1986). Rethinking equity theory: A referent cognition model. In H. W. Bierhoff, R. L. Cohen, & J. Greenberg (Eds.), *Justice in social relations* (pp. 145–162). New York: Plenum Press.
Folger, R., Konovsky, M. A., & Cropanzano, R. (1992). A due process metaphor for performance appraisal. In L. L. Cummings & B. M. Staw (Eds.), *Research in organizational behavior* (pp. 129–177). Greenwich, CT: JAI Press.
Folger, R. C., & Greenberg, J. (1985). Procedural justice: An interpretive analysis of personnel systems. In R. Rowland & G. Ferris (Eds.), *Research in personnel and human resources management* (pp. 141–183). Greenwich, CT: JAI Press.

Forte, S. (2006, Fall). Oklahoma City bombing creates workplace havoc. *River Academic Journal, 2*(2).
Fox, S., & Spector, P. E. (Eds.). (2005). *Counterproductive workplace behavior: Investigations of actors and targets*. Washington, DC: American Psychological.
Fraboni, M., Cooper, D., Reed, T. L., & Saltstone, R. (1990). Offense type and two-point MMPI code profiles: Discriminating between violent and nonviolent offenders. *Journal of Clinical Psychology, 46*(6), 774–777.
Frances, A. J. (1986). Introduction to personality disorders. In A. M. Cooper, A. J. Frances, & M. H. Sacks (Eds.), *Psychiatry–The personality disorders and neuroses* (Vol. I) (pp. 171–176). Philadelphia: Lippincott.
Franklin, F. P. (1991). Over the edge: Managing violent episodes. *Security Management, 35*, 138–144.
Frederiksen, L. W. (1982). Organizational behavior management: An overview. In L. W. Frederiksen (Ed.), *Handbook of organizational behavior management* (pp. 3–20). New York: Wiley.
Freud, S. (1968). *Character and anal eroticism*. London: Hogarth. (Original work published 1908).
Friedberg, A. (1983). *America afraid: How fear of crime changes the way we live*. New York: New American Library.
Frone, M. R., Russell, M. & Cooper, M. L. (1992). Prevalence of work-family conflict: Are work and family boundaries asymmetrically permeable? *Journal of Organizational Behavior, 13*, 723–729.
Fuqua, P., & Wilson, J. V. (1978). *Terrorism*. Houston: Gulf, Book Division.
Furlong, M., & Morrison, G. (2000). The school in school violence: Definitions and facts. *Journal of Emotional and Behavioral Disorders, 8*(20), 71.
Gaal, J., White, G. & Bond, Schoeneck & King. (2002). *Recent Developments in the Employment Torts of Hiring, Retention, and Supervision*. Paper presented at the 2002 Midwinter Meeting of the American Bar.
Gagliardi, M. M., & Freedman, F. F. (1986). Dispelling confusion about health promotion. *Journal of Compensation and Benefits, 2*(3), 166–168.
Garland, R. (1991). *Making work fun: Doing business with a sense of humor*. San Diego, CA: Shamrock Press.
Garland, S. B., & Harbrecht, D. (1995, May 8). In the wake of Oklahoma City, one nation–more indivisible. *Business Week*, 51.
Gaudin, S. (2000). Case study of insider sabotage: The Tim Lloyd/Omega case. *Computer Security Journal, 16*(3), 4.
Gelles. R. J. (1987). *Family violence*. Newbury Park, CA: Sage.
Gibbs, N. (1995, May 1). The blood of innocents. *Time*, 57–64.
Gill, M., Fisher, B., & Bowie, V. (Eds.). (2002). *Violence at work: Causes, patterns, and prevention*. Portland, OR: Willan.
Gilligan, G. (1992). *Violence*. New York: Grosset/Putnam.
Ginn, G. O., & Henry, L. J. (2002). Addressing workplace violence from a health management perspective. *Advanced Management Journal, 67*(4), 4.
Glick, E. (1995, May 1). Who are they? *Time*, 44–51.

Glomb, T. (2002). Workplace anger and aggression: Informing conceptual models with data from specific encounters. *Journal of Occupational Health Psychology, 7*(1), 20–36.

Goldman, A. (2006). High toxicity leadership: Borderline personality disorder and the dysfunctional organization. *Journal of Managerial Psychology, 21*(8), 733–747.

Goldman, A. (2008). Company on the couch. *Journal of Management Inquiry, 17*(3), 226–238.

Goldman, A. (2009a). *Destructive leaders and dysfunctional organizations.* Cambridge, UK: Cambridge University Press.

Goldman, A. (2009b). *Transforming toxic leadership in organizations.* Palo Alto, CA: Stanford University Press.

Goldstein, A. P. (1983). United States: Causes, controls, and alternatives to aggression. In A. P. Goldstein & M. H. Segall (Eds.), *Aggression in global perspective* (pp. 435–474). New York: Pergamon Press.

Goldstein, A. P., & Huff, C. R. (Eds.) (1993). *The gang intervention handbook.* Champaign, IL: Research Press.

Grahame-Smith, D. G., & Aronson, J. K. (1984). *The Oxford textbook of clinical pharmacology and drug therapy.* London: Oxford University Press.

Greenberg, J. (1996). *The quest for justice on the job.* Thousand Oaks, CA: Sage.

Greenberg, L., & Barling, J. (1999). Predicting employee aggression against coworkers, subordinates and supervisors and the roles of person behavior and perceived workplace factors. *Journal of Organizational Behavior, 20*(6), 897–913.

Greenhaus, J. H., & Beutell, N. J. (1985). Sources of conflict between work and family roles. *Academy of Management Review, 10,* 76–88.

Greenhaus, J. H., & Parasuraman, S. (1987). A work-nonwork interactive perspective of stress and its consequences. *Journal of Organizational Behavior Management, 8*(2), 37–60.

Griffin, R. W., & Lopez, Y. P. (2004). Toward a model of the person-situation determinants of deviant behavior in organizations. Paper presented at the 64th Annual Meeting of the Academy of Management.

Griffith, T. J. (1987). Want job improvement? Try counseling. *Management Solutions, 32*(9), 13–19.

Groebe, L. (1988, October). What's NeXT from Steven Jobs? *Fort Worth Star-Telegram: Tarrant Business,* 17–24.

Grote, R. C., & Harvey, E. L. (1983). *Discipline without punishment.* New York: McGraw-Hill.

Guyton, A. C. (1986). *Textbook of medical physiology* (7th ed.). Philadelphia: W. B. Saunders.

Hackworth, D. H., & Annin, P. (1995, July 3). The suspect speaks out. *Newsweek,* 22–26.

Hales, T., Seligman, P. J., Newman, S. C., & Timbrook, C. L. (1988). Occupational injuries due to violence. *Journal of Occupational Medicine,* 483–487.

Hall, C. S., & Lindzey, G. (1957). *Theories of personality*. New York: John Wiley & Sons.

Hare, R. D. (1999). *Without conscience: The disturbing world of the psychopaths among us*. New York: Guilford Press.

Hartley, D., Biddle, E. A., & Jenkins, E. L. (2005). Societal cost of workplace homicides in the United States, 1992–2001. *American Journal of Industrial Medicine, 47*(6), 518–527.

Harvey, J. H., & Weary, G. (1984). Current issues in attribution theory and research. *Annual Review of Psychology, 35*, 427–459.

Harvey, M. G. (1993). A survey of corporate programs for managing terrorist threats. *Journal of International Business Studies, 24*(3), 465–478.

Henderson-Loney, J. (1995). The crying game. *Training and Development, 49*(8), 54–58.

Hequet, M., & Picard, M. (1994). Violence: An ounce of prevention. *Training, 31*, 94.

Heskett, S. L. (1996). *Workplace violence: Before, during, and after*. Burlington, MA: Butterworth-Heinemann.

Hess, W. R. (1954). *Diencephalon: Autonomic and extrapyramidal functions*. New York: Grune & Stratton.

Hill, C. (1988). Protecting employees from attack. *Personnel Management, 20*, 34–39.

Hipp, E. (2000). *Understanding the human volcano: What teens can do about violence*. Center City, MN: Hazelden.

Hoffer, W. (1986, October). Business' war on drugs. *Nation's Business, 74*(10), 18–26.

Hofmann, D. A., & Tetrick, L. E. (Eds.). (2003). *Health and safety in organizations: A multilevel perspective*. San Francisco: Jossey-Bass.

Hofmann, M. A. (1995, January 23). Bomb threat exposure. *Business Insurance*, 1.

Hofmann, M. A. (1995, April 24). Bombing spurs heightened attention to security. *Business Insurance*, 1.

Holland, J. (1973). *Making vocational choices. A theory of careers*. Englewood Cliffs, NJ: Prentice-Hall.

Holmes, S. T., & Holmes, R. M. (Eds.). (2004). *Violence: A contemporary reader*. Upper Saddle River, NJ: Pearson Education.

Horton, T. R. (1987). Drugs in the workplace. *Management Review, 76*(2), 5–6.

Hotaling, G. T., & Sugarman, D. B. (1986). An analysis of risk markers in husband to wife violence: The current state of knowledge. *Violence and Victims, 1*, 101–124.

How the Oklahoma City bombing was planned. (1995, June 5). *Newsweek, 125*(23), 24.

Howard, J. L. (2001). Workplace violence in organizations: An exploratory study of organizational prevention techniques. *Employee Responsibilities and Rights Journal, 13*(2), 57–75.

Hutter, B., & Power, M. (Eds.) (2005). *Organizational encounters with risk.* New York: Cambridge University Press.

International Association of Chiefs of Police. (1979). *Clandestine tactics and technology: Tactics and countermeasures.* Gaithersburg, MD: The International Association of Chiefs of Police.

International Association of Chiefs of Police. (1996). *Combating workplace violence: Guidelines for employers and law enforcement.* Alexandria, VA: International Association of Chiefs of Police.

International Labour Organization. (2003). *Code of practice on workplace violence in services sectors and measures to combat this phenomenon.* Geneva, Switzerland: International Labour Organization.

Ivancevich, J. M., & Matteson, M. T. (1980). *Stress and work: A managerial perspective.* Dallas: Scott, Foresman.

Jackson, D. (1994, Winter). Prevention of terrorism: The United Kingdom confronts the European convention on human rights. *Terrorism and Political Violence, 6*(4), 507–535.

Jablonski, M. A., McCelellan, G., & Zdziarski, E. L. (Eds.). (2009, January). *In Search of Safer Communities: Practices for Student Affairs in Addressing Campus Violence: Supplement to New Directions for Student Services No. 124.* San Francisco: Jossey Bass.

Jacob, I. G. (2004). Defusing the explosive worker. *Occupational Health and Safety, 73,* 56.

Jacobs, J. L., & Porter, W. D. (1999). *Workplace violence in healthcare toolkit: A guide to establishing a prevention and training program.* New York: McGraw-Hill Professional.

Jacobson, M., & Royer, H. (2009, January). *Aftershocks: The impact of clinic violence on abortion services.* Paper downloaded from www.econ.ucla.edu/workshops/papers/Applied/JacobsonRoyer2.2.09.pdf.

Jawahar, I. M. (2002). A model of organizational justice and workplace aggression. *Journal of Management, 28*(6), 811–834.

Jeffrey, C. R. (1977). *Crime prevention through environment design.* Beverly Hills, CA: Sage Publications.

Jeffreys-Jones, R. (1974). Violence in American history: Plug uglies in the progressive era. In D. Fleming & B. Bailyn (Eds.). *Perspectives in American History* (Vol. VIII, pp. 465–583). Cambridge, MA: Charles Warren Center for Studies in American History/Harvard University.

Jenkins, B. M. (1985). *Terrorism.* Stoneham, MA: Butterworth.

Jenkins, B. M. (1985, Summer). Unconquerable nation: Knowing our enemy. *TVI Journal. 6*(1).

Jenkins, E. L., Layne, L. A., & Kisner, S. M. (1992, May). Homicide in the workplace: The U.S. experience, 1980–1988. *AAOHN Journal,* 215–218.

Johnson, D. L. (1994, March 1). Workplace violence: Why it happens and what to do about it. *EAP Digest, 14*(3), 18–22.

Johnson, P. (1986). The cancer of terrorism. In B. Netanyahu (Ed.), *Terrorism: How the West can win* (pp. 31–37). New York: Farrar, Straus, & Giroux.

Johnston, W. B., & Packer, A. H. (1987). *Work force 2000.* Indianapolis: Hudson Institute.

Jones, J., & Bogat, G. (1978). Air pollution and human aggression. *Psychological Reports, 43,* 721–722.

Jung, C. G. (1923). *Psychological types.* (H. Godwyn Baynes, Trans.). New York: Harcourt. Justin. (Original translation published in 1921).

Kazdin, A. E. (1978). *History of behavior modification: Experimental foundations of contemporary research.* Baltimore: University Park Press.

Kazdin, A. E. (1984). *Behavior modification in applied settings* (3rd ed.). Homewood, IL: Dorsey Press.

Kedjidjian, C. B. (1993, October). Is anyplace safe? *Safety and Health, 148*(4), 79–84.

Keeton, L. E., Pawlosky, M., & Tomsho, R. (1995, April 20). Terrorism hits home: U.S. building bombed; dead include children. *Wall Street Journal,* A-1.

Kemshall, H., & Pritchard, J. (Eds). (2000). *Good practice in working with victims of violence.* London: Jessica Kinsley.

Kennedy, D., Homant, R., & Homant, M. (2004). Perceptions of injustice as a determinant of support for workplace aggression. *Journal of Business and Psychology, 18,* 323–336.

Kenrick, D. T., & Funder, D. C. (1988). Profiting from controversy: Lessons from the person-situation debate. *American Psychologist, 43,* 23–34.

Kernberg, O. F. (1986). Narcissistic personality disorder. In A. M Cooper, A. J. Frances, & M. H. Sacks (Eds.). *Psychiatry (I) The personality disorders and neuroses* (pp. 219–230). Philadelphia: Lippincott.

Kilmann, R. H. (1985). Managing troublemakers. *Training and Development Journal, 39*(5), 102, 104, 106, 108.

Kinkade, P., Burns, R., & Fuentes, A.I. (2005). Criminalizing attractions: Perceptions of stalking and the stalker. *Crime & Delinquency, 51,* 3–25.

Kittrell, A. (1986). Public entities behind in cost control: Study. *Business Insurance, 20*(44), 10–14.

Klein, D. (1981). Violence against women: Some considerations regarding its causes and its elimination. *Crime & Delinquency, 27,* 64–80.

Kobetz, R. W., & Cooper, H. H. (1978). *Target terrorism: Providing protective services.* Gaithersburg, MD: International Association of Chiefs of Police.

Kolb, B., & Whishaw, I. Q. (1985). *Fundamentals of human neuropsychology* (2nd ed.). New York: Freeman.

Kossek, E. E., & Lobel, S. A. (Eds.) (1995). *Managing diversity: Human resource strategies for transforming the workplace.* Cambridge, MA: Blackwell.

Kramer, M. (1995, May 8). Why Guns Share the Blame. *Time,* 145.

Krebs, D. L., & Miller, D. T. (1985). Altruism and aggression. *Handbook of Social Psychology,* 1–71.

Kreidler, W. J. (1984). *Creative conflict resolution.* Glenview, IL: Scott Foresman & Company.

Kurland, O. M. (1993). Workplace violence. *Risk Management, 40,* 76–77.

Labig, C. E. (1995). *Preventing violence in the workplace.* New York: Amacom Books.

Landsbergis, P. A., Cahill, J., & Schnall, P. L. (1999). The impact of lean production and related new systems of work organization on worker health. *Journal of Occupational Health Psychology, 4,* 1–23.

Lansner, K. (1995, May 23). Aftershocks of terror. *Financial World,* 88.

Laqueur, W. (1977). *Terrorism.* Boston: Little, Brown.

Laqueur, W. (1987). *The age of terrorism.* Boston: Little, Brown.

Larson, E. (1994, October 13). A false crisis: How workplace violence became a hot issue. *Wall Street Journal,* p. A-1.

Leather, P. (1999). *Work-related violence: Assessment and intervention.* London: Routledge.

LeBlanc, M. M., & Kelloway, E. K. (2002). Predictors and outcomes of workplace violence and aggression. *Journal of Applied Psychology, 87,* 444–453.

Lefkowitz, M. M., Eron, L. D., Walder, L. O., & Huesman, L. R. (1977). *Growing up to be violent.* New York: Pergamon Press.

Leventhal, G. S. (1980). What should be done with equity theory? In R. J. Gergen, M. S. Greenberg, & R. H. Willis (Eds.), *Social exchange: Advances in theory and research* (pp. 27–55). New York: Plenum Press.

Levin, J., & Fox, J. (1985). *Mass murders.* New York: Plenum Press.

Levin, R. L. (1995). Workplace violence: Sources of liability, warning signs, and ways to mitigate damages. *Labor Law Journal, 46,* 418–428.

Levinson, D. (1978). *The seasons of a man's life.* New York: Knopf.

Lies, M. A. (1999, July–August). Disarming the threat of workplace violence. *Workplace Violence Prevention Reporter, 5,* 6–7.

Lineberry, W. P. (1977). *The struggle against terrorism.* New York: H. W. Wilson.

Lion, J. R. (Ed.). (1981). *Personality disorders: Diagnosis and management.* (2nd ed.). Baltimore: Williams & Wilkins.

Lipscomb, J., Silverstein, B., Slavin, T. J., Cody, E., & Jenkins, L. (2002). Perspectives on legal strategies to prevent workplace violence. *Journal of Law, Medicine & Ethics, 30*(3), 166–172.

Littler, M., Fastiff, T., & Mathiason, P. C. (1994). *Terror and violence in the workplace.* San Francisco: Littler, Mendelson, Fastiff, Tichy, & Mathiason.

Longshore, D., Chang, E., Hsieh, S., & Messina, N. (2004). Self-control and social bonds: A combined control perspective on deviance. *Crime & Delinquency, 50,* 542–564.

Lord, R. G., Klimoski, R. J., & Kanfer, R. (2002). *Emotions in the workplace: Understanding the structure and role of emotions in organizational behavior.* San Francisco: Jossey-Bass.

Lorenz, R. (1966). *On aggression.* New York: Harcourt, Brace & World.

Losey, J. F. (1994). Managing in an era of workplace violence. *Managing Office Technology, 39,* 27–28.

Louis, M. R. (1980). Surprise and sense making: What newcomers experience in entering unfamiliar organizational settings. *Administrative Science Quarterly, 25,* 226–251.

Lucero, M., Middleton, K., Finch, W., & Valentine, S. (2003). An empirical investigation of sexual harassers: Toward a perpetrator typology. *Human Relations, 56*(12), 1461–1483.

Lutz, S. (1995, April 24). Hospitals race to treat 400 bomb victims. *Modern Healthcare,* 2.

Lyncheski, J. E., & Hardy, W. S. (2001, May). Workplace violence: Practical advice for a problem with dire legal consequences. *Health Care Law Monthly,* 17–25.

Macauley A. J. (2006). Recent developments in workers' compensation and employers' liability law. *Tort Trial & Insurance Practice Law Journal, 41*(2), 783–798.

Machiavelli, N. (1952). *The prince.* New York: The New American Library of World Literature, Inc. (Original translation published 1903).

Madsen, R. B., & Knudson-Fields, B. (1987). Productive progressive discipline procedures. *Management Solutions, 32*(5), 17–24.

Mantell, M., & Albrecht, S. (1994). *Ticking bombs: Defusing violence in the workplace.* Burr Ridge, IL: Irwin Professional.

Mantell, M. R. (1994, April 5). Let's put a stop to workplace violence. *USA Today,* A-11.

Maslach, C., & Jackson, S. (1981). *The Maslach burnout inventory.* Pale Alto, CA: Consulting Psychologists Press.

Masland, T. (1995, May 1). Life in the bull's eye. *Newsweek,* pp. 57–58.

Masters, A., & Masters, J. (1995, Summer). Reflections on the Oklahoma City bombing. *The Journal of Psychohistory, 23*(1), 26–29.

Masterson, J. F. (1981). *The narcissistic and borderline disorders.* New York: Brunner/Mazel.

Mattman, J., & Kaufer, S. (Eds.). (1998). *The complete workplace violence prevention manual* (Vols. 1–2). Costa Mesa, CA: James.

McCaghy, C. (1980). *Crime in American society.* New York: Macmillan.

McCartney, S., & Evans, H. (1994, April 21). After the bomb, expert opinions flood the media. *Wall Street Journal,* B-1.

McClure, L. F. (1996). *Risky business: Managing employee violence in the workplace.* New York: The Haworth Press.

McConvile, J. (1995, April 24). The television link to terror. *Broadcasting and Cable, 125*(17), 1.

McCune, J. (1994). Companies grapple with workplace violence. *Management Review, 83*(3), 52–58.

McFadden, R. D. (1993, February 27). Blast hits trade center, bomb suspected; 5 killed, thousands flee smoke in towers. *New York Times,* p. 1, 22.

McGeehan, P. (1995, April 23). To insurers, terrorism is not like war. *New York Times*, III-14.

McKay, M., Rogers, P., & McKay, J. (1989). *When anger hurts*. San Francisco: New Harbinger.

Mefferd, R. B., Lennon, J. M., & Dawson, N. E. (1981). Violence—An ultimate noncoping behavior. In J. R. Hays, T. R. Roberts, & R. S. Solway (Eds.), *Violence and the violent individual* (pp. 273–296). New York: Spectrum.

Megargee, E. (1969). The psychology of violence: A critical review of theories of violence. In D. J. Mubihill & M. M. Tumin (Eds.), *Crimes of violence: A staff report to the U.S. National Commission on the causes and prevention of violence* (1969 [i.e. 1970]). (Vol. 12). Washington, DC: U.S. Government Printing Office.

Megargee, E. (1976). The prediction of dangerous behavior. *Criminal Justice Behavior, 3*, 3–21.

Megargee, E. (1981). Methodological problems in the prediction of violence. In J. R. Hays, T. K. Roberts, & K. S. Solway (Eds.). *Violence and the violent individual* (pp. 179–191). New York: Spectrum.

Mendell, R. L. (1994, December). A cause for concern. *Security Management, 38*(12), 7–19.

Mendoza, M. (2009, May 21). Economic stress may be intensifying domestic violence. *Houston Chronicle*, p. A-1.

Merchant, J. (2001). Researchers seek federal funds to study workplace violence. *Professional Safety, 46*(7), 10.

Mesnikoff, A., & Lauterbach, C. G., (1975). The association of violent dangerous behavior with psychiatric disorders: A review of the research literature. *Journal of Psychiatry and the Law, 31*, 415–445.

Methvin, E. H. (1995, July 10). Anti-terrorism: How far? *National Review, 47*(13), 32–34.

Miller, V. D., & Jablin, F. M. (1991). Information seeking during organizational entry: Influences, tactics, and a model of the process. *Academy of Management Review, 16*, 92–120.

Miller, W. H. (1986). Trouble at home? *Industry Week, 231*(4), 49–53.

Millon, T. (1986). The avoidant personality. In A. M. Cooper, A. J. Frances, & M. H. Sacks (Eds.), *Psychiatry I: The personality disorders and neuroses* (pp. 263–273). Philadelphia: Lippincott.

Minor, M. (1995). *Preventing workplace violence*. Hamilton, CT: Crisp.

Mischel, W. (1968). *Personality and assessment*. New York: Wiley.

Mischel, W. (1973). Toward a cognitive social learning reconceptualization of personality. *Psychological Review, 80*, 252–283.

Mohammed, Y. A., Scott, J., & Al-Khatib, J. A. (1994, March). Consumer ethics: The possible effects of terrorism and civil unrest on the ethical values of consumers. *Journal of Business Ethics, 13*(3), 223–231.

Monahan, J. (1975). The prediction of violence. In D. Chappel & J. Monahan (Eds.), *Violence and criminal justice* (pp. 15–31). Lexington, MA: Lexington Books.

Monahan, J. (1978). Prediction research and the emergency commitment of dangerous mentally ill persons. *American Journal of Psychiatry, 135,* 214–226.

Monahan, J. (1981). *The Clinical prediction of violent behavior.* Rockville, MD: National Institute of Mental Health.

Mr. X (1995). *Fired? Fight back!* New York: American Management Association.

Murphy, K. R. (1993). *Honesty in the workplace.* Belmont, CA: Brooks/Cole.

Myers, D. W. (1995). *Stop violence in the workplace: A guide to understanding and prevention.* Chicago: CCH.

Namie, G., & Namie, R. (2000). *The bully at work: What you can do to stop the hurt and reclaim your dignity on the job.* Naperville, IL: Sourcebooks.

National Organization for Victim Assistance. (1986). *Crisis response training manual.* Alexandria, VA: National Organization for Victim Assistance.

Near, J. P., & Miceli, M. P. (1986). Retaliation against whistle blowers: Predictors and effects. *Journal of Applied Psychology, 71*(1), 137–145.

Netanyahu, B. (Ed.) (1986). *Terrorism.* New York: Farrar, Straus Giroux.

Netanyahu, B. (1995). *Fighting terrorism: How democracies can defeat domestic and international terrorists.* New York: Farrar, Straus Giroux.

Newsfile. (1995, June 1) Oklahoma City bombing creates workplace havoc. *Personnel Journal, 74*(6), 11–14.

Nigro, L. G., & Waugh, W. L., Jr. (1996, June). Violence in the American workplace: Challenges to the public employer. *Public Administration Review, 56,* 27–31.

NIMH. (1984). *The neuroscience of mental health: A report on neuroscience research.* Rockville, MD: U.S. Department of Health and Human Services, National Institute of Mental Health, Public Health Service.

NIOSH. (1992, September). *Homicide in US workplaces: A strategy for prevention and research.* Morgantown, WV: U.S. Department of Health and Human Services, National Institute for Occupational Safety and Health.

NIOSH. (1993). *Preventing homicide in the workplace.* (Publication No. 93-109). Morgantown, WV: U.S. Department of Health and Human Services, National Institute for Occupational Safety and Health.

NIOSH. (1995, May). *Alert: Preventing homicide in the workplace.* Morgantown, WV: U.S. Department of Labor, National Institute for Occupational Safety and Health.

NIOSH. (June 1996). *Violence in the workplace: Risk factors and prevention strategies.* Morgantown, WV: U.S. Department of Labor, National Institute for Occupational Safety and Health.

Nixon, W. B. (2004). *The Financial impact of workplace violence.* Lake Forest, CA: National Institute for the Prevention of Workplace Violence.

O'Boyle, T. F. (1992, September 15). Disgruntled workers intent on revenge increasingly harm colleagues and bosses. *Wall Street Journal,* B-1, B-10.

Ofman, P. S., Mastria, M. A., & Steinberg, J. (1995, July). Mental health reponse to terrorism: The World Trade Center bombing. *Journal of Mental Health Counseling, 17*(3), 312–320.

O'Hare, D. (1994, July). Target: CEO. *Risk Management, 41*(7), 5.

Oklahoma City: The long road ahead. (1995, May 15). *Time, 145*(20), 43.

O'Leary-Kelly, A. M., Paetzold, R. L., & Griffin, R. W. (1995). Sexual harassment as aggressive action: A framework for understanding sexual harassment (pp. 453–457). *Best Papers Proceedings of the 1995 Academy of Management Meetings.*

Oldham, J. M., & Frosch, W. A. (1985). Compulsive personality disorder. In A. M. Cooper, A. J. Frances, & M. H. Sacks (Eds.), *Psychiatry (I): The personality disorders and neuroses* (pp. 219–230). Philadelphia: Lippincott.

Oliver, A. (1986). Burnout: Causes and cures. *Marketing Communications, 11*(9), 82–83.

O'Loughlin, M. A. (1996). Terrorism: The problem and the solution—The Comprehensive Terrorism Prevention Act of 1995. *Journal of Legislation, 22*(103), 106.

Olweus, D. (1979). Stability of aggressive reaction patterns in males: A review. *Psychological Bulletin, 86*, 852–875.

Olweus, D., Block, J., & Roadke-Yarrow, M. (Eds.) (1986). *Development of antisocial and prosocial behavior.* New York: Academic Press.

Orwell, G. (1949). *1984.* New York: Harcourt, Brace.

OPM. (1998). *Organizational recovery after an incident in dealing with workplace violence: A guide for agency planners.* (OWR 09). Washington, DC: U.S. Office of Personnel Management, Office of Workforce Relations.

Ostroff, C., & Kozlowski, S. W. J. (1992). Organizational socialization as learning process: The role of information acquisition. *Personnel Psychology, 45*, 849–874.

Overman, S. (1993, July). Be prepared should be your motto. *HRMagazine*, 46–49.

Paetzold, R. L., & O'Leary-Kelly, A. M. (1994). Hostile environment sexual harassment in the United States: Post-Meritor developments and implications. *Gender, Work and Organization, 1*(1), 50–57.

Pammer, W. J., Jr., & Killian, J. (2003). *Handbook of conflict management.* New York: Marcel Dekker.

Panniello, J. (Ed.). (2004). *Workplace violence: Wakefield responds.* Boston, MA: Northeastern University Center for Criminal Justice Policy Research.

Pasternak, D. (1955, May 1). Safer buildings at a price. *US News and World Report,* 170.

Patton, W. E., III, & Questell, M. (1986). Alcohol abuse in the sales force. *Journal of Personnel Selling and Sales Management, 6*(3), 39–51.

Pavlov, I. P. (1927). *Conditioned reflexes* (G. V. Anrep, Trans.). London: Oxford University Press.

Pawlik, V., & Kleiner, B. H. (1986). On-the-job employee counseling: Focus on performance. *Personnel Journal, 65*(11), 31–36.

Perlow, R., & Latham, L. L. (1993). Relationship of client abuse with locus of control and gender: A longitudinal study in mental retardation facilities. *Journal of Applied Psychology, 78*(5), 831–834.

Perrewé, P. L., & Ganster, D. C. (Eds.). (2002). Historical and current perspectives on stress and health. *Research in Occupational Stress and Well Being* (Vol. 2). New York: Elsevier.

Peter, L. J., & Hull, R. (1969). *The Peter Principle: Why things always go wrong.* New York: Morrow.

Peters, T. J., & Waterman, R. H., Jr. (1982). *In search of excellence.* New York: Harper & Row.

Petersen, D. J., & Massengill, D. (1989/90). The negligent hiring doctrine—A growing dilemma for employers. *Employee Relations Law Journal, 15*(3), 419–432.

Petrozzello, D. (1995, April 24). Radio, TV mobilize in Oklahoma City. *Broadcasting and Cable, 125*(17), 10–14.

Phalon, R. (1987). Sobering facts on Rehab. *Forbes, 139*(5), 140, 142.

Philson, C. S. (1994, August). A safe haven from violence emerges as another duty. *Occupational Health and Safety, 8*(5), 63.

Pisano, R., & Taylor, S. P. (1971). Reduction of physical aggression: The effects of four strategies. *Journal of Personality and Social Psychology, 19,* 237–242.

Poirot, C. (1988, November 25). Toxins are aimed at AIDS. *Fort Worth Star-Telegram,* p. 30.

Potter-Efron, R. T. (1998). *Work rage.* New York: Barnes & Noble.

Prince, J. (1993). Fuming over workplace violence. *Security Mangement, 35*(3), 64.

Programs tackle employees' personal problems. (1988). *Savings Institutions, 109*(1), 70–73.

Punch, M. (1996). *Dirty business: Exploring corporate misconduct.* London: Sage.

Quick, J. C., Murphy, L. R., & Hurrell, J. J. (Eds.). (1992). *Stress and well being at work: Assessments and interventions for occupational mental health.* Washington, DC: APA Books.

Quick, J. C., Quick, J. D., Nelson, D. L., & Hurrell, J. J. (1998). *Preventive stress management in organizations.* Washington, DC: APA.

Rachman, S., & Hodgson, R. J. (1980). *Obsessions and compulsions.* Englewood Cliffs, NJ: Prentice-Hall.

Randel, J. A., & Wells, K. K. (2003). Corporate approaches to reducing intimate partner violence through workplace initiatives. *Clinics in Occupational and Environmental Medicine, 3,* 821–841.

Rappaport, J., & Holden, K. (1981). Prevention of violence: The case for a nonspecific social policy. In J. R. Hays, T. R. Roberts, & R. S. Solway (Eds.), *Violence and the Violent Individual* (pp. 409–440). New York: Spectrum.

Rasco, E. (1987). Techniques: The floggings will continue until morale improves. *Management World, 16*(1), 33, 35.

Reid, W. H. (1983). *Treatment of the DSM-III psychiatric disorders.* New York: Brunner/Mazel.

Reid, W. H. (1986). Antisocial personality. In A. M. Cooper, A. J. Frances, & M. H. Sacks (Eds.), *Psychiatry (I): The personality disorders and neuroses* (pp. 219–230). Philadelphia: Lippincott.

Reiss, A. J., Jr., & Roth, J. A. (Eds.). (1993). *Understanding and preventing violence.* Washington, DC: National Academy Press.

Remboldt, C., & Zimman, R. N. (1996). *Respect and protect: A practical, step-by-step violence prevention and intervention program for schools and communities.* Minneapolis: Johnson Institute-QVS.

Rigdon, J. E. (1994, April 12). Companies see more workplace violence. *Wall Street Journal,* p. B-1.

Rinefort, F. C., & Van Fleet, D. D. (1993). Safety issues beyond the workplace: Estimated relationships between work injuries and available supervision. *Employee Responsibilities and Rights Journal, 6*(1), 1–8.

Rinefort, F. C., & Van Fleet, D. D. (1995, October). How Howard Pyle helped make America safer. *Safety and Health, 152*(4), 90–92.

Rinefort, F. C., & Van Fleet, D. D. (1998, June). Work injuries and employee turnover. *American Business Review,* 9–13.

Rinefort, F. C., & Van Fleet, D. D. (2000). The United States safety movement and Howard Pyle. *Journal of Management History, 6*(3), 127–137.

Rinefort, F. C., Van Fleet, D. D., & Van Fleet, E. W. (1998, September). Downsizing: A strategy that may be hazardous to your organization's health. *International Journal of Management, 15*(3), 335–339.

Roberts, T. K., Mock, L. T., & Johnstone, E. E. (1981). Psychological aspects of the etiology of violence. In J. R. Hays, T. K. Roberts, & K. S. Solway (Eds.), *Violence and the violent individual* (pp. 9–33). New York: Spectrum.

Robertson, D. (1993). *Violence in the workplace.* Santa Rosa, CA: Atrium.

Robinson, S., & Bennett, R. (1995). A typology of deviant workplace behaviors: A multi-dimensional scaling study. *Academy of Management Journal, 38,* 555–572.

Robinson, S. L., & O'Leary-Kelly, A. M. (1998). Monkey see, monkey do: The influence of work groups on the antisocial behavior of employees. *Academy of Management Journal, 41,* 658–672.

Roha, Ronaleen R. (1995, September 1). Business among the ruins. *Kiplinger's Personal Finance Magazine, 49*(9), 154–155.

Rosen, L. S. (2004). *The safe hiring manual.* Tempe, AZ: Facts on Demand Press.

Rosenfeld, R., & Fornango, R. (2007). The impact of economic conditions on robbery and property crime: The role of consumer sentiment. *Criminology, 45,* 735–770.

Ross, J. I. (1993, August). Structural causes of oppositional political terrorism: Towards a causal model. *Journal of Peace Research, 30*(3), 317–329.

Ross, J. I. (1994, Summer). The psychological causes of oppositional political terrorism: Toward an integration of findings. *Journal of Group Tensions, 24*(2), 157–185.

Rossi, A. M., & Perrewé, P. L. (Eds.) (2006). *Stress and quality of working life: Current perspectives in occupational health.* Charlotte, NC: Information Age.

Rotter, J. B. (1966). Generalized expectancies for internal versus external control of reinforcements. *Monographs of the American Psychological Association, 80*(1), 1–28.

Rouhi, M. (1995, May 1). Oklahoma bomb shows common items' power. *Chemical and Engineering News,* 2.

Rowe, D. C. (1987). Resolving the person-situation debate: Invitation to an interdisciplinary dialogue. *American Psychologist, 42,* 218–227.

Ruggless, R. (1995, May 1). Suppliers, operators rally in Oklahoma relief effort. *Nation's Restaurant News, 29*(18), 1,18.

Runyan, C., Zakocs, R., & Zwerling, C. (2000). Administrative and behavioral interventions for workplace violence prevention. *American Journal of Preventive Medicine, 18*(4), 116–127.

Ryckman, R. M. (1985). *Theories of personality.* (3rd ed.). Monterey, CA: Brooks/Cole.

Sachs, A. (1995, May). Bombing aftermath. *Advertising Age's Business Marketing, 80*(5), 1,45.

Sagie, A., Stashevsky, S., & Koslowsky, M. (Eds.). (2003). *Misbehaviour and dysfunctional attitudes in organizations.* New York: Palgrave Macmillan.

Salin, D. (2003). Ways of explaining workplace bullying: A review of enabling, motivating and precipitating structures and processes in the work environment. *Human Relations, 56*(10), 1213–1232.

Schat, A. C. H., & Kelloway, E. K. (2000). Effects of perceived control on the outcomes of workplace aggression and violence. *Journal of Occupational Health Psychology, 5,* 286–402.

Schat, A. C. H., & Kelloway, E. K. (2003). Reducing the adverse consequences of workplace aggression and violence: The buffering effects of organizational support. *Journal of Occupational Health Psychology, 8,* 110–122.

Schatzberg, A. F., & Cole. J. O. (1986). *Manual of clinical psychopharmacology.* Washington, DC: American Psychiatric Press.

Schein, V. E. (1985). Organizational realities: The politics of change. *Training and Development Journal, 39*(2), 37–41.

Schell, B. H, & Lanteigne, N. M (2000). *Stalking, harassment, and murder in the workplace: Guidelines for protection and prevention.* Westport, CT: Quorum Books.

Schermerhorn, J. R, Jr. (1982). *Managing organizational behavior.* New York: John Wiley & Sons.

Schumpeter, S. A. (1934). *The theory of economic development.* (R. Opie, Trans.). Cambridge, MA: Harvard University Press.

Schwab, D. (1980). Construct validity in organizational behavior. In B. Staw & L. Cummings (Eds.), *Research in Organizational Behavior, 2*, 3–43.

Schwartz, A. E. (1988). Counseling the marginal performer. *Management Solutions, 33*(3), 30–35.

Schwartz, G. G., & Neikirt, W. (1983). *The work revolution*. New York: Rawson.

Scism, L., & Davidson, J. (1995, May 4). Insurance losses in Oklahoma bombing seen topping several hundred million. *Wall Street Journal*, p. A-4.

Seligman, M. E. P. (1975). *Helplessness: On depression, development, and death*. San Francisco: W. H. Freeman.

Seligman, P. J., Newman, S. C., Timbrook, L. L., & Halperin, W. E. (1987). Assault of women at work. *American Journal of Industrial Medicine*, 445–450.

Selye, H. (1956). *The stress of life*. New York: McGraw-Hill.

Shapero, H. 2002. Pre-employment criminal background checks: Why employers should look before they leap. *Employee Relations Law Journal, 28*, 63

Shapiro, B. P. (1977, Sept/Oct). Can marketing and manufacturing coexist? *Harvard Business Review*, 104–114.

Shapiro, D. (1989). *Autonomy and rigid character*. New York: Basic Books.

Sherwood, A. (1987). How to identify and handle rivals. *Chief Executive, 4*, 38–40.

Shlachter, A. (1988, December 5–11). Texas blends: Family has given chili its spice for 118 years. *Fort Worth Star-Telegram: Tarrant Business*, pp. 8–9.

SHRM. (2003). *2004 Workplace Violence Survey Report*. Alexandria, VA: Society for Human Resources Management.

Simon, G. K. (1996) *In sheep's clothing: Understanding and dealing with manipulative people*. Little Rock, AR: A.J. Christopher.

Siljander, R. P. (1980). *Terrorist attacks*. Springfield, IL: Charles C. Thomas.

Siropolis, N. C. (1982). *Small business management: A guide to entrepreneurship* (2nd ed.). Boston: Houghton-Mifflin.

Skarlicki, D. P., & Folger, R. (1997). Retaliation in the workplace: The roles of distributive, procedural and interactional justice. *Journal of Applied Psychology, 82*, 416–425.

Skinner, B. F. (1938). *The behavior of organisms: An experimental analysis*. New York: Appleton-Century-Crofts.

Skinner, B. F. (1948). *Walden two*. New York: Macmillan.

Skinner, B. F. (1953). *Science and human behavior*. New York: Macmillan.

Skinner. B. F. (1988). A statement on punishment. *APA Monitor, 19*(6), 22.

Sloan. R. P., & Allegrante, J. P. (1985). Corporate health is more than a robust balance sheet. *Training and Development Journal, 39*(12), 57–59.

Slora, K. B., Joy, D. S., Jones, J. W., & Terris, W. (1991). In J. W. Jones (Ed.), *Preemployment honesty testing: Current research and future directions* (pp. 171–183). Westport, CT: Quorum Books.

Slora, K. B., Joy, D. S., & Terris, W. (1991). Personnel selection to control employee violence. *Journal of Business and Psychology, 5*(3), 417–426.

Smith, G. D. (1993, Summer). Sources of terrorism weaponry and major methods of obtaining weapons and techniques. *Terrorism and Political Violence,* 5(2), 123–129.

Smolowe, J., Allis, S., Barnes, E., Dawson, P., Jackson, D. S., Norvell, S., & Woodbury, R. (1995, May 8). Enemies of the state. *Time,* 145.

Snyder, W., III. (1994). Hospital downsizing and increased frequency of assaults on staff. *Hospital and Community Psychiatry, 45,* 378–379.

Solomon, J., & King, P. (1993). Waging war in the workplace. *Newsweek,* 30–34.

Sonkin, D., & Durphy, M. (1982). *Learning to live without violence.* San Francisco, CA: Volcano Press.

Southerland, M. D., & Collins, P. A. (1994). Workplace violence: A 'recent case' analysis. *Journal of Security Administration, 17*(2), 1–10.

Southerland, M. D., Collins, P. A., & Scarborough, K. E. (1997). *Workplace violence: A continuum from threat to death.* Cincinnati, OH: Anderson.

Spector, P. E. (1975). Relationships of organizational frustration with reported behavioral reactions of employees. *Journal of Applied Psychology, 60*(5), 635–637.

Spector, P. E. (1978). Organizational frustration: A model and review of the literature. *Personnel Psychology, 31,* 815–829.

Spector, P. E. (1982). Behavior in organizations as a function of employee's locus of control. *Psychological Bulletin, 91,* 482–497.

Speer, R. (2003). Workplace violence: A legal perspective. *Clinics in Occupational and Environmental Medicine, 3,* 733–749.

Speer, R. A. (1997). The legal implications of workplace violence. *Women Lawyers Journal, 83,* 13–19.

Sprouse, M. (1992). *Sabotaging the American workplace.* San Francisco: Pressure Drop Press.

Spruell, G. R. (1985). Love in the office. *Training and Development Journal, 39*(2), 21–23.

Steadman, H. J. (1986). Predicting violence leading to homicide. *Bulletin of the New York Academy of Medicine, 62*(5), 570–578.

Steinmetz. L. L. (1969). *Managing the marginal and unsatisfactory performer.* Reading, MA: Addison-Wesley.

Stone, R. A. (1995). Workplace homicide: A time for action. *Business Horizons, 38,* 3–10.

Storms, P. L., & Spector, P. E. (1987). Relationships of organizational frustration with reported behavioural reactions: The moderating effect of locus of control. *Journal of Occupational Psychology, 60,* 227–234.

Storr, A. (1968). *Human aggression.* New York: Atheneum.

Stuart, P. (1992). Murder on the job. *Personnel Journal, 71,* 79–88.

Stuart, R. B. (1981). Violence in perspective. In R. B. Stuart (Ed.), *Violent behavior: Social learning approaches to prediction, management, and treatment* (pp. 3–30). New York: Brunner/Mazel.

Stuckless, N., & Goranson, R. (1992). The vengeance scale: Development of a measure of attitudes toward revenge. *Journal of Social Behavior and Personality, 7*(1), 25–42.

Stussie, G. (2002). The real terror at work. *Risk Management, 49*(5), 30.

Super, D. (1957). *The psychology of careers.* New York: Harper & Row.

Swanson, D. L., & Paul, R. J. (2002–2003, Fall). Violations of ethical expectations: The toxicity of organizational pain and some remedies. *Journal of Individual Employment Rights, 10*(1), 25–39.

Tehrani, N. (2001). *Building a culture of respect: Managing bullying at work.* London: Taylor & Francis.

Tepper, B. J. (2007). Abusive supervision in work organizations: Review, synthesis, and research agenda. *Journal of Management, 33,* 261–289.

Terrazas, M. (1995, June 1). Guarding against another Oklahoma City. *American City and County, 110*(7), 50+.

Terrorism: The new corporate threat. (1990, October). *Management Review, 79*(10), 39.

Thibault, J., & Walker, L. (1975). *Procedural justice.* Hillsdale, NJ: Erlbaum.

Thibodeau, C. T. (2007). Staff training and development. In S. J. Davies & C. A. Hertig (Eds.), *Security supervision & management* (3rd ed., pp. 155–164). Woburn, MA: Butterworth-Heinemann.

Thomas, E. (1995, May 8). The plot: Oklahoma City bombing suspect Timothy McVeigh (cover story). *Newsweek,* 28–34.

Thomas, E. (1995, June 5). Inside the plot. *Newsweek,* 24–27.

Thomas, J. L. (1992, June). CPTED: A response to occupational violent crime. *Professional Safety Journal, 37,* b.

Thomas, J. L. (1992, Summer). Occupational violent crime: Research on an emerging issue. *Journal of Safety Research, 23,* 55–62.

Thomas, K. (1976). Conflict and conflict management. In M. Dunnette (Ed.), *Handbook of industrial and organization psychology* (pp. 889–936). Chicago, IL: Rand McNally.

Thornburg, L. (1993, July). When violence hits business. *HRMagazine,* 40–45.

Tiedeman, D., & O'Hara, R. (1963). *Career development: Choice and adjustment.* New York: College Entrance Examination Board.

Tobin, T. J. (2001). Organizational determinants of violence in the workplace. *Aggression and Violent Behavior, 6*(1), 91–102.

Toch, H. (1969). *Violent men.* Chicago: Aldine.

Toufexis, A. (1994, April 25). Fight firing with fire. *Time,* 35–37.

Trice, H. M., & Beyer, J. M. (1993). *The cultures of work organizations.* Englewood Cliffs, NJ: Prentice-Hall.

Turner, C. W., Fenn, M. R., & Cole, A. M. (1981). A social psychological analysis of violent behavior. In R. B. Stuart (Ed.), *Violent behavior: Social learning approaches to prediction, management and treatment* (pp. 31–67). New York: Brunner/Mazel.

Turner, J. T., & Gelles, M. G. (2003). *Threat assessment: A risk management approach.* Binghamton, New York: The Haworth Press.
United States Congress. House Committee on Post Office and Civil Service. (1992, June 15). *A Post Office Tragedy: The Shooting at Royal Oak* . (V 92-0397-P). One Hundred Second Congress, second session. Washington, DC: Government Printing Office.
Vaisman-Tzachor, R. (1991). Stress and coping styles in personnel of a terrorism prevention team. *Journal of Social Behavior and Personality, 6*(4), 889–902.
Van Fleet, D. D., in collaboration with G. Moorhead & R. W. Griffin. (1991). *Behavior in Organizations.* Boston: Houghton Mifflin.
Van Fleet, D. D., & Griffin, R. W. (2006). Dysfunctional organization culture: The role of leadership in motivating dysfunctional work behaviors. *Journal of Managerial Psychology, 21*(8), 698–708.
Van Fleet, D. D., & Peterson, T. O., in collaboration with R. W. Griffin (1994). *Contemporary Management* (3rd ed.). Boston: Houghton Mifflin.
Van Fleet, D. D., & Van Fleet, E. W. (2001, November). How terrorism affects companies. *Scottsdale Airpark News, 21*(11), 36–39.
Van Fleet, D. D., & Yukl, G. A. (1986). *Military leadership: An organizational behavior perspective.* Greenwich, CT: JAI Press.
Van Fleet, E.W., & Van Fleet, D. D. (1996). *Workplace violence: Moving toward minimizing risks.* (Special report for Minerva Education Institute (CM 96-02). Washington, DC: U.S. Department of Labor, Occupational Safety and Health Administration, Department of Education and Training,
VandenBos, G. R., & Bulatao, E. Q. (Eds.). (1996). Violence on the job. Washington, D.C.: *American Psychological.*
Vardi, Y., & Weitz, E. (2004). *Misbehavior in organizations: Theory, research and management.* Mahwah, NJ: Erlbaum.
Walker, S., Spohn, C., & DeLone, M. (2007). *The color of justice: Race and crime in America* (4th ed.). Belmont, CA: Wadsworth.
Walters, R. (1987). Chemical abuse and the employer. *Management Quarterly, 28*(3), 19–26.
Warren, J., Brown, D., Hurt, S., Cook, S., Branson, W., & Jin, R. (1999). The organizational context of non-lethal workplace violence: Its interpersonal, temporal and spatial correlates. *Journal of Occupational and Environmental Medicine, 41*(7), 567–581.
Watson, D., & Clark, L. A. (1984). Negative affectivity: The disposition to experience aversive emotional states. *Psychological Bulletin, 96,* 465–490.
Watson, D., & Pennebaker, J. W. (1989). Health complaints, stress, and distress: Exploring the central role of negative affectivity. *Psychological Review, 96,* 234–254.
Watson, J. B. (1914). *Behavior: An introduction to comparative psychology.* New York: Holt, Rinehart & Winston.
Watson, J. B. (1916). The place of the conditioned reflex in psychology. *Psychological Review, 23,* 89–116.

Weisinger, H. (1995). *Anger at work*. New York: William Morrow.

Weiss, D. H. (1988). How to handle difficult people. *Management Solutions, 33*(2), 33–38.

Weiss, R. M. (1985). Determining the effects of alcohol abuse on employee productivity. *American Psychologist, 40*(5), 578–580.

Wheeler, T. (1995, June 1). Behind the Oklahoma bombing. *Political Affairs, 74*(6), 9–14.

White, S. G., & Hatcher, C. (1988). Violence and trauma response. *Occupational Medicine, 3*(4), 677–694.

Why drug testing is needed. (1987). *Security Management, 31*(8), 47–48.

Why It Shouldn't Happen Here. (1995, May 1). *Business Insurance*, 1.

Wilkinson, C. W. (1998). *Violence in the workplace*. Rockville, MD: Government Institutes.

Willems, H. (1995, Spring). Development, patterns and causes of violence against foreigners in Germany: Social and biographical characteristics of perpetrators and the process of excalation. *Terrorism and Political Violence, 7*(1), 162.

Williams, W., & Miller, K. (1977). The role of personal characteristics in perceptions of dangerousness. *Criminal Justice and Behavior, 4*(3), 241–252.

Wilson, M., & Lynxwiler, J. (1988) Abortion clinic violence as terrorism. *Studies in Conflict & Terrorism, 11*(4), 263–273.

Winwood, P. C., Bakker, A. B., & Winefield, A. H. (2007). An investigation of the role of non-work time behaviour in buffering the effects of work strain. *Journal of Occupational and Environmental Medicine, 49*, 862–871.

Wolfgang, M. E., & Ferracuti, F. (1967). *The subculture of violence: Toward an integrated theory in criminology*. London: Social Science Paperback.

Woo, J. (1993, September 1). Businesses find suits on security hard to defend. *Wall Street Journal*, p. B-1.

Wood, W., Wong, F. Y., & Chachere, J. G. (1991). Effects of media violence on viewers' aggression in unconstrained social interaction. *Psychological Bulletin, 109*, 371–383.

Wooldredge, J. D., Cullen, F. T., & Latessa, E. J. (1992). Research note: Victimization in the workplace: A test of routine activities theory. *Justice Quarterly, 9*(2), 325–335.

Workers' Compensation Board of British Columbia. (1995). *Take Care: How to Develop and Implement a Workplace Violence Prevention Program (A Guide for Small Business)*. Vancouver, BC (Canada): Workers' Compensation Board of British Columbia.

Worthington, K. (2000). Violence in the health care workplace. *American Journal of Nursing, 100*(11), 69–70.

Worthington, K., & Franklin, P. (2001). Workplace violence: What to do if you're assaulted. *American Journal of Nursing, 101*(4), 73.

Wright, L., & Smye, M. (1996). *Corporate abuse: How "lean and mean" robs people and profits*. New York: Macmillan.

Wright, R. (1995, May 15). What do 167 Deaths Justify? *Time, 145*(20).
Zillman, D., Baron, R., & Tamborini, R. (1981). Social costs of smoking: Effects of tobacco smoke on hostile behavior. *Journal of Applied Psychology, 11*, 548–561.
Zimmerman, M. (1992) *The interview guide for evacuating DSM III-R psychiatric disorders and the imental health status examination.* Philadelphia: Psychology Press.
Zohar, D. (2000). A group-level model of safety climate: Testing the effect of group climate on microaccidents in manufacturing jobs. *Journal of Applied Psychology, 85*, 587–596.
Zubialde, J. P. (1995, August). Training the 'complete physician' for rural America: Lessons from the Oklahoma City federal building bombing. *The Journal of Family Practice, 41*(2), 118–120.
Zugelder, M. T., Champagne, P. J., & Maurer, S. D. (2007). Dealing with harassment in all of its forms. *Journal of Individual Employment Rights, 12*(3), 223–238.

LaVergne, TN USA
27 January 2010
171338LV00001B/46/P